What others are saying about this book

"I'm not sure why, but I suddenly star book. It's not any particular story, but men just a little bit better. I have never read a history book like this about the Founding Fathers - one with such personal stories and conversations. They are becoming real men to me instead of the mythical heroes they usually seem to be."

- Jennifer Green, Portland Oregon

"I started reading this book and could not put it down - The first chapter completely captured me."

- Juli Woodall, Mesa Arizona

"What a wonderful book! It is clear to me now why our country has always been and remains such a great nation. This book has opened my eyes on such a personal level to the amazing men who founded this country. They were men of character and integrity. As I read page after page, I felt that I was not only learning "about" these great individuals, but that I was getting to know them. Steven W. Allen succeeds in bringing them to life by relating many personal stories from their lives that I've never read in any other historical work about the Founding Fathers. I loved it!"

- Tricia Graves, Houston, Texas

"From cover to cover, this book thrilled me. From sea to shining sea, as I see our stars and stripes wave over this land, choice above all other lands, I give gratitude. As I read each account of our Founding Fathers, I became better acquainted with greatness and goodness and so appreciative of our uncommon heroes who pledged their lives and their sacred honor to our freedom and liberty.

It was exciting to read the appendix that refuted the base rumors that are so prevalent in the world today to discount the moral integrity of these men. These were written to get gain and arouse media attention. I appreciate Mr. Allen's research and insights.

This is an uncommon history of uncommon heroes fighting on the battleground of freedom, who, wearing the armor of God and bearing the shield of faith, win the victory. May we honor their lives, their names, and the liberty for which they stand."

- Marilyn Adams, Salt Lake City, Utah

"I have read your book and enjoyed it!! I plan to keep it available for reference."

- Marge Price, Mesa, Arizona

"As I finished reading your book about our Founding Fathers, I was so impressed with the dignity, faith and courage that these men had. Your book brought to remembrance many things I had previously known, and brought to my understanding so many good works I was previously not aware of. You write clearly, in detail and yet simply. I am very impressed. A GREAT book. My only question...when is Volume II expected for release?"

-Chuck Kober, Mesa, Arizona

"Reading Founding Fathers—Uncommon Heroes reminded me just how fascinating American history truly is, and how rich a heritage we have. So many of the freedoms we enjoy today we owe to sacrifices these men and women made, yet they faced many of the same personal challenges and crises we encounter today. The book reveals many interesting, humorous and touching tidbits about their lives, bringing them to life like never before. I couldn't put it down and I hope it is followed by another profiling others who helped make America the great country it is today!"

- Valliere Jones, Gilbert, Arizona

"This book should be used as a text book in all of our schools. It is such an inspiring and awesome true history of our great nation, which can be a sacred guideline for our present and future generations."

- Buck & Sylvia Caruthers, Tallahassee, Florida

"These books have made great gifts while at the same time helped teach some of the fundamental truths from our founding fathers. Thanks for taking the time to compile such great stories/historical accounts and publish them in one book."

- Dave Allen, Peoria, Arizona

"My wife and I have both read this really great book. Every American should know this information by heart. It makes us even more proud to be an American and to appreciate what our "Founding Fathers" went through to give us such a wonderful heritage. They were truly dedicated, intelligent men who were willing to sacrifice everything, if need be, in order to get their new nation started on Godly principles.

Our Constitution is as valid today (maybe even more so) as it was when ratified in spite of many court decisions which have tried to change the original intent of the framers.

We recommend that this book be past of every school's history curriculum"

- Bill Howard,Prescott, Arizona

"Not only is your book the most informative work I have ever read on our founding fathers, it was wonderful to see that you were able to really capture the Christianity of these men and the scriptural basis for their decisions and actions. It was also good to see the dispelling of many of the myths that have shrouded them for the last 200 plus years. I absolutely believe that this book should be mandatory reading for all children at some point during their educational years."

- Stephen J. Rockwell, D.D., LL.B, Mesa, Arizona

Founding Fathers
Uncommon Heroes

by

Steven W. Allen

Legal Awareness Series, Inc.
Mesa, Arizona

Legal Awareness Series, Inc.
Mesa, AZ 85203
www.legalawareness.com

Founding Fathers–Uncommon Heroes

This book is available for educational use. For information or to purchase additional copies, contact Legal Awareness Series, Inc. 1-800-733-5297 or www.uncommonheroes.us.

Page layout and design by Tracy Grace and Wendi Lee

Library of Congress Control Number: 2002094381

ISBN 1-879033-76-3

ACKNOWLEDGMENTS

I wish to thank the many people whose help enabled this work to come to fruition.

First, I have to thank my mother, Marjorie Allen, for initially suggesting that I put some of my thoughts and stories about the Founding Founders of the United States of America on paper. That was the "bud" that has blossomed into this book.

I thank the many followers of my lectures who have repeatedly urged me to compile my thoughts and references into a single volume of information and inspiration.

Thanks to Mark L. McConkie for his friendship and for giving me the encouragement and motivation to dedicate myself to the writing of this book.

I thank Rosemary Green for her patience with me, her care in bringing this book into its final form, and for her ability to turn a phrase or thought into a meaningful expression.

Thanks also to Amy Hardison for her generosity in reviewing the manuscript and for her invaluable suggestions.

Special thanks to my daughter Wendi Lee for her many hours of cheerfully checking reference sources, her enthusiastic assistance in research, her many timely comments and insightful suggestions, and her help with the cover design.

Thanks also to my paralegal daughter, Kari VanNoy for "holding down the fort." With care and persistence, she made certain my law office continued to function in an orderly fashion during the production of this book.

Thanks to Glen Hopkinson who, while in the middle of producing his own book, painted the stirring cover of this book.

And most of all, I wish to thank my wife, Linda, for her tireless days and nights at the computer, putting this book together for the publisher, and for her love, faith, support, and confidence in me during the whole process. Without her it simply couldn't have been done.

This book is dedicated
to all those great men and women
who pledged their lives, their fortunes,
and their sacred honor to the establishment
of the United States of America—
especially to those memorialized
in this book.

TABLE OF CONTENTS

Foreword vii

Preface ix

Benjamin Franklin 1

George Washington 37

John Adams 81

Patrick Henry 115

Thomas Jefferson 145

James Madison 183

Timeline 213

Appendix - Debunking the Rumors 253

Endnotes 265

Bibliography 289

FOREWORD

The Founding Fathers of our nation were, indeed, "uncommon heroes." Uncommon in the sense that they were remarkable and exceptional men, the kind one would rarely encounter. Heroes in the sense of legendary figures who were endowed with divine character, ability, and strength. When reading Allen's book Founding Fathers – Uncommon Heroes, I appreciated anew these legendary figures, these men of great faith, inspired vision, acute understanding, unrivaled integrity, and dogged perseverance. Beyond that, I appreciated in a new light the divine miracle that brought these brilliant, courageous men together at the same point in time to stand nobly by their beliefs until their united efforts and actions brought forth a new nation that would literally change the world. With a profound understanding of what had to be done, and at great personal sacrifice, they established a government that would lead their fledgling nation to become the greatest in the history of mankind.

Founding Fathers – Uncommon Heroes is a fascinating look at the lives of six of the Founding Fathers of our nation. It is filled with anecdotes and stories not often told, and gives readers a glimpse of what truly made these men uncommon heroes. This book brings to light the physical, spiritual, and philosophical characteristics that propelled these men to greatness. I thoroughly enjoyed reading about some very "uncommon heroes" whose courage, convictions, and fortitude shaped the fabric of our nation and established the greatest democracy on earth. My many years of service in the United States Senate has helped me understand better than ever what a monumental undertaking the Founders of the nation pursued and then remarkably achieved.

Immediately after the new Constitution of the United States was signed in Philadelphia in 1787, Benjamin Franklin was asked, "Well Doctor, what have we got, a Monarchy or a Republic?" He responded, "A Republic—if we can keep it." The responsibility to "keep it" now devolves upon us, the citizens of today. We will be better able to do so if we are familiar with the noble character traits and beliefs which our Founding Fathers possessed, and which they affirmed were indispensable to the maintaining of a free nation. This book is a fascinating and educating reminder of the character traits and beliefs that made our Founding Fathers incredibly "uncommon heroes."

Orrin G. Hatch
United States Senator

PREFACE

At the age of 21, having been overseas for two years, I returned home to the United States in the winter of 1967. I arrived at the airport in Washington, D.C., to find the city beautifully decorated for Christmas. I spent the first night back in my country at a hotel near the government mall. As I walked down the mall from the Capitol Building to the White House, I was emotionally overcome by the great blessings of freedom the Capitol Mall represents. It was late. The trees were all lighted with red, white, and blue lights. Red, white, and blue . . . I was *home*. What a wonderful feeling to return to America. My love for this great country reached a patriotic peak at that moment.

When I returned to college, I studied some political science, some history, some law. After graduating from college, I entered law school. Shortly after graduation from law school and passing the bar exam, I was appointed by the mayor of Phoenix to be a member of the Phoenix Citizens Crime Commission. In 1976, I was elected to represent the city of Phoenix at the National Convention of the Citizens Crime Commissions to be held in Philadelphia. Philadelphia in 1976. The Bicentennial of the signing of the Declaration of Independence. While in Philadelphia, I visited Independence Hall, the Liberty Bell, Carpenter's Hall, the Betsy Ross House, and the Graff House—where Thomas Jefferson stayed while attending the Continental Congress. The Graff House—where he wrote the Declaration of Independence without notes or reference books. Standing close to the spot where that inspired document was first penned, I was once again emotionally overcome. It was as if I were visiting a sacred shrine.

I had always been a patriotic American. From time to time, I shared stories with my parents, brothers, and sister about the founders of the United States. Mother, always interested in my stories, suggested that I write them down in an outline form. She encouraged me to share them with church groups, civic groups and others to help people understand the amazing lives and sacrifices of the Founding Fathers. So I did.

My presentations about Benjamin Franklin, George Washington, John Adams, Patrick Henry, Thomas Jefferson, and James Madison were always well attended and well received. After the presentations, many of the attendees asked me where certain stories were found. They often requested that I put these inspiring stories into a book to create one source of information. It became apparent that such a book might be a good idea.

I have loved learning about the Founding Fathers. It is interesting to find a story about General Washington that is no longer general knowledge. I am convinced that Americans are hungry to hear more about the lives of these great men. I have experienced deep humility as I assembled some of my favorite stories from my lectures into this volume. But this book was really written over two hundred years ago, when a handful of men decided—against all odds—to follow their own professed inspiration and pledged their life, liberty, and sacred honor for the noblest cause on earth . . . freedom.

Chapter 1

Benjamin Franklin

January 17, 1706 – April 17, 1790

BENJAMIN FRANKLIN

Benjamin Franklin. Even if his face weren't on the one-hundred-dollar bill, his name evokes an overwhelming sense of worth and importance. Often, great men are not fully appreciated in their own time. But during the 1700's, Benjamin Franklin was held in greater esteem throughout the entire world than any of his contemporaries. Considering his contemporaries included the likes of George Washington, Thomas Jefferson, John Adams, King George III, and Napoleon, he was indeed revered. He was treated with great respect in any country he visited. Thomas Jefferson called Benjamin Franklin "the greatest man and ornament of the age and country in which he lived."[1]

The accomplishments of Benjamin Franklin are staggering. He seemed to live his life in direct answer to one of his own witty sayings: "If you would not be forgotten as soon as you are dead and rotten, either write things worth reading, or do things worth the writing."[2] He wrote much that was, is, and always will be well worth reading. And he did things, many things, amazing things! Franklin was an inventor, a scientist, a statesman, a diplomat, a public servant, a philosopher, a humorist, an economist, a printer, a writer, and even a musician.

As an American inventor, he was unparalleled until Thomas Edison. Franklin loved to improve the quality of life for himself and for humankind. Among other things, he invented the Franklin stove, which used less wood and was safer than the traditional fireplace; bifocal eyeglasses; the lightning rod; an odometer to measure the distance traveled by a carriage; a long arm which helped a person reach an object otherwise out of his reach; and watertight bulkheads which allowed ships to work more efficiently and safely. He also developed America's first urinary catheter to help his older brother who suffered from kidney stones.

Franklin was an undeniable, creative genius. Yet perhaps even more amazing than his innate, phenomenal brilliance was the fact that he refused to profit from his inventions. He preferred to have them used freely for the comfort and convenience of everyone.

Franklin had an intense interest in the world around him. He was constantly trying to answer his own questions about how things worked. And that is why he was an outstanding scientist. In this field, he is most famous for his study on electricity—the well-known kite and key story. But he was also involved in many other scientific endeavors. Because of his belief that it was possible to plot the course of a storm, he once actually rode horseback three-fourths of a mile pursuing a whirlwind. During his many voyages, he charted the Gulf Stream—probably the first man to do so. And he was at the right place at the right time to witness the world's first hot-air balloon flight, which took place in Paris. He predicted that eventually such balloons would be used by the military . . . and he lived to see his own prediction fulfilled.

Even though the group of Founding Fathers were beyond impressive, few rivaled the incredible wisdom and wit of Franklin. He epitomized the ultimate statesman and diplomat, and his unequaled diplomatic skills were critical to the American cause. Perhaps no other single person could have secured the vital assistance of the French during the Revolutionary War. He was the only one of the

Founding Fathers who helped prepare and sign all four of the important documents which led to the establishment of the United States: The Declaration of Independence (1776); The Treaty of Alliance with France (1778); The Treaty of Paris (1782), a peace agreement with England which ended the Revolution; and the United States Constitution (1787). It seems a fitting tribute to a phenomenal man that Franklin alone signed all of them. He, like Washington, could have been king, but he had no desire to do so.

As a philosopher and humorist, Ben had little competition either in his day or throughout history. His clever, witty, provocative sayings are quoted around the world: "A penny saved is a penny earned." "Well done is better than well said." "Early to bed, early to rise, makes a man healthy, wealthy, and wise." "He that falls in love with himself will have no rivals."[3] But more than merely pronouncing clever thoughts, Franklin made a determined, organized, documented effort to improve his life . . . to actually embrace his own advice.

Although he is not often cited as an economist, he often spoke on the subject. His philosophy can be fairly accurately summed up by one of his own quotes: "The way to wealth . . . depends chiefly on two words, industry and frugality: that is, waste neither time nor money." "Ben Franklin's personal ideas about economy helped to shape our country's economy . . . Franklin believed that the only true way to wealth was through hard work. This noble idea became the soul of the 'American Dream,' the idea that all people are created equal and each person has the same opportunity to achieve success."[4]

As a printer, as in nearly everything else to which the man laid a hand, Franklin was unusually successful. Perhaps much of his success in his many and varied endeavors can be attributed to his philosophy that successful people had to work just a little harder than any of their competitors. Franklin bought the *Pennsylvania Gazette* in 1729 and published it for many years. It was in the *Gazette* that he published the first newspaper cartoon. But his greatest fame as a publisher came from *Poor Richard's Almanac*, which he published annually from 1733 until 1758. Ben also used his printing skills to print paper money, helping to establish the paper currency system in America.

Franklin was a profound and prolific writer. He was deeply appreciated, not only in his own country, but throughout much of Europe. Some of his writings were translated into French, German, and Italian. His writings helped him to earn the distinction of being inducted into the Royal Society of London, a major honor for a colonist.

Little is heard of Benjamin Franklin the musician.

> [He] found simple beauty in simple tunes. He played several musical instruments, including the violin, harp, and guitar. His great interest in music lead him to build his own glass armonica. This simple musical instrument was played by touching the edge of the spinning glass with dampened fingers. The armonica's beautiful tones appealed to many composers, including Mozart and Beethoven.[5]

In addition to inventor, scientist, statesman, diplomat, public servant, philosopher, humorist, economist, printer, writer, and musician, Franklin was also involved in various civic improvements. He set up the first subscription library in the world. He organized the first city hospital in America. He founded the academy which later became the University of Pennsylvania. He served as postmaster and helped Philadelphia establish a postal system. He organized the Union Fire Company and even established the first fire insurance company in America. When he saw criminals getting away without punishment, he also reformed the city's police department, and he began a program to pave, clean, and light city streets. Benjamin Franklin also proposed the idea of daylight savings time.

One historian said:

> Mind and will, talent and art, strength and ease, wit and grace met in him as if nature had been lavish and happy when he was shaped. Nothing seems to have been left out except a passionate desire, as in most men of genius, to be all ruler, all soldier, all saint, all poet, all scholar, all some one gift or merit or success. [6]

Benjamin Franklin was born in Boston on January 17, 1706. His father, Josiah Franklin, emigrated to America at the age of 25, seeking religious freedom. Josiah was a dissenter from the Church of England. He married Abiah Folger, after the death of his first wife. She bore the last 10 of his 17 children. Ben was the 15th child and 10th son. He described himself as "the youngest son of the youngest son for 5 generations back."[7]

Although Ben received only two years of formal education, he reports in his autobiography that he can't recall a time when he couldn't read. He remembers always having a book at hand and always trying to improve himself. He taught himself the basics of algebra and geometry, navigation, logic, history, science, English grammar, and five other languages—French, German, Italian, Spanish, and Latin.

Like George Washington, when Ben was a young boy, he had a desire to be a sailor. His father, who had already lost one son to drowning, discouraged him from that ambition. After making candles with his father for two years, Ben was certain he did not want to make that his profession. Josiah wanted to consecrate Ben, as the tithe son, to his Father in Heaven, to be a minister. But Ben didn't want to be a minister, and Josiah wouldn't force him. Instead, he took Ben with him to view various vocations that were practiced in the city. Together they watched the bricklayers, masons, and carpenters. They visited the merchants to see the storekeepers at work. They listened to the lawyers at court, and observed the doctors. All so that Ben could see where his interests were, so that he could grow up with a desire to improve in the talents necessary for the occupation of his choice.

Ben's older half brother James was a printer by trade. Ben found that he had acquired some interest in that particular craft. So, at the tender age of 12, Ben was allowed to be indentured to his brother. He had to sign the "article of indenture," which stated he would serve his brother until age 21. Ben was to work 12 hours a day as James taught him the printing trade and provided him with food, clothing, and a place to live. Ben would not receive any pay until his last year with his brother, when he would receive a small journeyman's wages. He could not buy or sell anything without James' prior approval. He could not gamble, drink, or get married. While the rules of indenture were strict, this job did provide Ben a greatly increased access to books. And it afforded him contact with great writers, speakers, and leaders of the Boston area. So Ben learned how ideas were spread through a newspaper and how a community could be influenced for the good.

Ben's brother James had established the fourth newspaper printed in the colonies: *The New England Courant. The Courant* printed letters of editorial comment which added to the popularity of the newspaper. Ben enjoyed the editorial letters and wanted to participate in this editorial process. But he was afraid that James would not allow him, at the age of 16, to submit anything he wrote. So Ben invented a fictional widow, named her Silence Dogood, and submitted his editorials in her name.

For seven months, posing as a widow, Ben secretly wrote letters every two weeks and slipped them under the door of the printing house. He advocated timely improvements. He expressed good-natured criticism. He editorialized about such topics as freedom and government, immorality and drunkenness, hypocrisy and pride, and other such subjects until he ran out of ideas.

All of Silence Dogood's letters were printed. Ben took great pride in hearing people discuss these articles as they tried to guess who the real author was. "None were named but men of some character among us for learning and ingenuity."[8]

This was a great source of confidence for a boy of 16 years. Ben had begun to express some of his ideas that would later help develop some of the fundamental principles of our future government. When Ben eventually revealed to James the true identity of Silence Dogood, James was jealous of his little brother's obvious ability and talent for writing. From that point on, their relationship began to deteriorate. Though they were brothers, James considered himself Ben's master and treated him as his apprentice. When James began to beat him, Ben began to look for ways to shorten his apprenticeship.

When some articles insulting the colonial government in Massachusetts were printed in *The Courant*, James was arrested and thrown into prison. Eventually, he had to flee Boston. In order to keep the paper alive, James tore up Ben's articles of indenture, and Ben was the editor and publisher of the newspaper for the next eight months. When James came back, Ben refused to act as an indentured servant again, and the brothers quarreled. James requested of other Boston printers that they not hire Ben, so, at the age of 17, Ben sold most of his books and boarded a ship to New York. Since he was already a skilled printer, he was sure he could get a job in some print shop.

Ben traveled by sea or foot until he finally arrived at Philadelphia. After his long journey in his work clothes, he was dirty, disheveled, and dismal in appearance. He was also hungry and short of money. Upon entering the city, he saw a young man eating some bread and asked where he could get a similar loaf. He was pointed toward the bakery. Ben asked the baker for a "3 penny loaf" and was informed that there was no such thing in Philadelphia. So he asked for whatever he could get for 3 pennies. He was surprised when he was given 3 great "puffy rolls" or loaves of bread. He stuck one under each arm and ate the other as he walked up Market Street.[9]

This was Ben's first introduction to many of the people of Philadelphia, including Deborah Read, whom he would marry some seven years later. Deborah was a native of Philadelphia, from a family of not much prominence. Shortly after arriving in Philadelphia, Ben began working for a printer named Samuel Keimer at the *Pennsylvania Gazette*, which Franklin later took over and provided a way for him to make his fortune. He lodged for a time with the Reads and began to court Deborah. But then there came a trip to London which lasted nearly two years. Not until sometime after Ben's return from London was their mutual affection revived.

Ben and Deborah were married on September 1, 1730. "She proved a good and faithful helpmeet; assisted me much by attending the shop; we throve together and have mutually endeavored to make each other happy."[10] They lived happily together for 44 years, even though for at least 11 of those years, Ben was living in England or France on assignments. "Mrs. Franklin was a handsome woman of a comely figure, yet nevertheless an industrious and frugal one," writes one biographer.[11]

Mrs. Franklin died of paralysis on December 19, 1774, while her husband was still in England. She had suffered a stroke the year before, and now a second stroke carried her into eternity. Sadly, she died before she was able to witness many of Benjamin's most notable achievements.

Early in life, Ben developed what he termed his "First Principles" or "Articles of Belief and Acts of Religion." He remarked that:

> [God] has in himself some of these passions he has planted in us. He has given us the ability to reason. We are capable of observing the wisdom in His creations. We know that He is pleased by our praise, and offended when we neglect His glory. He is a Good being.
>
> I should be happy to have so wise, good, and powerful a being my friend, [so] let me consider in what manner I shall make myself most acceptable to Him. . . .
>
> I believe He is pleased and delights in the happiness of those He has created; and since without virtue men can have no happiness in this world, I firmly believe He delights to see me virtuous, because He is pleased when He sees me happy. . . .
>
> I love Him, therefore, for His goodness, and I adore Him for His wisdom. Let me, then, not fail to praise my God continually, for it is His due, and it is all I can return for His many favors and great goodness to me; and let me resolve to be virtuous, that I may be happy, that I may please Him who is delighted to see me happy.[12]

It is a rather simple line of thinking: God wants us to be happy. The only way we can be happy is to be virtuous. If we are virtuous, we will be happy, and God will be pleased. Ben once additionally stated, "For my own part, when I am employed in serving others, I do not look upon myself as conferring favors, but as paying debts."[13]

Benjamin Franklin's quest for bettering himself was an integral part of his life. From his autobiography, in his own words, he explains why he began his plan for moral perfection:

> It was about this time [1728] that I conceiv'd the bold and arduous project of arriving at moral perfection. I wish'd to live without committing any fault at any time; I would conquer all that either natural inclination, custom, or company might lead me into. As I knew, or thought I knew, what was right and wrong, I did not see why I might not always do the one and avoid the other.[14]

Early in his life, in order to facilitate his "plan," Ben prepared a notebook that he carried around with him. In this notebook, he made seven columns—one for each day of the week. Then he listed in a row his 13 virtues. At the end of the day, Franklin would put a little black spot in that day's column for every fault which he had committed against the virtue upon which he was working. He had a different page for each week, and each week he would diligently strive to perfect one virtue . . . then he would move on to the next one. This was his plan for progressing, for improving himself, for capturing a particular characteristic and virtue until he could almost master all of them.

Form of the Pages
This example is for the week Benjamin worked on Temperence.

TEMPERENCE
Eat not to dullness; drink not to elevation.

	Sunday	Monday	Tuesday	Wednesday	Thursday	Friday	Saturday
Tem.							
Sil.	●	●		●		●	
Ord.	●	●			●	●	●
Res.		●				●	
Fru.		●				●	
Ind.			●				
Sinc.							
Jus.							
Mod.							
Clea.							
Tran.							
Chas.							
Hum.							

The following is Benjamin Franklin's list of virtues as recorded in his autobiography, with an anecdote from his own life about each virtue.

1. TEMPERANCE: Eat not to dullness. Drink not to elevation.

During his stay in England, Franklin enjoyed some time in Scotland with Lord Kames, a Scottish jurist. On one occasion, Ben and his son, William, joined the Kames for a long visit at their home. Ben enjoyed the company of his host. They exchanged stories, tall tales, and tried a few practical jokes on each other. They also sampled much of the Kames wine cellar. One evening, as they were working on finishing one bottle of wine, Lady Kames shot her husband a dark look of disapproval. Franklin noticed and remarked that the world would be much better off if it followed the Bible's teaching on tolerance.

Kames, a trained Presbyterian, demanded to know what passage in the Good Book taught tolerance. If anything, the Bible taught intolerance. Franklin asked for a Bible, assuring Kames that he would find the passage in a moment. A Bible was produced, Franklin flipped the pages for a minute, and then gave a satisfied exclamation and began to read:

> 1. And it came to pass after these Things, that Abraham sat in the Door of his Tent, about the going down of the Sun.
>
> 2. And behold a Man, bowed with Age, came from the Way of the Wilderness, leaning on a Staff.
>
> 3. And Abraham arose and met him, and said unto him, Turn in, I pray thee, and wash thy Feet, and tarry all Night, and thou shalt arise early on the Morrow, and go thy Way.
>
> 4. And the Man said, Nay, for I will abide under this Tree.
>
> 5. But Abraham pressed him greatly; so he turned, and they went into the Tent; and Abraham baked unleavened Bread, and they did eat.
>
> 6. And when Abraham saw that the Man blessed not God, he said unto him, Wherefore dost thou not worship the most high God, Creator of Heaven and Earth?
>
> 7. And the Man answered and said, I do not worship the God thou speakest of; neither do I call upon his Name; for I have made to myself a God, which abideth alway in mine house and provideth me with all Things.

In the same carefully cadenced Biblical prose, the story told how Abraham, in a fit of righteousness, drove the old man out of his house. For this he was sternly rebuked by God, and warned that his seed would be afflicted "Four hundred years in a strange land."

Kames jaw sagged. Lady Kames looked bewildered. They thought, as good Presbyterians, that they knew their Bible. Yet not a word of the story that Franklin had just read to them was familiar. So they asked from what book of the Bible he was reading.

Ben's son William had been sitting quietly to one side, and now his eyes met his father's and they both burst out laughing. Franklin himself had written this parable on persecution, imitating the style of the Good Book, and then committed it to memory. Whenever he felt someone was too dogmatic in his religious opinions, or too pretentious in his knowledge of the scriptures, Franklin treated him to this little performance.

Franklin and Kames both enjoyed their times together. Back in London, Franklin told Kames: "On the whole . . . I think the time we spent [in Scotland] was six weeks of the densest happiness I have met with in any part of my life."[15]

2. SILENCE: Speak not but what may benefit others or yourself; avoid trifling conversation. Seek not to dispute or contend.

Ben first applied this virtue in his editorial letters from "Silence Dogood," in which he desired to benefit others without causing any contention. He was wary of the possible repercussions accompanying undue disputes or contention. He once observed:

> [Gouverneur Morris] had been brought up to it from a boy, His father, . . . accustoming his children to dispute with one another for his diversion, while sitting at table after dinner; but I think the practice was not wise; for, in the course of my observation, these disputing,

> contradicting, and confuting people are generally unfortunate in their affairs. They get victory sometimes, but they never get good will, which would be more use to them.[16]

Ben made these comments about his own experience in battling with words:

> There was another bookish lad in the town, John Collins by name, with whom I was intimately acquainted. We sometimes disputed, and very fond we were of argument, . . . [but] it is apt to become a very bad habit. . . . Besides souring and spoiling the conversation, it is productive of disgusts and perhaps enmities where you may have occasion for friendship. . . . Persons of good sense, I have since observed, seldom fall into it, except lawyers [and] university men . . .[17]

Franklin would rather reason things out than dispute and contend. He did not like to hurt anyone or anything. Franklin's noncombative nature helps explain his relationship with others. He generally avoided hostilities; rather than insisting on the menu he preferred, he withdrew from the table of battle.

3. ORDER: Let all your things have their places; let each part of your business have its time.

Perfecting this character trait gave Ben the most trouble. He was well aware that this trait was critically necessary in running a business, or the business could take control of the owner's time. Even though Ben had an exceeding good memory that enabled him to easily recall where he should be or exactly where he left an item, his concentration in his attempts at perfecting this virtue cost him so much painful attention that he almost gave it up. He was willing to have a faulty character in this one area.

Working towards perfecting this character trait reminded Ben of the man who went to buy an ax. He desired the whole surface to be as bright as the highly polished edge. The smith said he would be glad to polish the whole surface of the ax if only the man would turn the grinding wheel.

The man turned the wheel, and the smith pressed heavily on the stone. This pressure made it difficult to turn the wheel and the man quickly grew weary. He stopped once in a while to see how bright it was becoming. Finally, the man pronounced that he'd take the ax now—as it was—with no further grinding.

The smith replied, "No, turn on, turn on; we shall have it bright by and by; as yet, it is only speckled."

"Yes," observed the man, "But I think I like a speckled ax best."[18]

In this virtue, Benjamin Franklin experienced the frustration of the struggle for perfection, and so he chose the "speckled ax." He concluded (or maybe rationalized), ". . . a perfect character might be attended with the inconvenience of being envied and hated; and that a benevolent man should allow a few faults in himself, to keep his friends in countenance."[19]

4. RESOLUTION: Resolve to perform what you ought; perform without fail what you resolve.

"[Ralph Watson] and I had made a serious agreement, that the one who happened first to die should, if possible, make a friendly visit to the other, and acquaint him how he found things in that separate state. But he never fulfill'd his promise."[20]

Franklin resolved to always fulfill his promises and perform his duties. As deputy postmaster general, Franklin was often required to travel. Traveling was a difficult matter in the 1750's. Bad weather created rutted, muddy, or dusty roads. Rivers had to be forded or ferried. A sparsity of taverns and inns insured overcrowding and discomfort. But in spite of the difficulties involved, Franklin resolved to fulfill the duties of the job. On one of his trips, he stopped at a Rhode Island inn on a cold, blustery, rainy day. When he walked in, he observed two dozen locals and travelers crowding around the room's only fire.

"Boy," said Franklin to the innkeeper's son, "get my horse a quart of oysters."

"A quart of oysters?" gasped the boy.

"You heard me, a quart of oysters," Franklin boomed.

The boy obeyed, and there was a general stampede out the door to see this incredible horse who ate oysters. The horse snorted and snuffled in indignation and refused to have anything to do with the oysters. Baffled, the curiosity seekers trooped back into the tavern, to find Deputy Postmaster General Franklin sitting comfortably in the chair nearest the fire.[21]

5. FRUGALITY: Make no expense but to do good to others or yourself; that is, waste nothing.

Benjamin Franklin wrote in *Poor Richard's Almanac*: "A penny saved is a penny earned." Ben was about seven years old when he experienced his first lesson on the value of money. At that time, some visitors to his father's house gave him ten pennies. A few hours later, he came upon another boy playing with a whistle. Charmed with the sound, Ben gave the boy all his pennies for the whistle.

When his older brothers and sisters heard him blowing on his whistle, they asked him where he got it, so he told them about his purchase. They laughed at him and informed him that he could buy that same whistle for only two pennies. Instantly the whistle lost all its charm. When Ben thought of what he could have bought with the rest of the pennies, and as he heard his family laugh, he cried with vexation.

He never forgot the experience, and as he grew older, whenever he was tempted to buy something, he would stop and remind himself not to "give too much for the whistle." Gradually, the memory generalized to an even broader principle. When Ben saw a man too fond of political popularity, neglecting his own affairs, and ruining himself, he would say: "He pays too much for his whistle." If he saw a miser who spent all his money for life's comforts, and, for the sake of accumulating wealth, lost the pleasure of doing good to others, he drew the same conclusion: "Poor man, you pay too much for your whistle." When he met a man of pleasure who ignored all opportunities to improve his mind or his fortune, abandoning himself to sensuality, again the childhood voice would say, "You pay too much for your whistle."

"In short, I conceived that the great part of the miseries of mankind," Franklin said, "were brought upon them by the false estimates they had made of the value of things, and by their giving too much for the whistle."

In Franklin's opinion, one of the greatest vices was the "pursuit of wealth to no purpose." He felt that once a man had accumulated enough money to assure himself and his family of independence and comfort, a good citizen should turn his hand to public service.[22]

6. INDUSTRY: Lose no time; be always employed in something useful; cut off all unnecessary actions.

Franklin was a well-rounded citizen of the world. In an age when it was possible to become a master of more than one discipline, Ben surpassed all his contemporaries. He became a superb athlete and a proficient swimmer. He was so strong that as a young man he could carry two forms of type, one in each hand, when most carried but one in both hands. He was second to none as a statesman. He was the oldest by a whole generation of the Founding Fathers, and in some respects he was the most radical, the most devious, and the most complicated. He proved to be a talented printer, and an enterprising newspaper editor and publisher. He was a tireless promoter of cultural institutions. He was America's first great scientist, whose book on electricity turned out to be the most influential volume to come out of America in the 18th century.

He often used his discoveries to mystify and entertain others. Once, strolling with friends through the park, he declared that his study of science had given him powers which he seldom revealed. For instance, he said, pointing to a nearby stream, where a brisk breeze was causing a good deal of turbulence, he had learned how to calm storm-tossed waters. The friends wanted a demonstration, so he left them and went to the edge of the stream and made a series of magical passes over it with his cane. Suddenly, to the disbelieving eyes of his friends, the surface of the water became as smooth and glassy as a sheltered puddle. The friends rushed to the bank but saw nothing to explain the miracle. One of them was convinced Franklin had supernatural powers.

After letting his friends rack their brains for an hour or two, Franklin smilingly revealed his secret. In the hollow bottom of his cane, he carried a small vial of oil. He had been experimenting for two years on calming water by pouring oil on it. It hadn't worked on the ocean, as he had hoped, but it did work on smaller bodies of water.[23]

During the War for Independence, Franklin was a Minister to France. He knew the British were spying on him, and he used that knowledge against them. Because of his experiments with electricity and other things, Franklin was world famous as an inventor and scientist. He left clues that he was turning his genius to making war machines. Soon, London learned that he had set up giant mirrors on the French coast to reflect the sun's rays across the English Channel to burn the British fleet in its harbors. Other spies reported that he'd invented a huge chain connected to an electrical machine to be stretched from France to England. When the machine was turned on, the chain would electrocute the whole island. Today, we know these ideas were nonsense, but they made the British waste time and money trying to find out more about nothing.[24]

Franklin was also a master at issuing false news stories that couldn't be traced to him. He once used the name of a New England militia captain to write a letter describing the capture of a shipment of scalps. These scalps had been sent by the Seneca Indians to the British in Canada. "The packages contained 954 salted scalps of 'American' men, women and children. Each scalp was elaborately marked with symbols indicating the age and sex of the person, where they were killed, and how." The letter appeared in newspapers throughout Europe, shocking people at the cruelty of Britain's "savage" allies.[25]

7. SINCERITY: Use no hurtful deceit; think innocently and justly, and if you speak, speak accordingly.

Franklin wrote a little work for the benefit of youth, titled, *The Art of Virtue*. In it, he proposed that one of the principles for happiness is truth and honesty. He remarked elsewhere, "If the rascals knew the advantage of virtue, they would become honest men out of rascality." For himself, speaking the truth served admirably. "That is my only cunning."[26]

While in France, Franklin was bombarded with appeals for interviews and letters of recommendation. His old friend Jacques Barbeu' Duborg would often send total strangers to Ben for a letter of recommendation they could take with them to America. Finally, Franklin could stand it no longer and spoke his mind with undiplomatic bluntness:

> These applications are my perpetual torment. . . . Officers in all ranks, in all departments; ladies great and small . . . worry me from morning to night. The noise of every coach now that enters my court terrifies me. I am afraid to accept an invitation to dine. . . . If therefore, you have the least remaining kindness for me, if you would not help to drive me out of France . . . my dear friend, let this your twenty-third application be your last.

As usual, Franklin kept his sanity by seeing the funny side of the situation. Not long after Duborg's twenty-third application, he wrote out this "Model of a Letter of Recommendation of a Person You are Unacquainted With:"

> *The bearer of this, who is going to America, presses me to give him a letter of recommendation, tho' I know nothing of him, not even his name. This may seem extraordinary, but I assure you it is not uncommon here. Sometimes indeed, one unknown person brings another equally unknown, to recommend him; and sometimes they recommend one another! As for this gentleman, I must refer you to himself for his character and merits, with which he is certainly better acquainted than I can possibly be. I recommend him however to those civilities which every stranger of whom one knows no harm has a right to; and I request you will do him all the good offices and show him all the favour that, on further acquaintance, you shall find him to deserve.*[27]

8. JUSTICE: Wrong none by doing injuries, or omitting the benefits that are your duty.

After Bunker Hill, Franklin had no doubt whatsoever that all-out war had begun. It was time to form a nation out of the13 colonies. Franklin was ideally suited to draft the master plan. A full year before Congress took the step, Franklin had written his own Declaration of Independence. Since he was the elder statesman, and because of his vast experience as writer, editor, and publisher, and also as civic leader, he was the likely choice to draft the document. And he was on the committee to do so. He probably would have been chosen, except that his son, William, had remained loyal to the crown during all the hostilities, and Franklin's bluntness verged on rudeness.

Jefferson's inspired prose seems the better choice when compared to the scathing language used by Franklin:

> Whereas the British nation, through great corruption of manners and extreme dissipation and profusion, both private and public, have found all honest resources insufficient to supply their excessive luxury and prodigality, and thereby have been driven to the practice of every injustice, which avarice could dictate or rapacity execute; . . . and, grudging us the peaceable enjoyment of the fruits of our hard labour and virtuous industry, have for years past been endeavoring to extort the same from us. . . . And whereas, impatient to seize the whole, they have at length proceeded to open robbery . . . and have even dared . . . to declare, that all the spoilings, thefts, burnings of houses and towns, and murders of innocent people . . . were just actions, and shall be so deemed, contrary to several of the commandments of God (which by this Act they presume to repeal).[28]

9. MODERATION: Avoid extremes; forbear resenting injuries so much as you think they deserve.

Ben practiced moderation in all his habits, including his eating. His ability to reason helped him to solve most problems with moderation. Even his abandonment of the faddish vegetarian diet shows his pride in rational decisions. On a voyage from Boston to Philadelphia, his ship became "becalmed." The crew used the time to fish for cod. As the fish were opened, he saw that smaller fish came out of the stomachs of the larger cod. "Then, thought I, if you eat one another, I don't see why we mayn't eat you." He then enjoyed a meal of fresh cod, and returned to a normal diet.[29] Franklin added this comment: "So convenient a thing it is to be a reasonable creature, since it enables one to find or make a reason for everything one has a mind to do."

Except as expressed in his own Declaration of Independence, Franklin favored avoiding "resenting injuries so much as you think they deserve." Franklin sought nearly always to avoid conflicts with others. He said:

> *I made it a rule to forbear all direct contradictions to the sentiments of others, and all positive assertion of my own.* I even forbid myself, agreeably to the old laws of our Junto, the use of every word or expression in the language that imported a fixed opinion, such as *certainly*, *undoubtedly*, etc., and I adopted, instead of them, *I conceive, I apprehend, or I imagine* a thing to be so or so; *or it so appears to me at present.* When another asserted something that I thought an error, I denied myself the pleasure of contradicting him abruptly, and of showing immediately some absurdity in his proposition; and in answering I began by observing that in certain cases or circumstances his opinion would be right, but in the present case there appeared or seemed to me

> some difference. *I soon found the advantage of this change in my manner; the conversations I engaged in went on more pleasantly. The modest way in which I proposed my opinions procured them a readier reception and less contradiction; I had less mortification when I was found to be in the wrong, and I more easily prevailed with others to give up their mistakes and join with me when I happened to be in the right.*
>
> And this mode, which I at first put on with some violence to natural inclination, became at length so easy, and so habitual to me, that perhaps for these 50 years past no one has ever heard a dogmatical expression escape me. And to this habit (after my character of integrity) I think it principally owing that I had early so much weight with my fellow citizens when I proposed new institutions, or alterations in the old, and so much influence in public councils when I became a member; for I was but a bad speaker, never eloquent, subject to much hesitation in my choice of words, hardly correct in language, yet I generally carried my points.[30]

10. CLEANLINESS: Tolerate no uncleanliness in body, clothes or habitation.

Franklin had a habit of engaging in a daily "air bath." A French admirer of Franklin's, Jacques Barbeu' Duborg, had advised Franklin of a new and novel method for treating smallpox that involved cold baths. In his response to Mr. Duborg, Franklin wrote on July 28, 1768, "I have found it much more agreeable to my constitution to bathe in another element, I mean cold air. With this view I rise early almost every morning, and sit in my chamber without any clothes whatever, half an hour or an hour, according to the season, either reading or writing. This practice is not in the least painful, but on the contrary, agreeable." So Franklin arose, opened all the windows in his room, and sat around for an hour or so in the altogether. Not even winter weather discouraged him.[31]

He frequently recommended the practice to other people, and explained to John Adams that this practice was the reason he rarely caught a cold. John Adams, though, couldn't quite adapt to it. In September of 1776, at the request of General Lord William Howe, Adams and Franklin were sent by Congress to meet with General Howe for a conference at Staten Island. They were to discuss the position of the United States regarding independence. The journey from Philadelphia took two days. At New Brunswick, the inn was so full that Adams and Franklin had to not only share a room, but also sleep in the same bed. The room had only one small window. Before turning in, Adams started to close the window against the cold night air. Franklin objected, complaining they would both suffocate.

> Contrary to convention, Franklin believed in the benefits of fresh air at night and had published his theories on the question. "People often catch cold from one another when shut up together in small close rooms," he had written, stressing "it is the frowzy corrupt air from animal substances, and the perspired matter from our bodies, which, being long confined in beds not lately used, and clothes not lately worn . . . obtains that kind of putridity which infects us, and occasions the cold observed upon sleeping in, wearing, or turning over, such beds [and] clothes." He wished to have the window remain open, Franklin informed Adams.
>
> "I answered that I was afraid of the evening air," Adams would write, recounting the memorable scene. Dr. Franklin replied, "The air within this chamber will soon be, and indeed is now worse than that without doors. Come, open the window and come to bed, and I will convince you. I believe you are not acquainted with my theory of colds."

Adams assured Franklin he had read his theories; they did not match his own experience, Adams said, but he would be glad to hear them again.

So the two eminent bedfellows lay side-by-side in the dark, the window open, Franklin expounding, as Adams remembered, "upon air and cold and respiration and perspiration, with which I was so much amused that I soon fell asleep."[32]

Dr. Franklin's penchant for air baths was one reason that Thomas Jefferson did not like to travel with or share a room with Benjamin Franklin.

11. TRANQUILITY: Be not disturbed at trifles, or at accidents common or unavoidable.

Ben never allowed himself to get upset over trifles. In fact, even when major problems were imminent, he rarely became disturbed. He believed that things would usually work out for the best.

> "The malice of our adversaries I am well acquainted with," [he wrote to a friend, Samuel Rhodes, July 8, 1765, who had just been defeated for an Assembly election] "But hitherto it has been harmless, all their arrows shot against us have been like those that Rabelais speaks of which were headed with butter hardened in the sun. As long as I have known the world I have observed that wrong is always growing more wrong, till there is no bearing, and that right, however opposed, comes [out] right at last."[33]

Ben also had advice for those who sought to stir up trouble during the Stamp Act crisis:

> Instead of raving (with your correspondent of yesterday) against the Americans as "diggers of pits for this country," "lunatics," "sworn enemies," "false,"

> "ungrateful," "cut-throats," &c. which is a treatment of customers that I doubt is not like to bring them back to our shop, . . . I would recommend to all writers on American affairs (however *hard* their *arguments* may be) *soft words*, civility, and good manners.[34]

12. CHASTITY: Rarely use venery [35] but for health or offspring, never to dullness, weakness, or the injury of your own or another's peace or reputation.

Many spurious accounts have been written about the supposed illegitimate children of Benjamin Franklin. Such claims have become increasingly popular in recent years, even creeping into textbooks. One story claims as many as thirteen.

> The first child to enter the Franklin family was William, apparently born in the spring of 1731. He is commonly said to have been illegitimate—at least most historians think so, although "the only evidence that has been cited is that 'everybody knew it.'" The identity of William's mother has long been debated by the scholars; many believe that Deborah conceived the child before she assumed the name of Mrs. Franklin, but that Benjamin took "all the blame" himself in order to "save Deborah's honor." In any event William was welcomed into the Franklin household and was reared and educated as the legitimate son. He later became the governor of New Jersey.[36]

His relationship, or lack of one, with William, was the one major disappointment of Benjamin Franklin's life. William wanted to make sure his political aspirations weren't affected by his famous father's reputation. In 1774, William pledged to the British Secretary of State for American affairs that "no attachments or connections shall ever make me swerve from the duty of my station."[37] The gulf between Benjamin and William continued to widen. William remained a loyalist and left the United States for England—even after his father had helped produce the Declaration of Independence. In 1784, after the Revolutionary War was over, William wrote to his father, hoping to resume their relationship as it had been before the war. Obviously still brokenhearted, Benjamin wrote back:

> I received your letter of the 22nd past, and am glad to find that you desire to revive the affectionate intercourse that formerly existed between us. It will be very agreeable to me. Nothing has ever hurt me so much and affected me with such keen sensations as to find myself deserted in my old age by my only son; and not only deserted, but to find him taking up arms against me, in a cause wherein my good fame, fortune and life were all at stake.
>
> You conceived, you say, that your duty to your King and regard for your country required this. I ought not to blame you for differing in sentiment with me in public affairs. We are men, all subject to errors. Our opinions are not in our own power; they are formed and governed much by circumstances that are often as inexplicable as they are irresistible. Your situation was such that few would have censured your remaining neuter, *though there are natural duties which precede political ones, and cannot be extinguished by them.*

Franklin underlined these last words, which went to the heart of the issue—and to the heart of Franklin himself. They never did resume a father-son relationship.[38] Franklin noted that nothing had ever hurt him so much as having his son remain a loyalist. But his faith in the people never wavered.

13. HUMILITY: Imitate Jesus and Socrates.

Franklin originally listed only twelve virtues, but was soon compelled to add another:

> My list of virtues contain'd at first but twelve; but a Quaker friend having kindly informed me that I was generally thought proud; that my pride show'd itself frequently in conversation; that I was not content with being in the right when discussing any point, but was overbearing, and rather insolent, of which he convinc'd me by mentioning several instances; I determined endeavoring to cure myself, if I could, of this vice or folly among the rest, and I added *Humility* to my list.[39]

About his success with this virtue, he adds, "I cannot boast of much success in acquiring the reality of this virtue, but I had a good deal with regard to the appearance of it." And then he adds this morsel about pride:

> In reality, there is, perhaps, no one of our natural passions so hard to subdue as pride. Disguise it, struggle with it, beat it down, stifle it, mortify it as much as one pleases, it is still alive, and will every now and then peep out and show itself; you will see it, perhaps often in this history [speaking about his autobiography]; for, even if I could conceive that I had completely overcome it, I should probably be proud of my humility.[40]

It must have been nearly impossible for Franklin to retain any semblance of humility in light of the constant recognition he received. Consider, for example, this paragraph from his friend George Washington:

> If to be venerated for benevolence, if to be admired for talents, if to be esteemed for patriotism, if to be beloved for philanthropy can gratify the human mind, you must have the pleasing consolation to know that you have not lived in vain. And I flatter myself that it will not be ranked among the least grateful occurrences of your life to be assured that, so long as I retain my memory, you will be

recollected with respect, veneration, and affection by your sincere friend, George Washington.[41]

Benjamin Franklin's list of virtues is an amazing tribute to his own attempt at striving to be a better person. He himself acknowledged that when he started out on his project for arriving at moral perfection, he was "surpris'd to find myself so much fuller of faults than I had imagined; but I had the satisfaction of seeing them diminish."[42]

At first, Franklin worked through the entire plan at least four times a year. Then one course in a year, then once through the list in several years. He always carried his little book with him. To avoid having to replace the pages each time he completed a course, he eventually began to use pages made of ivory, already imprinted with indelible red lines. He marked his mistakes with a lead pencil, which marks could easily be removed with a wet sponge. A remarkable, simple little plan of self-improvement created by one of the most remarkable men to ever walk the earth.

About three years before his death, Benjamin Franklin participated in yet another critical American experience. He attended the Constitutional Convention. At 81, he was the oldest person in audience . . . but one of the most venerated. His wisdom and wit were legendary. Often in great pain, he sometimes had to be carried to Independence Hall in a sedan chair. But he came. And his thinking was clear, his insights important, and his influence invaluable.

Franklin humbly asked the assembly to consider prayer as a means to facilitate better communication among them. The picture is a stirring one: long white hair outlining the sides of his bald head, slightly crippled, in knee breeches, eloquently imploring:

> Mr. President, [he said, after days of bickering over the principles of the new constitution at the Constitutional Convention], The small progress we have made is, methinks, a melancholy proof of the imperfection of the human understanding. . . . In this situation of this assembly, groping . . . in the dark to find political truth, and scarce able to distinguish it when presented to us, how has it happened, Sir, that we have not hitherto once thought of humbly applying to the Father of Lights to illuminate our understandings? In the beginning of the contest with Britain, when we were sensible of danger, we had daily prayers in this room for the divine protection. Our prayers, Sir, were heard—and they were graciously answered. . . .
>
> I have lived, Sir, a long time; and the longer I live, the more convincing proofs I see of this truth, that *God governs in the affairs of men.* And if a sparrow cannot fall to the ground without his notice, is it probable that an empire can rise without his aid?
>
> I therefore beg leave to move that, henceforth, prayers imploring the assistance of heaven and its blessings on our deliberations be held in this assembly every morning before we proceed to business . . .[43]

During the Convention, there was much debate on many issues. As the men in that room penned the words of the Constitution, the Spirit breathed life into it. None of them could realize the magnificence of what they had created under Divine directive. As the Convention drew to a close, Benjamin Franklin made one of the most important speeches of his life as he encouraged all present to sign along with him. Because of the deep regard that nearly everyone had for him, Franklin's words were listened to with deep respect. His humility was obvious, his sincerity beyond doubt when he uttered:

> I confess that I do not entirely approve of this constitution at present. But, Sir, I am not sure I shall never approve it; for, having lived long, I have experienced many instances of being obliged, by better information or fuller consideration, to change my opinions even on important subjects, which I thought right but found to be otherwise. It is therefore that, the older I grow, the more apt I am to doubt my own judgment. . . .
>
> Thus I consent, Sir, to this Constitution, because I expect no better and because I am not sure that it is not the best. . . .
>
> On the whole, Sir, I cannot help expressing a wish that every member of the convention who may still have objections to it would, with me, on this occasion doubt a little of his own infallibility and, to make manifest our unanimity, put his name to the instrument.[44]

It is possible that without Benjamin Franklin's inspired speech, and his timely display of humility, an agreement would never have been reached.

After the draft of the Constitution had been accepted, Ben Franklin came forward to sign. He had been looking at the back of the chair in which George Washington had presided over the proceedings. On that chair was a carving of half of a sun. "I have . . . often and often in the course of the session . . . looked at that [sun] behind the president without being able to tell whether it was rising or setting. But now at length I have the happiness to know that it is a rising and not a setting sun." Ben was helped forward to sign, and he wept as he signed it.[45]

Amazingly, participating in the Constitutional Convention was not Franklin's last act of public service. The man truly did live by his sixth virtue, *Industry: Lose no time; be always employed in something useful.* Besides attending the Convention in 1787, that same year he was elected president of America's first anti-slavery society. Signing an appeal to Congress to abolish slavery was his last public act. Years earlier he had penned these powerful words that seemed to come alive with his gift of expression and so aptly declared the message of anti-slavery, of freedom for all: "God grant," he said in writing to a friend, "that not only the love of liberty but a thorough knowledge of the right of man may pervade all the nations of the earth, so that a philosopher may set his foot anywhere on its surface and say, 'This is my country.'"[46]

Early in April, 1790, Franklin complained of a pain in his chest which endured for at least ten agonizing days. Then it subsided long enough for him to arise and let his daughter Sally make the bed up fresh for him so that he might "die in a decent manner." When Sally avowed she was praying that he would get well and live for many more years, Franklin quietly replied, "I hope not."[47]

A few hours later an abscess in his lungs burst, and it became more difficult for him to breathe. At eleven o'clock in the evening on April 17, 1790, at the age of 84, he passed quietly into history. The largest crowd yet assembled in America, more than 20,000 mourners, paid tribute to their beloved Benjamin Franklin—printer, editor, publisher, inventor, civic leader, Governor, statesman, and Founding Father of a new nation.

As a young man, Franklin had prepared an epitaph for himself:

The body of
B. Franklin, printer
(Like the cover of an old book,
Its contents torn out
And stripped of its lettering and gilding),

Lies here, food for worms.
But the work shall not be lost;
For it will (as he believed) appear once more
In a new and more elegant edition,
Revised and corrected
By the Author.[48]

Even upon his death, Benjamin Franklin did not quit serving others. Among other directives in his will, he left 2,000 pounds (the dollar didn't become the official currency until 1792) to the cities of Philadelphia and Boston, and to the states of Pennsylvania and Massachusetts. This money came from his tenure as President of the Commonwealth of Pennsylvania. Franklin had refused to accept his salary because he didn't believe that public servants should be paid for their service.

The funds were not to be finally distributed until the 200th anniversary of his death. He figured that at the end of the second century, each fund should total more than 4,000,000 pounds. Franklin decreed that the Boston fund should then be divided one-fourth to the city of Boston, and the remainder to the state of Massachusetts. The Philadelphia fund should be similarly split between Philadelphia and the state of Pennsylvania. "At the bicentennial of his death the Boston fund amounted to $4.5 million, and that of Philadelphia, which had been less well managed, $2 million."[49] Franklin became the quintessential example of his own, now-famous maxim. His "pennies saved" were worth in excess of $6.5 million. These funds were distributed to the proper cities and states in 1991.

Benjamin Franklin—inventor, scientist, statesman, diplomat, Governor, public servant, philosopher, humorist, economist, printer, editor, publisher, writer, and even musician. ". . . the greatest man and ornament of the age and country in which he lived." "Mind and will, talent and art, strength and ease, wit and grace met in him as if nature had been lavish and happy when he was shaped." Yet perhaps beyond all of this, perhaps even greater than his greatest accomplishments and discoveries and inventions, was the simple plan of action Benjamin Franklin created for his own self-improvement. He took seriously, as few other mortals have, the words of the Savior: "Be ye therefore perfect, even as your Father which is in Heaven is perfect."[50] That is what Benjamin Franklin tried to do with his "Project of Arriving at Moral Perfection." A brilliant lesson, an outstanding example for all of us. "Be ye therefore perfect." And, perhaps, his burning desire to obey that commandment is the key to much of his success.

Chapter 2

George Washington

February 22, 1732 – December 14, 1799

GEORGE WASHINGTON

On a cold February day in 1732,[1] an infant son is born to Mary and Augustine Washington . . . and the world is forever changed. This newborn bundle of joy is arguably the most important figure that is ever to grace the Americas, certainly the critical figure of the 1700's. One biographer justly stated:

> The story of [George Washington's] life is the story of the founding of America. His was the dominant personality in three of the most critical events in that founding: the Revolutionary War, the Constitutional Convention, and the first national administration. Had he not served as America's leader in those three events, all three would likely have failed. And America, as we know it today, would not exist.[2]

Early Years

George Washington was born into a family whose ancestors had lived in America for some 75 years, a considerable duration in the year 1732. His great-grandfather, John Washington, had landed in Virginia in 1657, the first of the Washington family to live in America. John's son, Lawrence, was George's grandfather. George's father was Augustine. George Washington was a fourth-generation American.

Augustine Washington's disposition was mild and his character was without reproach, but his frame was large and his strength was widely known. George inherited his father's large frame and strength. Thankfully, George learned to emulate his father's character. The Reverend Mason Locke "Parson" Weems, a biographer and storyteller, recorded the following powerful words that George's father recited to him before he was six years old:

> Truth, George, is the loveliest quality of youth. I would ride fifty miles, my son, to see the little boy whose heart is so honest and his lips so pure, that we may depend on every word he says. . . . But oh, how different, George, is the case with the boy who is so given to lying that nobody can believe a word he says. He's looked at with aversion wherever he goes. . . . Oh, George! my son! rather than see you come to this pass, dear as you are to my heart, gladly would I assist to nail you up in your little coffin and follow you to your grave. Hard, indeed, would it be to me to give up my son, whose little feet are always so ready to run about with me, and whose . . . sweet prattle makes so large a part of my happiness. But still, I would give him up, rather than see him a common liar.[3]

After that masterful message to his son, it is indeed easy to believe the famous story of George Washington and the cherry tree. It was first told by Reverend Mason Weems. While we can't confirm or deny the story in fact, Weems did sit at George Washington's table for many a dinner. Since he had first-hand knowledge of Washington, it is possible that Weems' version of the incident is true (although it has been embellished by others). It occurred when George was only six or seven years old. On this particular day, Augustine Washington was making a trip into town. George had resolved to get his chores done quickly so that he might be permitted to ride into town with his father. One of his tasks was to restock the woodpile. But George did not complete the chore in time and was not allowed to accompany his father. Augustine left without him.

George had a little temper which he had not yet learned to control. When his father left for town, the hatchet was still in George's hand. In frustration, George struck out at the nearest available target: a cherry tree which his father had recently planted near the kitchen door.

Upon arriving home from his trip, Augustine put his horse in the stable and walked toward the house. When he saw the cherry tree, he called his son. "George, do you know anything about what has been done to this tree?"

The reply was hardly audible, "Yes, father. I can't tell a lie, Pa, I did cut it with my hatchet." As Augustine believed in swift and certain punishment, it is likely that there was a trip to the woodshed . . . not just the embrace that some of the storytellers would include in the tale. After the discipline, big, softhearted Augustine was completely undone and welcomed the repentant youth back into his arms.[4]

Besides his father, George experienced another incredibly influential teacher in his life. A most unusual one. This "teacher" was a list titled "110 Rules of Civility and Decent Behavior in Company and Conversation." In 1745 George was attending school at Fredericksburg, Virginia, and his teacher was a native of France. George spent hours of his youth practicing penmanship by transcribing this list of rules from dictation in his school exercise book. These maxims are recognized as rules from an old Jesuit College in France. This practice served several purposes. It improved penmanship, while at the same time, polished manners, impressed moral virtues, taught how to treat others in social situations, and inculcated self-control. These rules, these maxims, were so unmistakably exemplified in George Washington's life that biographers have regarded them as a formative influence in the development of his character. Here are 24 of them with spelling and punctuation as written in George's "Copy-book":[5]

1. Every Action done in Company ought to be with Some Sign of Respect, to those that are Present.
2. In the Presence of Others sing not to yourself with a humming Noise, nor Drum, with your Fingers or Feet.
3. Sleep not when others Speak, Sit not when others stand, Speak not when you should hold your Peace, walk not when others Stop.
4. At Play and at Fire its Good manners to give Place to the last Commer, and not affect to Speak Louder than ordenary.
5. Read no Letters, Books, or Papers in Company but when there is a Necessity for the doing of it you must ask leave: come not near the Books or Writings of Another so as to read them unless desired or give your opinion of them unask'd also look not nigh when another is writing a Letter.
6. Shew not yourself glad at the Misfortune of another tho he be your enemy.
7. Superfluous Complements and all Affectation of Ceremony are to be avoided, yet where due they are not to be Neglected.

8. Strive not with your Superiers in argument, but always Submit your Judgment to others with Modesty.
9. Use no Reproachfull Language against any one neither Curse nor Revile.
10. Associate yourself with Men of good Quality if you Esteem your own Reputation; for 'tis better to be alone than in bad Company.
11. Speak not injurious Words neither in Jest nor Earnest.
12. Be not apt to relate News if you know not the truth thereof.
13. Undertake not what you cannot Perform but be Carefull to keep your Promise.
14. Speak not Evil of the absent for it is unjust.
15. When you Speak of God or his Attributes, let it be Seriously & with Reverence.
16. Honour & obey your Natural Parent Altho they be Poor.
17. Labour to keep alive in your Breast the Little Spark of Celestial fire called Conscience.
18. Let your Countenance be pleasant, but in Serious Matters Somewhat grave.
19. Do not laugh too much or too loud in public.
20. Take all admonitions thankfully in what time or place soever given, but afterwards, not being culpable, take a time & place convenient to let him know it that gave them.

21. Think before you speak; pronounce not imperfectly nor bring out your words too hastily, but orderly & distinctly.
22. When your superiors talk to any body, hearken not neither speak nor laugh.
23. Put not your meat to your mouth with your knife in your hand; neither spit forth the stones of any fruit pie upon a dish nor cast anything under the table.
24. If others talk at the table, be attentive; but talk not with meat in your mouth.

Undoubtedly, these "110 Rules of Civility and Decent Behavior in Company and Conversation" had a profound impact upon the life of George Washington.

On April 11, 1743, when George was 11 years of age, he was away from home, playing with some of his friends. Suddenly, a messenger arrived and announced that George was to return home immediately; his father was very ill and anxious for him to come. When George arrived home, he found his father in bed—in great pain. The doctors had diagnosed Augustine's sickness as "gout of the stomach."[6] It proved fatal. Shortly before he died, Augustine uttered this declaration: "I thank God that in all my life I never struck a man in anger; for if I had, I am sure that, from my remarkable muscular powers, I should have killed my antagonist, and then his blood, at this awful moment would have lain heavily upon my soul. As it is, I die at peace with all mankind."[7]

His father's dying statement had a powerful and lasting effect on the child George. As a youngster, George never bullied or mistreated his contemporaries. As Commander in Chief in the Revolution, he never misused his great physical strength or his enormous influence. As President of the Constitutional Convention, he never abused his unquestioned authority. And most important, as the first President of the United States of America, he never misused his power or position. And that last fact alone is rather amazing, as he wielded untried and unknown power in a field in which no precedents existed to limit him.

Yes, George Washington's father had a powerful impact on George, even though Augustine died on April 12, 1743, while George was still only 11 years old. Augustine seemed to have had a premonition about his death; on April 11, he made out his will. As the second son, George did not inherit the homestead. Mount Vernon would become the property of the first-born son, Lawrence, who was four years older and a half brother to George.

After his father's death, young George continued to live by the precepts that his father had taught him. Many of George's friends smoked tobacco, and almost all of the field hands did. Sometime during his early teen years, George, like his friends, tried smoking. But he found the taste unpleasant and showed his strength of character by not taking up the habit. He was smart enough to not be unduly influenced by what "everyone else" was doing. After that first youthful attempt, Washington never again tried smoking.

At a young age, George became interested in exploring the frontier. Becoming a surveyor and marking out new farms in the wilderness would give him a chance to leave home and seek adventure. George had a natural aptitude for surveying, and mathematics was his favorite subject. He easily picked up an understanding of fractions and geometry. He retrieved his father's old set of surveying instruments from storage and began to practice. At age 15 he started earning money as an assistant to local surveyors.

In 1743, Lawrence Washington inherited the land owned by Augustine, and lived there with his wife, Ann Fairfax Washington.

This land was known as "Little Hunting Creek." Lawrence renamed the site "Mount Vernon" after Admiral Vernon, under whose command he had served in the West Indies. Lawrence also built a new cottage, which became the nucleus of the present mansion. George was living with his mother at their home known as "Ferry Farm" about 30 miles south of Mount Vernon. George was very fond of his brother Lawrence and often visited Mount Vernon.

On one of his frequent visits to Mount Vernon, George met Lord Thomas Fairfax, the largest property holder in Virginia. Fairfax owned more than 5,000,000 acres of land in northern Virginia, extending to the Allegheny Mountains and including much of the Shenandoah Valley. He was a cousin to Lawrence Washington's wife, Ann. Lord Fairfax was planning an expedition to survey his western lands. Sixteen-year-old George Washington was invited to go along as an assistant to the expert surveyor in charge of the expedition. George was able to persuade his mother to let him go along on his first long trip away from home.

The month-long expedition set out in March 1748. They traveled on horseback into the unsettled wilderness. Washington learned to sleep in the open, to hunt game for food, and be self-sufficient. By the time he returned to Mount Vernon, he felt he had grown into a man. He had certainly learned many skills critical to his later successes in leadership and survival.

In the summer of 1749, Washington helped lay out the newly established town of Alexandria, Virginia. Later that same year, he was appointed the official surveyor for Culpepper County. In November, Lord Fairfax hired him to make a surveying trip into the Shenandoah Valley. His surveying work paid well. It was one of the few businesses in which a man could expect to be paid in cash, as opposed to barter. With these proceeds, he supported himself and gave assistance to his mother. Washington kept track in his account book of small loans he made to relatives and friends.

Washington's reputation as a surveyor increased in the 1750's. His services were in demand more and more as people continued to move into the Shenandoah Valley. George carefully saved his money. When a particularly good piece of land became available, he bought it. By the end of 1750, he owned nearly 1,500 acres of his own land.

In 1751, when Lawrence contracted a serious case of tuberculosis, his doctor advised him to sail to Barbados, an island in the Caribbean, in an attempt to recover from the much dreaded disease. At Lawrence's request, George accompanied his brother to the island. George was 19 years old. This was the only time he ever left the American continent. While in Barbados, George became infected with smallpox. It seemed an unfair price to pay for his selfless effort to help his brother recover from tuberculosis. But, as in many times in George Washington's life, the hand of Providence was watching out for this great man. Years later, smallpox ravaged the Revolutionary Army. Smallpox was the greatest killer of soldiers during the Revolutionary War. And because of his earlier encounter, George Washington was immunized from the killer disease. This certainly saved him from weeks of inability to function as Commander. It likely saved him his life.

Tragically, Lawrence never fully recovered from tuberculosis. He died in 1752, almost exactly one year after he and George had returned to Mount Vernon. Lawrence was only 35. Lawrence's widow, Ann, retained use of the property for her lifetime. It was only after Ann's death that Mount Vernon and other lands were to go to George. But in December of 1752, Ann married George Lee, and shortly after, in 1754, George Washington bought all the rights, titles, and interests from Ann and became the sole owner of Mount Vernon.

George and his younger brother, John Augustine, lived there as bachelors. John married Hannah Bushrod in 1756, and the couple stayed at Mount Vernon and managed the estate while George was away serving in the French and Indian War.

When his brother Lawrence died, George inherited his post as adjutant in the Virginia Militia. Earlier in his life, George had wanted to join the navy. However, because of his mother's strong objections, he had given up that idea. This unasked-for inheritance offered him another opportunity to prepare for his future, critically important leadership positions.

George Washington grew into adulthood. He did most things a little better than the average man. He was very tall for his era, 6 feet 3½ inches.[8] As he always stood erect, he was a most imposing individual. His very demeanor and physical presence marked him as a potential leader.

Yet Washington was not a vain man. Although he was unusually tall, he never recorded an accurate measurement of his own height and weight. But other contemporaries left us their observations of his physique with expressions such as: "He was remarkably tall, . . . wide shouldered, . . . His stature is noble and lofty, he is well made and exactly proportioned."[9] Lafayette reported that Washington had larger hands than any man he had ever known.

While many artists attempted to paint Washington, the failure to portray him as he really appeared was well recognized. In 1791, one observer wrote: "His modesty is very astonishing. He is without pretension. There is an expression on his face that no painter has succeeded in taking." Another said: "There are few portraits which resemble him." And another: "No picture accurately resembles him in the minute traits of his person."

Even the portrait of Washington that most Americans visualize when they refer to "the Father of our Country," painted by a contemporary, Gilbert Stuart, did not capture a true likeness. Members of Washington's own family, and others, such as John Marshall, refused to give it their approval as his likeness. (Stuart actually painted more than 120 pictures of Washington. But they differed so markedly in facial contour, and in the size and relationship of the features, that one would be justified in concluding that Stuart's pictures were of several different men.)[10]

Possibly the best likeness of George Washington is the marble statue of him located in the rotunda at the Capitol Building, in Richmond, Virginia. In 1784, the General Assembly commissioned a statue to be made of "the finest marble and best workmanship" as a tribute to the great Commander in Chief. Thomas Jefferson, then a Minister to France, was requested to engage a sculptor for this project. Jefferson hired Jean-Antoine Houdon, a noted French artist who is now widely regarded as the best sculptor of his time. In the fall of 1785, Houdon traveled to America with three assistants. They spent three weeks in Washington's home, taking measurements, making plaster casts, and sketching the General, before returning to France.

The statue was not completed until three years later, 1788. But at the time of its completion, France was embroiled in internal difficulties, and the statue couldn't be shipped to Virginia until 1796.[11] During that eight-year interval, it was on display at the Louvre in Paris. Even though Washington did not die until 1799, he never saw the statue. However, it was viewed by many of his contemporaries, who attested to its perfect likeness of the General. With tears in his eyes, Washington's close friend Lafayette declared, "That is the man himself. I can almost realize he is going to move."[12] This statue is very detailed. There are buttons missing from his military coat, symbolizing that the war was long but is now over. There is "something" in one of his coat pockets, causing it to bulge. His head is uncovered, his hair braided. (Washington usually wore his hair natural instead of donning the customary powdered wig, although he did often powder his own thick hair). He has the appropriate wrinkles. His sword hangs on his left side while he brandishes a cane in his right hand—depicting what Washington had so forcibly expressed to the General Assembly of Virginia: the military should be subordinate to the civil power. He stands by a bundle of 13 rods. The rods are similar to those borne before ancient Roman magistrates as a badge of authority and an emblem of official power. While the rods themselves represent power and honor, the number 13 represents the 13 colonies. Located on the other side of Washington is a ploughshare that represents the peaceful arts—the arts most congenial to his taste and feelings. The plowshare is also an acknowledgment of his life as a farmer and his contribution to the improvement of the plow.[13]

The French and Indian War

The colonies were embroiled in the French and Indian War between 1754 and 1763. Because of his status as adjutant in the Virginia militia, Washington served as an officer. He seems to have been providently prepared for military leadership. His years as surveyor gave him invaluable knowledge of the territory. In addition, he was smart enough to rely upon the advice of other officers, and he also experienced some plain good luck.

During the French and Indian War, Washington appears to have been divinely protected, avoiding many close calls with death. In one particular battle toward the end of the war, almost a thousand British soldiers were killed. Every mounted officer, except Washington, was slain, including the commanding officer, General Edward Braddock.

Braddock lived only long enough to get back to camp and receive some attention to his wounds. Of this battle George wrote: "By the all-powerful dispensations of Providence, I have been protected beyond all human probability or expectation; for I had four bullets through my coat and two horses shot under me, yet escaped unhurt, although death was leveling my companions on every side of me!"[14]

About 16 years after this battle, a most interesting sequel to this experience occurred. While Washington and a group of men were surveying a wilderness area, they were approached by a band of Indians. One of the members of that band was an old chieftain. This chief had fought in that bloody battle where a thousand British soldiers were killed, where Washington had received four bullet holes in his coat, where two horses were shot out from under him. This chief made a special effort to meet General Washington. They rendezvoused around a campfire, where the chief spoke through an interpreter:

> I am a chief and ruler over my tribes. My influence extends to the waters of the great lakes and to the far blue mountains. I have traveled a long and weary path that I might see the young warrior of the great battle. It was on the day when the white man's blood mixed with the streams of our forest that I first beheld this chief [Washington]. I called to my young men and said, mark yon tall and daring warrior? He is not of the red-coat tribe—he hath an Indian's wisdom, and his warriors fight as we do—himself is alone exposed. Quick, let your aim be certain, and he dies. Our rifles were leveled, rifles which, but for you, knew not how to miss—'twas all in vain, a power mightier far than we, shielded you. Seeing you were under the special guardianship of the Great Spirit, we immediately ceased to fire at you. I am old and soon shall be

> gathered to the great council fire of my fathers . . . but ere I go, there is something bids me speak in the voice of prophecy. Listen! The Great Spirit protects that man [pointing at Washington], and guides his destinies—he will become the chief of nations, and a people yet unborn will hail him as the founder of a mighty empire. I am come to pay homage to the man who is the particular favorite of Heaven, and who can never die in battle.[15]

Martha Dandridge Custis Washington

In the late autumn of 1758, George was traveling from Mount Vernon to Williamsburg, the capital of the colony, where he had some business with the Governor. On his way, he was invited to stop and dine with a Mr. Richard Chamberlayne. Since Washington assumed that he would leave shortly after the meal, he informed his servant to have his horse ready for his continued trip in the early afternoon. This servant faithfully held the horse at ready until the sun sank. When George didn't come at the appointed time, the servant remarked: "Twas strange, . . . he was not wont to be a single moment behind his appointments, for he was the most punctual of all men."[16] The servant didn't know that a certain widow by the name of Martha Dandridge Custis was also a visitor at the Chamberlayne house that afternoon. She was the loveliest widow in Virginia. They were mutually pleased on their first meeting. The lady was fair to behold, of fascinating manners, and splendidly endowed with worldly benefits. The colonel was a hero, fresh from the fields of battle, with fame and glory, and held an impressive bearing. Mr. Chamberlayne would not allow a guest to depart from his house after sunset, so George and Martha spent the night of their first meeting under the same roof.[17]

Martha had been married to Daniel Parke Custis, a 37-year-old bachelor who had inherited his father's large White House Plantation on the Pamunkey River. Martha and Daniel established their home at White House, as it was called. During the eight years of their marriage, they had four children; only two (John Parke and Patsy) survived to adulthood. When Daniel died unexpectedly in 1758, Martha and the two children were left to manage the large estate. It was only eight months later that the wealthy widow would visit the home of Mr. and Mrs. Richard Chamberlayne and meet the man with whom she would fall deeply in love, the man who would later become the first President of the United States of America.

Several days after their first meeting, George rowed across the Pamunkey River, in order to visit Martha at her own home. At this meeting, they became engaged to be married. They did not meet again until their wedding day, January 6, 1759. George was 26 years old, Martha was 27. At barely five feet, Martha stood only as tall as Washington's chest.

It was a brilliant wedding party which assembled on that winter day. The guests were all decked out in their finest clothes. The bride was dressed in silk and satin, laces and brocade, with pearls on her neck and in her ears. The bridegroom was attired in blue and silver, trimmed with scarlet, with gold buckles at his knees and on his shoes. Their future life together looked very bright and promising.

The couple did enjoy a good and happy marriage, with Martha giving full support to her husband's numerous and critically important activities and endeavors. Devoted to her, George always wore "a miniature painting of her under his shirt, next to his heart."[18] It is a sad irony that George Washington is called "the Father of our Country," but had no children of his own.

Washington had already experienced much well-earned fame when he took a leave from the army to go home and get married. Together, he and Martha would enjoy the goodwill and respect of all men. After a six-week honeymoon at Martha's White House, Washington took his new family to Williamsburg.

In 1759, while he was away fighting his last campaign in the French and Indian War, Washington was elected to the House of Burgesses. When he took his seat at Williamsburg, the Speaker of the House, Mr. Robinson, thanked him publicly for his services to his country. Washington rose to reply, but he was so unable to talk about himself, that he stood before the House stammering and stuttering. The speaker finally said, "Sit down, Mr. Washington; your modesty equals your valor, and that surpasses the power of any language I possess."[19]

When his term in the legislature was completed, Washington brought his wife and family to Mount Vernon[20] to live. They found the plantation run down due to the neglect of its overseers. But Washington began to buy farms that lay around his estate, and by 1773 he owned about 40,000 acres of land. He also controlled the vast Custis estate of his wife and her children. He rented much of his land to tenant farmers. Washington was an astute businessman who kept his own accounts and carefully recorded all his profits and expenses.

As the owner of vast amounts of land, Washington had to supervise many different activities. To learn more about farming techniques, he bought many of the latest books on the subject. When he saw that he couldn't grow the best grade of tobacco at Mount Vernon, he switched to wheat. He built flour mills to turn his wheat into flour and saw his profits increase. Washington experimented with tree-grafting to improve his fruit orchards. He hired out his carpenters, bricklayers, and blacksmiths to other plantation owners, creating more business income for himself. Mount Vernon also became well known for the barrels of salted fish it produced from the large schools of fish in the Potomac River. Weekends were often times of large social events, from fox hunting to barbecues, from dances to games. The time passed quickly and pleasantly for George and Martha.

George Washington's Political Career

The French and Indian War ended in 1763. During the next 11 years (until 1774), Washington was elected time after time to serve Virginia in the House of Burgesses. Here he learned the process of representative government. He seldom made speeches and didn't present any bills of importance to the legislature. He saw the difficulties in getting legislation passed. This experience helped him learn the patience that later served him so well in presiding over the Constitutional Convention and in his service as the first President of the United States of America. Here he also became acquainted with Richard Henry Lee, Thomas Jefferson, Patrick Henry, and other great leaders serving in the Virginia House of Burgesses.

When Britain passed the Boston Port Bill and the Massachusetts Government Act in 1774, it became clear to Washington that Britain was not going to allow self-government in the colonies. Instead, Britain wanted the colonists to forever be subject to her imperious rule. In May of 1774, Washington joined other Virginia Burgesses in proposing that a continental congress should be held. It is no surprise that he was elected as one of the delegates to the First Continental Congress, which met in Philadelphia in September.

A critical decision was made at that First Continental Congress that forbade importing to the colonies all British goods and all goods subject to British taxes.

> Moreover, it authorized all towns and counties to set up committees empowered to enforce its provisions. The Continental Congress thus enacted law and created a new government dedicated to resisting British rule. Washington spent the winter of 1774-1775 in Virginia, organizing independent military companies which were to aid the local committees in enforcing the Continental Association and, if need be, to fight against British troops.[21]

The Second Continental Congress was held in 1775, again in Philadelphia, and again George Washington was a delegate from Virginia. He was the only one to attend the convention dressed in full military uniform. Congress had been in negotiations with Britain to achieve an end to their unhappy disputes. Negotiations were progressing far too slowly. On June 14, 1775, John Adams of Massachusetts took the floor. In his opinion, they had wasted too much time already. More than 50 New Englanders had already lost their lives in skirmishes. Were they to sit composing humble addresses to the King while British ships of war were drawing nearer? In one of his most impassioned speeches, Adams urged that the troops at Cambridge be recognized as a Continental Army by the Continental Congress. He was ready to arm the army, appoint a commander, vote supplies, and proceed to the business of independence.

Commander in Chief

After weeks of heated debate, Congress adopted Adam's recommendation to form an army. The next problem was the election of a commander.

> The scene was intensely dramatic, and the eyes of all the assembly were fixed upon the speaker. At his right was seated George Washington, clad in his uniform of a Virginia colonel, and he, too, was leaning

> forward with breathless interest, eager to hear the name of the man whom John Adams would propose.
>
> More quietly, then, John Adams went on to portray the qualifications the new commander must have. Becoming more eloquent as his speech drew to an end, he closed with these words,
>
> "Gentlemen, I know these qualifications are high, but we all know they are needful in this crisis in this chief. Does anyone say they are not to be obtained in this country? In reply, I have to say they are; they reside in one of our own body, and he is the man whom I now nominate,—GEORGE WASHINGTON OF VIRGINIA."
>
> The startled Washington as he heard the words leaped to his feet and rushed into an adjoining room. The entire body sat silent and astonished. In the midst of the silence, Samuel Adams, acting on a promise he had previously given his cousin [John Adams], rose, and moved for an adjournment, that time for consultation and deliberation might be had. The motion prevailed, and the assembly was dismissed.
>
> [On June 15,] two days before the battle of Bunker Hill, Congress formally adopted all the colonial troops that had been raised; and on the very day on which the Yankees started for Bunker Hill and a glorious history, Delegate Washington of the Continental Congress was informed of his unanimous election as commander in chief.[22]

The next day, June 16, Washington stood on the floor of Congress and accepted his commission. Of course, hostilities between the Americans and the British had already commenced with the

Battles of Lexington and Concord on April 19, 1775. The Battle of Bunker Hill and of Breed's Hill were fought on June 17, the day after George Washington officially became Commander in Chief. Washington was still en route to Cambridge when he heard the good news of the Battles of Bunker Hill and Breed's Hill. Although the British won these battles, it was at great cost, suffering numerous casualties before the colonial forces abandoned the hills for lack of ammunition.

Washington's problem was unique. He was required to raise and train an army on the battlefield on the one hand, while attempting to recruit and replace it on the other hand. Consistent replacement was necessary because continental soldiers believed in going home after a battle. They had short-term enlistments, usually for six months, and sometimes as short as three months. They had little discipline or order. The untrained militia believed that all they had to do was get their dander up and grab their muskets. The militia, known as minutemen, were seldom crack shots. They were mostly plowboys, clerks, or mechanics, and were too far from the frontier to develop prowess with firearms.[23]

In September 1775, King George III of England and his cabinet met again. They were growing weary of the skirmishes and agreed upon a new strategy for putting down the rebellion in the American colonies. The cabinet selected which British officers would command the continued prosecution of the war and agreed on the armed forces that would be necessary to finally put down the uprisings.

In February 1776, Washington determined that the time was right to test his strength against the British garrison at Boston. But he kept his plan secret until the hour for execution. Since Dorchester Heights was strategically important, an advance party of some 800 men swarmed over Dorchester Heights to take up defensive positions. They were followed by 1,200 men under the command of General John Thomas. During this battle, the Americans obtained and retained the strong possession of Dorchester Heights, Massachusetts, overlooking Boston Harbor.

"If the Americans retain possession of the Heights," said British Admiral Shuldam, "I cannot keep a ship in the harbor." Another officer observed, "Perhaps there never was as much work done in so short a space. They were raised with an expedition equal to that of the Genii [sic] belonging to Aladdin's lamp." General William Howe wrote to Lord Dartmouth, describing the battle at Dorchester Heights, "It must have been the employment of at least twelve thousand men." Then he added, "The rebels have done more in one night than my whole army would have done in a month." But Washington had pulled off this coup with only 2,000 men. On March 17, 1776, General William Howe evacuated his British troops from Boston.[24] The evacuation made Washington a hero by proving that the Americans could overcome the British in a major contest.

Even though the battle at Dorchester Heights was a huge success for the American troops, other difficulties were besetting the Commander in Chief. He had troubles not only with the British, but with Congress, with his own officers, with inexperience in this kind of war, with the weather, and even with the food and lodging. These weighty problems troubled Washington for many weeks. He made a valiant effort to keep up the appearance of military preparation while in the midst of extreme confusion. Throughout his troubles, Washington often acknowledged the hand of Providence, as did other leaders of the Revolution.

One moment of unseen protection occurred in June 1776. A plot to assassinate General George Washington and other American officers and to destroy American munitions was uncovered. It was determined that Thomas Hickey, one of General Washington's bodyguards, was one of the conspirators. Hickey had accepted money to kill the General. He was given a court martial, found guilty, and was publicly hanged on June 28, just two days after his conviction. Some 20,000 people, including the army, witnessed the execution. Thirteen others were arrested but never tried. The conspiracy became known as the "Hickey Plot." Afterward, General Washington issued general orders giving solemn "warning to every soldier in the army to avoid those crimes . . . so disgraceful to the character of a soldier and pernicious to his country, whose pay he received and the bread he eats."[25]

Washington did not attribute this kind of protection to be mere accident. He wrote to a clergyman friend: "No man has a more perfect reliance on the all-wise and powerful dispensations of the Supreme Being than I have, nor thinks His aid more necessary."[26]

On June 25, 1776, General William Howe arrived in the New York area to take command of all British forces in the colonies. On July 4, 1776, the Declaration of Independence was adopted by the Continental Congress in Philadelphia. On July 9, General Washington ordered the Declaration of Independence to be read publicly to the entire American command, as well as the citizens in the New York area. In response to the boldness of the Declaration, on July 20, 1776, General Howe sent an officer to offer pardon to General Washington and all American patriots who would cease their rebellion and pledge their allegiance to the Crown. The offer was refused.

By late August, a British armada of over 400 ships and 32,000 troops had arrived in the New York area. On August 27, the battle of Long Island was fought with disastrous results for the Americans. On August 29 and 30, General Washington was forced to abandon

Brooklyn. Under cover of night, he moved his entire army from Long Island, across the East River to Manhattan Island. On September 15, the battle of Kip's Bay on Manhattan Island was fought, resulting in another disaster for the Americans. But the next day, September 16, the American forces prevailed in the battle of Harlem Heights. Only five days later, September 21, a fire of unknown origin burned about one-fourth of the city of New York.

Elsewhere, on October 11, General Benedict Arnold (who was a hero in this battle, but later became a traitor) lead a tiny fleet of 15 hastily constructed ships to stall the British fleet of 25 ships on Lake Champlain. This heroic action delayed the movement of 13,000 British troops, saving General George Washington's Continental Army from certain defeat.

On November 16, the battle of Fort Washington was fought in New York. It was another catastrophe for the Americans. While Fort Washington, located on the Hudson River, was lost in battle, Fort Lee, located on the opposite side of the Hudson on the shores of New Jersey, was simply abandoned. The Americans surrendered this fort to the British without firing a single shot.

On December 2, the situation was grim when Washington's bedraggled army reached Trenton, New Jersey, located on the banks of the Delaware River. They were virtually fleeing from the British. But escaping from the British was not the only problem facing the American army. The number of troops was shrinking daily from disease, desertion, and death. And now a river lay before them. Options were few. General Washington ordered the army to gather every boat they could find. Washington's army used these boats to cross the Delaware into Pennsylvania. The British would be unable to follow, as there were no more boats available. The American troops camped on the Pennsylvania shore. When the river froze,

Washington expected the British to advance across the river, squash his army, and move on to victory in Philadelphia.

Washington commanded only 6,000 men, and these were almost naked, dying of cold, without blankets, and very ill-supplied with provisions.[27] To make matters worse, enlistments were about to expire. On January 1, Washington would be left with fewer than 2,000 poorly equipped men.

On December 14, General Howe made a decision that would radically relieve Washington's fears. Howe decided to close the winter campaign and return to New York. Strangely, Howe directed the British troops to retire into winter quarters, intending to suspend further fighting until spring. He stationed General James Grant with a small force of British soldiers at Princeton, New Jersey. Howe then decided to quarter some of his British and Hessian soldiers in Trenton, just across the Delaware River from the American camp. The Hessians were German mercenaries who had been retained by the British and were among the finest soldiers in the world. The Trenton forces totaling 1550 men were put under the command of Colonel Johann Gottlieb Rall.

At this point, winning the war seemed hopeless for the Americans. They had lost major battles in New York. Food, shelter, and supplies were highly inadequate. Morale was crumbling. "If every nerve is not strained to recruit the New Army with all possible expedition, . . . I think the game is pretty near up,"[28] wrote General Washington to his brother Samuel Washington on December 18.

But once again, the hand of God dramatically directed the affairs of this budding nation, this time through the power of the pen. In January of 1776, Thomas Paine had written a best-selling pamphlet titled "Common Sense." In a few pages, he had awakened the heart of a nation and stirred it to declare independence. Still a fiery supporter of the Revolution, Thomas Paine traveled with Washington's army. Though subject to the same bitter cold, small rations, and cankerous discouragement, he refused to give in to the despair surrounding him. Instead, he wrote another soul-stirring piece of prose which he called "The American Crisis." It was published on December 19, 1776. Washington's weary troops were inspired and uplifted when they heard the words of Paine's newest essay:

> These are the times that try men's souls. The summer soldier and the sunshine patriot will, in this crisis, shrink from the service of their country; but he that stands it now, deserves the love and thanks of man and woman. Let it be told to the future world, that in the depth of winter, when nothing but hope and virtue could survive, that the city and the country, alarmed at one common danger, came forth to meet and to repulse it![29]

General Washington knew this was his last chance to act. No doubt encouraged by Paine's words, he formed a courageous plan. A nearly impossible plan. He would cross the Delaware with 40 percent of his army, about 2,400 men. The crossing would take place some nine miles north of Trenton. He knew from his spies that the town of Trenton had not been adequately fortified. He hoped to surprise the Hessian garrison well before dawn. On December 23, Washington sent word to Colonel Joseph Reed: "Christmas day, at night, is the time fixed upon for our attempt on Trenton. For Heaven's sake keep this to yourself, as the discovery of it may prove fatal to us."[30] The Revolution would have ended in defeat if the British had gotten wind of this bold plan. Washington's men were exhausted and discouraged. They would have been an easy target for the well-trained, well-fed, and well-armed enemy.

Colonel Rall, Commander of the British garrison in Trenton, had nothing but disdain for the patriot army. He was proud that he had once served and fought for the Russian Czar and regarded the Americans as "nothing but a lot of farmers." He considered an attack so unlikely that he refused to even prepare for the possibility of one. His arrogance proved his demise. An unprepared, unsuspecting enemy was exactly what Washington needed to give his plan even a slight chance.

The crossing of the Delaware began at six o'clock in the evening on December 25. The patriots made their way across the ice-choked river through a punishing gale of sleet and snow. The crossing was under the direction of Colonel John Glover. Marbleheaders, a remarkable troop of fishermen from Massachusetts, manned the shallow boats. For nine long hours, the Marbleheaders rowed, transporting boatload after boatload of men, canon, and ammunition. The last soldier stepped on to the bank of the New Jersey shore at about three o'clock in the morning.

After the crossing, the already exhausted soldiers marched the nine miles to Trenton through freezing wind and hail. "It will be a terrible night for soldiers who have no shoes," noted John Fitzgerald, a member of General Washington's staff. "Some of them have tied old rags around their feet, others are barefoot, but I have not heard a man complain."[31] Bloody footprints marked the way of the harrowing trek to Trenton.

Providence smiled on those brave troops on that freezing Christmas night in 1776. Colonel Rall spent the night drinking and playing cards with others who were on duty. When a local farmer knocked on Colonel Rall's door with a warning that the Americans were coming, the servant refused to interrupt the festivities to inform the Commander. So the loyalist farmer scribbled a warning note to the Commander. But Rall only stuffed it into his pocket, unread—an unintentional Christmas gift to the patriots.

After marching through the early morning hours, General Washington and his troops arrived at Trenton and fell upon the Hessians shortly after dawn. A sentry at the entrance to the town fired a warning shot, but it was too late. Two separate columns of the Americans converged on the town from different directions. The gunners from the American artillery unit under the command of a young American officer named Alexander Hamilton lit the touchholes of the cannon. Clusters of small cast iron balls known as "grapeshot" roared from the cannons' mouths, and the screaming Hessian soldiers fell back. The Hessian army was completely surprised. Frantically, they rolled out their own cannon and fired back. Captain William Washington, cousin of the Commander in Chief, and a young Lieutenant named James Monroe courageously led the charge toward the enemy. Lieutenant James Monroe fell with serious injuries from the battle. He would likely have bled to death had a doctor not been present. Through the doctor's careful attention, Monroe survived to become the fifth President of the United States.[32]

The fighting was all over in about two hours. Of the 1,000 Hessian soldiers in Trenton, 948 were taken captive. Colonel Rall was fatally injured in the melee. Another 115 of the Hessians were killed or wounded. But the Americans suffered few casualties. General Washington reported that four soldiers were wounded in the battle, but none of his soldiers were killed. Only two of his soldiers had died in the campaign, and they had tragically frozen to death. It was an incredible victory—nothing short of a miracle. But the troops did not simply march away with 948 prisoners . . . the Americans also carried with them numerous supplies of food, clothing, bedding, and ammunition that they had commandeered.

General Washington led his men hurriedly back across the Delaware River, exhausted but exhilarated by their triumph. The battle of Trenton was a complete rout. Continental General Henry Knox, chief of artillery, wrote to his wife: "The hurry, fright, and confusion of the enemy was [not] unlike that which will be when the last trump shall sound."[33] Against all odds, they had struck the enemy and scored a victory. Only one week later, they would re-cross the Delaware to fight the British at Princeton, where they would score another astonishing triumph.

The Christmas victories at Trenton and Princeton marked the psychological turning point of the War for Independence. The effect on the morale of the troops and the nation was considerable. Those pitiful colonials had taken on the King's own army . . . and whipped them. As word of the victory spread, confidence in the Revolution and in General George Washington was revived.

However, as winter gave way to spring in 1777, the British prepared a knockout blow. They intended to end the war in just a few months. General Howe was to use his forces against Washington, who they presumed would feel compelled to fight for Philadelphia, the American Capital. Then Howe would continue on and capture the rest of Pennsylvania, New Jersey, and Delaware. At the same time, Gentleman Johnny Burgoyne would lead a large army from Canada and capture New York and the rest of New England. To this end, on July 20, Howe put to sea from New York with 260 ships and 1700 soldiers. The fleet headed south for Philadelphia. Washington broke camp and moved quickly to block the southern approaches to the city.

They needn't have hurried, for what would normally have been a week's voyage turned into a month-long ordeal for the British. Once at sea, the wind died down, becalming the fleet in hundred degree temperatures. The vessels stank of melting tar, rotting food, and unwashed bodies. Horses, cramped belowdecks, went mad in the heat and had to be shot. Then came thunderstorms. Masts were split by lightning and sails torn to shreds. Finally, the fleet anchored off Head of Elk, Maryland, on Chesapeake Bay, fifty miles south of Philadelphia, August 25, 1777.[34]

All of the problems incurred on that voyage could hardly be coincidence. A powerful force was aiding the patriots. Then, on the very day that the British vessels landed in Maryland, divine intervention once more preserved the life of General George Washington. Historian Albert Marrin relates:

> The commander in chief had a close call himself that day. British Major Patrick Ferguson, nicknamed "Bulldog," was resting with some men in a clump of trees when a party of American officers rode past without seeing them. One of Ferguson's men happened to have a rifle of the major's design, as fine a weapon as any frontiersman's. A crack shot, he aimed at the easiest target, the back of the biggest man on the biggest horse. He was squeezing the trigger when the major, who thought it ungentlemanly to shoot a fellow officer from hiding, motioned for him to lower the gun. Next day Ferguson learned from an American prisoner that the officer was George Washington. "I am not sorry that I did not know at the time who he was," he said, relieved. Not knowing made it unnecessary to choose between doing something he thought dishonorable and possibly ending the war by killing the enemy commander.[35]

The winter of 1777-1778 was a bleak time for the Commander in Chief, probably the darkest period of the war. Washington had retreated to Valley Forge, where he resolved to pass the winter of

1777. Martha joined him there in his quarters for a few months. She was driven in her carriage through miles of the camp and saw the filth, the dead horses lying about, the open latrines, and the terrible shape of the soldiers. Then she was escorted through the hospital which was nothing more than a barn with some cots and some helpers. She was appalled at the death and squalor. She was able to scrounge up just a little bit of meat to make some broth and enough flour to make a dozen loaves of bread. She took the pitifully small amount of food to the hospital to feed the dying soldiers. That was the first meal many of them had had for several days. They loved her from then on and called her Lady Washington.[36]

One of the "nurses" took Martha to see an extremely sick soldier who had been sent to a small cottage where he could experience some privacy as he died. His wife was in the room with him. Martha brought some of her bread and broth to them. It was apparent that this soldier would not live long. As he approached death, his last thoughts showed loving concern for his wife. He asked Martha to watch out after her for him. Martha promised that she would, and the dying man whispered his thanks. Martha started to withdraw, then turned back and asked if she could leave a prayer with them. She bowed her head and clasped her hands together as she knelt beside him. She pronounced an inspired blessing. The soldier died the next day. Martha made an effort to live up to her promise and ensure that the soldier's wife was cared for.[37]

Like Martha, George Washington frequently offered prayers—many uttered in secret—for aid and comfort from God. There were at least 67 "desperate moments when Washington acknowledged that he would have suffered disaster had not the hand of God intervened in behalf of the struggle for independence."[38] On approximately December 24, 1777, Washington was alone in prayer when he received a marvelous vision.[39] As recorded in his own words, he was visited by an angel, who told him many times to "look and learn." Washington then beheld the birth, progress, and destiny of the United States. George Washington received the wondrous blessing of knowing that his army would prevail and his country would become great.[40]

The night after this vision, on December 25, 1777, the tide turned, and, as if by a miracle, the spirit of America was raised once again, and the patriots went on to win the war. But it was not a quick and easy victory. There were almost four more years of fighting and sacrifice required to achieve their ambitious goal "of life, liberty, and the pursuit of happiness."

In February 1778, like an angel coming to help the American cause, a German soldier arrived at the camp in Valley Forge to assist in training the troops. "He called himself Lieutenant General Friedrich Ludolf Gerhard Wilhelm Augustin von Steuben, aide-de-camp to King Frederick the Great of Prussia, the greatest soldier of the age."[41] When von Steuben had heard about the war in America, he went to France, where he met Benjamin Franklin. Franklin, deeply impressed, had given him a letter of introduction to John Hancock. Hancock had provided him with a sleigh, horses, a carriage, servants, and uniforms, and sent him to Washington at Valley Forge.

Von Steuben was a show in himself. He didn't speak English, and so his instructions had to be translated. The troops became used to his guttural accent and his soldier-like chant. Within four weeks, the baron had transformed the ragged troops into a unit more resembling European troops. He even surprised himself. He wrote:

> My enterprise succeeded better than I had dared to expect and I had the satisfaction . . . to see not only a regular step introduced in the army, but I also made maneuvers with ten and twelve battalions with as

> much precision as the evolution of a single company. . . . The genius of this nation is not the least to be compared with that of the Prussians, Austrians, or French. You say to your [European] soldier, "do this" and he doeth it. But [to an American] I am obliged to say, "This is the reason why you ought to do that," and then he does it.[42]

The American soldiers were schooling their Prussian leader about democracy. Washington had expected much from von Steuben, but even he admitted that the miracle wrought by the General went beyond his wildest hopes. The men began to perform their duties with a spring in their step. Several battles were still lost to the British, but the troops' morale and attitude had now improved dramatically.[43]

Finally on October 19, 1781, Washington experienced the greatest triumph of his military career. Exactly six years and six months from the day when that first fatal shot was fired in Lexington (April 19, 1775), General Lord Charles Cornwallis surrendered his entire British army of more than 7,000 men at Yorktown. The blow was decisive. The fighting was over—although it was almost two years before a formal peace treaty was signed.

In this interlude, Washington had many problems with his army. They were disgruntled with the reluctance of Congress to vote adequate pay for the soldiers. In May 1782, one of Washington's Colonels, Lewis Nicola, openly advocated that America should become a monarchy with Washington as king! Washington reacted in his singularly typical fashion:

> With a mixture of surprise and astonishment, I have read with attention the sentiments you have submitted to my perusal. Be assured, sir, no occurrence in the course of the war has given me more painful sensations than your information of there being such

> ideas existing in the army as you have expressed, and which I must view with abhorrence and reprehend with severity. . . . I am much at a loss to conceive what part of my conduct could have given encouragement to an address which to me seems big with the greatest mischiefs which can befall my country. . . . You could not have found a person to whom your schemes are more disagreeable.[44]

All the same, in March 1783, officers of the army were on the verge of overthrowing Congress and setting up their own government. Washington called them together and persuaded them that they must have patience. The emotional climax of his talk came when he put on eyeglasses and commented, "Gentlemen, you must pardon me. I have grown gray in your service and now find myself growing blind."[45] Washington was 51 years old.

On December 4, 1783, the day the British fleet sailed out of New York harbor, the War for Independence was over. A mighty, amazing, even miraculous, victory had been won. A victory that would change history in a way that none of those involved could ever imagine. As the British ships sailed away, Washington met with his few remaining officers, embraced them individually, and left the city at once. He was eager to return home to Mount Vernon. But his progress was slow. Each city through which he passed on his way home made the event a celebration.

Sadly for Washington, his visit home was brief. On December 23, 1783, he needed to attend a meeting of Congress held in Annapolis, Maryland. When Washington addressed this meeting, he turned back to them his commission as Commander in Chief. At the close of his remarks, he humbly stated, "Having now finished the work assigned me, I retire from the great theater of action; and bidding an affectionate farewell to this august body under whose orders I have so long acted, I here offer my commission and take my leave of all the employments of public life."[46]

This noble man would not be allowed his sincere desire to fade into the background to live out the remainder of his days. Simply. As a farmer. At his family home, Mount Vernon. His country needed him. More now, perhaps, than during the dark days of war. His destiny had not yet been fulfilled.

Constitutional Convention

On May 14, 1787, delegates from the states met in the Constitutional Convention in Philadelphia for the sole purpose of revising the Articles of Confederation. The Articles granted independence to each state, but there was no authority declared for the states to work together to solve national problems. Understanding the critical importance of the meeting and the impact of George Washington's presence, James Madison knew that Washington must be in attendance. Madison worked very hard to persuade Washington to simply appear at the meeting. He did appear and, not surprisingly, Washington was elected president of the Convention.

The magic of George Washington's unselfish leadership and his dynamic sincerity also began to have effect. For years he had talked and written, urging a new government. It seems rather ridiculous to think that he would now cease working to obtain his objectives. True, he made only one or two speeches on the floor of the Convention; his method was much more effective. He took advantage of the noon or the evening meal to discuss points of difference with individual delegates. This personal approach frequently made a convert.

Delegates often sought Washington's opinion and advice. His position as presiding officer required that he maintain an impartial attitude while presiding. Still, many of the delegates wrote that when he was meeting with a committee, and was not in the presiding chair, he frequently showed by his face and gestures when he approved or disapproved of a proposal. More important, every delegate knew where Washington stood on every issue.

It is worth noting that 30 of the 55 delegates had been officers under Washington's command during the Revolution. Three of them had served as his closest, most trusted aides. John Dickinson of Delaware had served as a brigadier general. Alexander Hamilton of New York had served as Washington's lieutenant colonel on his staff and had been a heroic leader in his own right. Edmund Randolph, then the Governor of Virginia, had served as an aide-de-camp to General Washington.[47] As each new subject came up, these men, who had lived with Washington during the long war years, told the other delegates what Washington had said or written about the issue. Moreover, during the years prior to the Convention, most of the delegates had received letters from Washington stressing the need for union, urging a strong central government, and emphasizing the necessity for an executive with well-defined powers. He had been tireless in urging that the central government must have control of all aspects of commerce, the currency, and other significant matters.

As president of the Constitutional Convention, Washington exhibited the same type of leadership that had been incredibly effective during the war. He wisely realized that the first few months of the Convention should be largely educational. He appreciated that the Constitution should be made for the coming centuries, and thus, as close to perfect as possible. He demonstrated a readiness to listen, a willingness to allow every person to express himself completely, and a patient temperament which permitted a delegate to reopen the same subject as many times as he wished. These qualities worked a noticeable effect. Just as Washington himself was always willing to listen to the ideas of any person, so the members of the Convention found themselves listening to each other, trying to understand each viewpoint. In addition, Washington showed exemplary patience and willingness to consider all opinions. For example, Washington permitted the convention to vote *60 times* on the method to be used in selecting a president. This eventually led to the creation of the Electoral College to protect the rights of the smaller states from the power of the larger ones.

A good example of Washington's desire to be fair was demonstrated when all the other delegates from Virginia, including Madison, wanted both the House and Senate to be organized on the basis of population. Washington felt that way, too. The less populous states objected. Eventually, Connecticut delegates proposed their so-called Great Compromise. It would provide a dual system of congressional representation. All states would have the same number of seats in the Senate, but in the House of Representatives, the number of seats would be determined by the population of the state. In 1787, it was a phenomenally unique idea.

Washington listened carefully to the plan proposed for a compromise: the House would be elected by the people in each state, while the Senators would be selected by the respective state legislatures. When this compromise carried, Washington was not altogether happy with the solution, but he wisely wrote: "To please all is impossible, and to attempt it would be vain. The only way, therefore, is . . . to form such a government as will bear the scrutinizing eye of criticism, and trust it to the good sense and patriotism of the people to carry it into effect."[48]

While Washington was a giant among men, perhaps the only person alive who could have lead such a delegation, the real phenomenon of the Constitutional Convention was the intricate web of brilliance that was woven by the many incredibly intelligent and wise men in attendance. That these men should be brought together at just this time in history is beyond coincidence.

George Washington was one of those wise men. There were many others. James Madison has been called the "Father of the Constitution." He had an excellent knowledge of governments and their structures. Madison's own notes record that he made rather lengthy speeches on most of the subjects of importance. His notes also bring out clearly that the Convention did not always follow his leadership.

John Adams, who was still in Europe at the time of the Convention, wrote his brilliant book, *A Defence of the Constitutions of the Government of the United States of America*, which was critical as a building block from which to begin. Many of the speakers at the Convention used it as a repertory from which they gleaned ideas.

Benjamin Franklin, arguably the most famous man in the world at the time, was in attendance at the Convention. He noted that no document could ever be drawn up which would suit everyone perfectly. But he declared to George Washington, "Thus, I consent, sir, to this Constitution because I expect no better, and because I am not sure that it is not the best."[49] His profound statement, perhaps, is what swayed the delegates to finally vote in approval.

When all the necessary decisions had been made, a massive amount of material was turned over to Gouverneur Morris and his committee. They were to put the document into final form. Gouverneur Morris deserves credit for accomplishing the monumental task of producing the dignified and precise language which is in our Constitution.[50]

Our inspired Constitution has stood the test of time better than any other similar document in the history of the world. William Gladstone, Prime Minister of England for 17 of the years between

1868 and 1894, characterized our Constitution as "the most wonderful work ever struck off at a given time by the brain and purpose of man."[51]

On April 30, 1789, when Washington was sworn in as President, he held his arm to the square. After repeating the oath of office, he spontaneously added the words, "so help me God." Since that day, those simple, powerful words, "so help me God" have been considered a part of the Presidential oath of office.

Washington was unanimously elected for a second term as President. He is the only man to be unanimously elected, not once, but twice! When asked to serve a third term, he declined. In his Farewell Address, George Washington declared:

> Of all the dispositions and habits which lead to political prosperity, religion and morality are indispensable supports. In vain would that man claim the tribute of patriotism, who should labor to subvert these great pillars of human happiness, these firmest props of the duties of men and citizens. . . . Let it simply be asked, where is the security for property, for reputation, for life, if the sense of religious obligation desert the oaths which are the instruments of investigation in courts of justice? And let us with caution indulge the supposition that morality can be maintained without religion. Whatever may be conceded to the influence of refined education . . . reason and experience both forbid us to expect that national morality can prevail in exclusion of religious principle.[52]

Retirement Years

George Washington finally left public life and returned to his beloved Mount Vernon. Here, he continued to show his love for life and for people, and continued to be held in great awe by his countrymen.

On one occasion, George and Martha organized a ball at Mount Vernon. George loved young people and was anxious to observe their enjoyment. In his unassuming manner, he entered the hall. Suddenly, everyone stopped dancing, and a pall came over the room. Realizing the festivities had come to an abrupt halt due solely to his presence, he quickly left the ballroom, feeling chagrined that his mere appearance could so markedly dull the sparkle of the young spirits. The dancing resumed after he left, so he peeked through a crack in the doorway and enjoyed the rest of the dance.[53]

On Thursday, December 12, 1799, only three short years since his retirement from public life, the General rode about his farms. The weather became severe. Rain, hail, and snow fell alternately with a cold wind. When Washington came in to dinner, his hair and neck were wet with snow. Friday, he complained of a sore throat, but still went out to mark some trees that were to be cut down. That evening, a hoarseness developed, but he was still quite cheerful. When offered something for his cold, he replied, "No, you know I never take anything for a cold. Let it go as it came."[54]

Between two and three o'clock on Saturday morning, George awakened Martha and told her he was very "unwell." She observed he could barely speak and was breathing with difficulty. That morning, he asked for a doctor to come to "bleed" him. A mixture of molasses, vinegar, and butter was prepared to soothe his throat, but he could not swallow a drop. Doctor Albin Rawlins came and began to bleed him. Martha asked that not much blood be taken, but the General asked that it be continued. The bleeding was stopped after taking about one-half pint. No relief was obtained from the bleeding.

Nothing would go down his throat. Finally, a bathing with smelling salts was administered.

A second doctor, Dr. James Craik, was called in. He placed a blister of Cantharides (a preparation of dried beetles used as a counter-irritant) on George's throat. More blood was let, then he was told to gargle with vinegar and hot water. In trying to gargle, George almost suffocated. This led to still more bleeding and the placement of another blister. But no relief.

At approximately four o'clock in the afternoon, Washington asked for the two wills that he had previously prepared. He reviewed them and asked that one be burned. It was. The other will was one that he had drawn up himself, without any help, and signed on July 9, 1799. It was put into Martha's closet. After this was done, Washington said to his secretary, "I believed from the first that the disorder would prove fatal. . . . Arrange and record all my late military letters and papers. Arrange my accounts and settle my books, as you know more about them than anyone else, and let Mr. Rawlins finish recording my other letters which he has begun."[55]

In late afternoon, George appeared to be in great pain and distress because of his difficulty in breathing and his need to frequently change positions on his bed. About five o'clock in the evening, Dr. Craik came again. George told him, "I die hard; but I am not afraid to go; I believed from my first attack that I should not survive it; my breath can not last long."[56] In all his distress he uttered not a sigh nor a complaint. At about ten o'clock in the evening, with great difficulty, he finally said, "I am just going. Have me decently buried." He passed on between ten and eleven o'clock, without a struggle or sigh. He was 67 years old. As he had requested, he was buried without any funeral oration.[57]

One of the greatest and most beloved men in history died on that cold December day in 1799. In spite of all his monumental accomplishments, there was one goal that Washington was not able to achieve. Martha remarked that he did not intend "to quit the theater of this world" until the new century had been rung in.[58] His life ended in the century in which he had profoundly played the starring role.

Congress honored the life of George Washington, and, after other tributes, "the House passed the resolutions written by Henry Lee, one of Washington's calvary officers, which ends: ' . . . to the memory of the MAN, first in war, first in peace, and first in the hearts of his countrymen.'"[59]

George Washington is rightfully remembered with honor. As historian Richard Brookhiser has written: "Washington was the most important man in America, whether he was on stage or off, for twenty-four years; for seventeen of those years, he was front and center. It is a record unmatched in our history . . ."[60]

Perhaps the greatest tribute ever paid to George Washington was given by another man who is also greatly revered by his country. A man whose name is often tied in reverence with the leader he so admired. Abraham Lincoln declared, "To add brightness to the sun or glory to the name of Washington is . . . impossible. Let none attempt it. In solemn awe pronounce the name and in its naked deathless splendor, leave it shining on."[61]

Chapter 3

John Adams

October 19, 1735 – July 4, 1826

JOHN ADAMS

John Adams was a short and stubby man, sometimes called "His Rotundity" by his enemies. He was brash, outspoken, and, at times, cranky and temperamental. But his brilliance and fervency in defense of America's interests overwhelmingly outweighed his negligible appearance and various undesirable personality traits. This fact was made obvious when Adams was appointed as a diplomat to three different countries and when he was elected as the second President of the United States of America.

John Adams was born October 30, 1735, just outside of Boston, Massachusetts, in a little town called Braintree (now Quincy). He came from pilgrim stock. His grandmother, Hannah Bass, descended from the Honorable John Alden, who sailed to Plymouth on the Mayflower in 1620. As a child, John Adams was athletic, loving to ice skate, wrestle, and swim. He grew to be a man of passion, intellect, and vanity—with an unlimited need for approval and recognition. He was a zealous student of the scriptures, and he wanted to be a farmer.

John entered Harvard College at the typical-for-the-time young age of 15. He was the first from his family to graduate from Harvard, the only one of three brothers to do so. John described his years at Harvard as "total and complete happiness."[1] After graduation, he became a schoolmaster. He taught for only one year, then decided to continue at Harvard to study law.

Education wasn't the only thing occupying the mind of John Adams. As he grew into manhood, he described one of his personal weaknesses when he admitted that "his enjoyment of the society of females 'engaged' him too much."[2] Yet his taste for the ladies was not easily satisfied. Sometime in about 1759, John was introduced to the Smith girls, one of whom was 15-year-old Abigail.[3] In his diary, John concluded that "the 'S girls' did not measure up: 'Not fond, not frank, not candid.'"[4] But a short two years later, his opinion had altered dramatically! John enlisted the help of Abigail's sister to get messages to Abigail. Even though John was nine years older than Abigail, her sister Mary seemed eager to facilitate the romance.

Now 17, Abigail was tall, slender, and beautiful. Her face displayed a becoming symmetry of bone structure with her high and agreeably curved forehead being balanced by prominent cheekbones, a slender but resolute oval of a jaw-line and a strongly molded chin. Her mouth was small but full-lipped, with precisely set, small white teeth. Her eyes were the best part of her visage: large, a warm brown, luminously liquid and friendly under slender arched brows. Her nose was a miniature of her father's Roman nose. Her skin was smooth and lovely, and her hair was a soft chestnut color, alive with light.

John and Abigail shared a passion for learning, even though the way they each obtained their education was strikingly different. His was a rigorous formal education; hers was a matter of bits and pieces. While John was already involved in his higher education, Abigail became concerned about beginning her schooling. Abigail loved to learn. "She prized learning perhaps a shade less than morality."[5] Her mother, however, shielded Abigail because she was delicate and the little one of the family.

On the afternoon of her eighth birthday, Abigail boldly announced that she wanted to attend the neighboring "Dame School," where her sister Mary had studied for several years. But Abigail's mother prohibited her, saying that she needed her health more than she needed book learning. Later that same night, knowing that Abigail was upset, her father went to her room and carried her downstairs to his library. He had already taught Abigail to read and write. Now she wished her father could somehow convince her mother to let her go to the dame school. However, realistically she knew he would not bring contention into the family. Family fights produced nothing good. But he did promise to see that she would get the best education this side of Harvard College. But they were not to let her mother know. She would be worried about the strain on Abigail's weak body.

There were three good libraries in their family: the one at their own home, the one at the Smith home in Boston, and the fine collection at Mount Wollaston. Her father promised that between her Uncle Isaac Smith, her Grandfather John Quincy, and himself, slowly and carefully, they would see her educated. Parson Smith kept his birthday promise to little Abigail. He taught her not only from the Bible and his extensive collection of sermons, but also from the plays of Shakespeare and Ben Johnson, in between assignments of grammar, arithmetic, geography, and such history books as the *Discourses of Virginia*. Between the rigorous minds of her father, her uncle, and her grandfather, and from her natural thirst for knowledge, which she slaked by exploratory reading, she had achieved a rudimentary education along with the valuable tools of logic and objective thinking.

Marriage and Family

When John and Abigail began courting, they fell deeply and passionately in love. Yet, Abigail's mother was against the match, feeling that Abigail would be marrying beneath her status. "John Adams is nothing but a lawyer!" her mother had cried scornfully. "Lawyers are the most despicable group in New England. Everybody agrees. They ought to be outlawed."[6]

In her marriage plans, as in her desire for an education, Abigail showed her determination. Soon, after both their mothers had been won over to the couple's intentions to wed, Abigail married John Adams on October 25, 1764. As for John, his marriage to Abigail was the most important decision of the years to come. Abigail proved to be the ballast John needed in his life.

Within a short nine months, their daughter was born on July 14, 1765. Abigail asked John if he was disappointed the new baby was not a boy. He assured her he was content with his new baby girl, that he'd always hoped for a daughter, and that they had many years ahead of them to have sons. When choosing a name for their new little one, they settled on Abigail. It was a name to which John was partial. And apparently there had been an Abigail in nearly every generation of the Smith family. When John was asked which Abigail should come running when he called, he responded that both should come . . . as the master of the house had a right to expect such response.

When her husband called himself "the master of the house," Abigail Adams was not offended because she understood the important role that women play in the home. "How 'miserable' must that woman be, Abigail supposed, who allowed herself to be confined to a narrow circle of domesticity with no higher sites in mind. More to be pitied, however, was the woman of both genius and taste who could not 'cheerfully' leave her intellectual pursuits to tend to the daily cares of the prudent housewife."[7]

When they were first married, Abigail created a little study for herself in an alcove of their bedroom. In preparing for their second child, she moved her small desk and bookcase in order to make a "borning room" out of her study. Their second child, a son, was born July 11, 1767. Two days after the birth of the boy, Abigail's grandfather, Colonel John Quincy, died at Mount Wollaston. Naturally, Abigail was excused from attending the funeral, but when John returned from it, he proposed they name their new son after Abigail's grandfather. She agreed to the name, John Quincy Adams. Her grandfather Quincy was a good man. With their son carrying his name, he would remain alive.

In an effort to help John's law practice grow, the couple determined to move from Braintree to Boston. They chose to lease a house on Battle Street that was called the "White House." John suggested that one of the rooms would serve adequately as his study. He agreed that he wouldn't attempt to cart in his whole library, only the books he should need. Abigail knew that the books he didn't need had yet to be printed!

On December 28, 1768, a second daughter, Susanna, was born to John and Abigail. It was only 17 months since their son, John Quincy, had come into the world. In the mid-1700's, midwives were normally the only medical help requested at the birth of a child. But Abigail knew this pregnancy was not proceeding well. Her cousin, Dr. Cotton Tufts, had recommended a specialist in the new field of obstetrics be called in to attend to her at the birth. This was a fortunate decision since Susanna's birth was not easy. It was long and painful for Abigail. She was at the end of her strength before the baby was born. But she realized that if she gave in to exhaustion, both she and the baby would die. Because of her determination to save the child's life, she also saved her own.

The baby was finally born, but was not breathing. The doctor began compressing and squeezing the child's chest. But the infant did not breathe for some 15 or 20 minutes. Little Susanna, or "Suky," was a puny baby. She didn't move around much and was content with a minimum of milk. Abigail, too, was slow to recover from the difficult birth and return to health.

In the winter of 1769, the "White House" was sold out from under John and Abigail by the owner. But the Adams found a new, even nicer house to lease. Their new home, also in Boston, was a handsome, two-story wood house with dormer windows. There were eight main rooms, seven of them with fireplaces. John had a front room of their house remodeled into a law office and went about expanding his law practice. Their marriage proved happy, and they found they worked well together through all their highs and lows. Tragically, baby Susanna died on February 4, 1770. She was only 14 months old. There was no particular reason for her death. Her life just seemed to flicker out like a candle at the end of its wick. John and Abigail had two more children, both sons. On May 29, 1770, less than four months after poor Susanna died, baby Charles was born. And on September 15, 1772, their last child, Thomas Boylston, came into the world. Abigail was now 28 years old; John was 37.

Sparks of Revolution

Earlier, while struggling as an obscure lawyer in Boston, John became better acquainted with his older second cousin, Samuel Adams. Sam, a member of the Harvard class of 1740, was already well known for his stiff resistance to British colonial policies. He had a major influence on John's becoming involved in the revolutionary movement.

On March 22, 1765, the British Parliament passed the Stamp Act. By this law, all American colonists were required to pay a tax on every piece of printed paper they used. There was to be a stamp affixed to every clearance paper of every ship that entered or left the harbor, every newspaper, every almanac, every pamphlet, every sheet of writing paper, every indenture, bill of sale, signed will, deed, every writ, and every decision handed down in the courts. In the past, taxes and duties on colonial trade had been measures to regulate commerce, but the Stamp Act seemed a measure designed purely to raise money for the English. John Adams was immediate in his stern condemnation of the Stamp Tax. He referred to it as an "unconstitutional" incursion in the natural rights of Americans. Sam Adams was also incensed when the British passed the Stamp Act. To oppose it, he organized a radical group called the "Sons of Liberty." John Adams, together with James Otis and John Hancock, became charter members.

John Adams was selected to serve on a committee to write "Instructions to Parliament" concerning the feelings of Bostonians about the stamps. His draft of these instructions was accepted unanimously. He titled his draft *Instructions from the freeholders (landowners) of the town to the General Court*, the legislative body of Massachusetts. Later, this became known as the "Braintree Instructions." In it, John wrote: "We have always understood it to be a grand and fundamental principle of the [English] constitution that no freeman should be subject to any tax to which he has not given his own consent. There must be 'no taxation without representation.'"[8] One newspaper said Adams' words were "worthy . . . to be wrote [sic] in letters of gold."[9] On Monday, May 19, 1766, there were "rejoicings" in the colonies when the Stamp Act was at last repealed—due in no small measure to the "Instructions to Parliament" written by John Adams.

In July 1767, just 14 months after the repeal of the Stamp Act, the British Parliament issued the Townshend Acts. One of these acts placed duties on glass, lead, paint, paper, wine, and tea imported into the colonies. Another act established a customs agency in Boston to collect them efficiently. The Townshend Acts led to renewed protests in the American colonies and had a major impact on John Hancock, and, in turn, John Adams. John Hancock (about 15 months younger) and John Adams had been close friends for the three years that they attended Harvard College together. The Boston Hancocks were among the richest shipowners and merchants in America. When his father, Thomas, died in 1764, John Hancock inherited most of the family's vast estate. This included more than 80,000 pounds, huge areas of land in Massachusetts and Connecticut, ships, shops, wharfs, and warehouses. Adams observed it was remarkable that Hancock's inheritance of that tremendous fortune made little change in him. He was always steady, punctual, industrious, and an indefatigable man of business. And he continued to be generous with his money. John found this a rarity among the rich in New England.

The Townshend Acts also included duties on wine, which John Hancock often imported. Sometimes Hancock cleverly invited the customs officer into his cabin for a friendly drink before the officer checked the cargo on the boat. Since Hancock's cabin was at the far end of his wharf, this "friendly drink" provided time for his men to unload the undeclared wine and other goods.

It wasn't a foolproof plan. In 1768, when a customs officer came on board unannounced, the crew locked him in a cabin and unloaded the wine without paying the duty. In response, boats from the British warship *Romney* rowed to the wharf, cut the ropes to the *Liberty* (Hancock's ship), and towed her out to the *Romney*.

Now Hancock was in trouble. The British were in the process of declaring the *Liberty* contraband, and thus confiscating her. They planned to levy a fine of 100,000 pounds. This was an outrageous fine, all out of proportion to the charge. It was also most of the wealth of John Hancock. Hancock asked John Adams to represent him. Adams agreed, even though Hancock was indeed guilty of smuggling goods to shore without paying duties on them. Adams believed the Townshend Acts to be unconstitutional, and, therefore, the seizing was unlawful.

But the British were also very clever. They didn't seize the *Liberty* for smuggling, as the wine had already vanished into Boston. Instead, they had caught Hancock loading tar and oil without a Customs Commission permit. On a technical legality, they had him in violation of law. John sought and received a postponement of the trial to allow things to settle down. Through intensive study he came up with his plan and strategy.

At trial, the prosecution made a good case against John Hancock. John Adams then attacked the Townshend Acts for enabling the case against Mr. Hancock to be tried in an Admiralty court, not by a jury, not by the law of the land, but by a single judge. The judge arose after Adams' statements, banged his gavel, and said, without notice or reason, "His Majesty's Court is adjourned. Hearings will be continued." The court was never reconvened. On March 26, 1769, the prosecution announced that the case was dropped. His Majesty would not pursue the matter. It appeared to John Adams that the Crown officials were afraid of the verdict going either way, and were waiting for outside events to render the trial obsolete. The decision to drop the case meant that the Crown wouldn't fine Hancock the 100,000 pounds, but neither would they declare him innocent. They also wouldn't release his confiscated ship. John Hancock never again saw the *Liberty* . . . but the British never again seized another of his ships. John Adams was glad to be done with the whole business. "I was thoroughly weary and disgusted," he wrote, "with the court, the officers of the crown, the cause, and even with the tyrannical bell that jangled me out of my house every morning."[10]

In 1770, John Adams once again strode into the public eye. British troops had been assigned to Boston for two years, but on March 5, 1770, a riot began when a number of drunken, angry Bostonians threatened some soldiers with clubs and sticks. Captain Thomas Preston, a British officer, brought several soldiers to his assistance. But the crowd had grown to about 400 and was pressing close to the soldiers. The soldiers fired into the crowd, killing five Americans. Speechmakers of the day invented the name "Boston Massacre," but it was really only a street clash in which a squad of British soldiers killed five colonists. Nine soldiers were jailed and charged with murder. No lawyer in Boston dared to touch their case.

John Adams knew that the British had fired in self-defense. He also knew that without adequate counsel, they would surely be executed. Even though he detested the British occupation, John consented to represent the soldiers in court. Friends warned Adams that the case would destroy him. But his sense of justice compelled him "to differ in opinion from all my friends, to set at defiance all their advice, their remonstrances, their raillery, their ridicule, their censures, and their sarcasms, without acquiring one symptom of pity from my enemies."[11] Working with his partner, Josiah Quincy, Adams was able to win complete acquittal for Captain Thomas Preston and his soldiers, except for two who were convicted of manslaughter, branded on the hand, and then released.

The fears of Adams' fellow lawyers never came to pass. As a result of defending Preston and his soldiers, young John Adams gained the reputation of being a man of true character and a lawyer with the highest principles. A few weeks after the trial, John Adams was elected by the people of Boston to be a representative to the Massachusetts General Court. Exhausted by the trial, John and Abigail moved their little family back to their farm in Braintree.

The Declaration of Independence

On September 5, 1774, Massachusetts sent John Adams to the First Continental Congress. And the following year, May 10, 1775, he returned to the Second Continental Congress. Here he argued that all America must unite behind the ragged armies that were assembling in Massachusetts. After a heated debate, the Congress adopted the army, giving it official recognition. But that decision demanded another immediate action: the selection of the new army's Commander in Chief. Just as Adams had fervently argued for the adoption of the army, he now eloquently argued for its leader and the specific qualifications that the new Commander must have. The Commander should be a gentleman with excellent character who could command the favorable regard of all Americans and whose talents would unite the colonies better than any other person could. He closed his speech with these words:

> Gentlemen, I know these qualifications are high, but we all know they are needful in this crisis in this chief. Does anyone say they are not to be obtained in this country? In reply, I have to say they are; they reside in one of our own body, and he is the man whom I now nominate,—GEORGE WASHINGTON OF VIRGINIA.[12]

George Washington and John Adams had served together as delegates in the First Continental Congress. Adams was fully acquainted with Washington's reputation as a military leader in the French and Indian War. By their service together in Congress, Adams was aware of George Washington's character and personality.

Adams felt a twinge of regret as he proposed Washington's name. Adams was mindful of the historical importance of what this little group of men was about to do. He knew that others in the assembly were setting their course for fame and acclaim, whether or not they intended to do so. He was also painfully aware that several of them would receive their fame due to more than a little help from John Adams. He was afraid he would remain behind, unknown, and, as he said in a letter to Abigail: "Worn out with scribbling, for my Bread and my Liberty, low in Spirits and weak in Health, must leave others to wear Laurells which I have Sown; others, to eat the Bread which I have earned."[13]

By January 9, 1776, an anonymous pamphlet called *Common Sense* had been published in Philadelphia. A month later, when John Adams resumed his seat in the Second Continental Congress, this pamphlet was already in its third printing and sweeping the colonies. In a letter to Abigail, John commented that he expected *Common Sense* to become the common faith in the colonies. He was flattered when he learned that Bostonians considered him to be the author. However the author was later revealed to be an English immigrant named Thomas Paine. He had landed at Philadelphia a year earlier with little more than a letter of introduction from Benjamin Franklin. *Common Sense* was written in simple language, written to be understood by anyone. It attacked the idea of a hereditary monarchy as absurd and evil. It was a call to arms.

Adams, however, was the author of a pamphlet called *Thoughts on Government*. These thoughts were first set out in a letter to a fellow congressman, William Hooper. Hooper was returning home to help write a new constitution for the state of North Carolina and had asked Adams for a "sketch" of his views. Some people who had seen what Adams had written out for Hooper wanted copies for themselves. After hand writing an additional three copies, Adams had the letter published as a pamphlet by a Philadelphia printer. The essay began:

> It has been the will of Heaven, that we should be thrown into existence at a period when the greatest philosophers and lawgivers of antiquity would have wished to live. . . . A period when a coincidence of circumstances without example has afforded to thirteen colonies at once an opportunity of beginning government anew from the foundation and building as they choose. How few of the human race have ever had an opportunity of choosing a system of government for themselves and their children? How few have ever had anything more of choice in government than in climate.[14]

It was a profound statement. It was an amazing concept upon which these Founding Fathers were embarking. A government based on freedom for all. It was unheard of before these divinely inspired men were brought together by the hand of God. Truly, as John Adams gloriously stated, before now, humanity had no more choice in their form of government than they did in their weather conditions.

Paine's pamphlet called for a tearing down. In his pamphlet, John Adams responded by proposing to build up a new form of government. Adams stressed the concept that separation of judicial power from both the legislative and executive powers was essential to the stability of government and to the able and impartial administration of justice. "Little that Adams ever wrote had such effect as his *Thoughts on Government*. Yet he felt it was too rough, too 'crude' in execution. He regretted insufficient time to write 'more correctly.'"[15]

On June 7, 1776, Richard Henry Lee of Virginia, acting on a resolution of the delegation meeting at Williamsburg, and proposed by Patrick Henry, stood before the Continental Congress to make the momentous Resolution:

> That these United Colonies are, and of right ought to be, free and independent States: that they are absolved from all allegiance to the British Crown; and that all political connection between them and the State of Great Britain is, and ought to be, totally dissolved.[16]

Before a dissenting vote could be heard, John Adams jumped to his feet to second the resolution. Some of the colonies were not yet ready to accept this resolution. After heated debate, it was agreed that a vote on the resolution would be postponed for three weeks. A committee would be appointed immediately to work on the language of a Declaration of Independence. This way, no time would be lost in the drafting of a document . . . should the resolution pass. John Adams was appointed to the committee assigned to write a Declaration of Independence. He sat on the committee with Thomas Jefferson, Benjamin Franklin, Roger Sherman, and Robert R. Livingston. Although Thomas Jefferson was asked to prepare the draft, because of his "felicity of expression,"[17] Adams was the man who carried the burden of defending the Declaration in the debate. Jefferson said, "John Adams was our Colossus on the floor. He was not graceful nor elegant, nor remarkably fluent but he came out occasionally with a power of thought and expression, that moved us from our seats."[18]

When others were vacillating on whether to adopt the Declaration of Independence, the sentiments of John Adams were these:

> Sink or swim, live or die, survive or perish, I give my hand and my heart to this vote. It is true, indeed,

that in the beginning we aimed not at independence. But there's a Divinity that shapes our ends. . . . Why, then, should we defer the Declaration? . . . You and I, indeed, may rue it. We may not live to see the time when this Declaration shall be made good. We may die; die Colonists, die slaves, die, it may be, ignominiously and on the scaffold. Be it so. Be it so. If it be the pleasure of Heaven that my country shall require the poor offering of my life, the victim shall be ready. . . . But while I do live, let me have a country, or at least the hope of a country, and that a free country.

But whatever may be our fate, be assured . . . that this Declaration will stand. It may cost treasure, and it may cost blood, but it will stand and it will richly compensate for both.

Through the thick gloom of the present, I see the brightness of the future as the sun in heaven. We shall make this a glorious, and immortal day. When we are in our graves, our children will honor it. They will celebrate it with thanksgiving, with festivity, with bonfires, and illuminations. . . .

Before God, I believe the hour is come. My judgment approves this measure, and my whole heart is in it. All that I have, and all that I am, and all that I hope, in this life, I am now ready here to stake upon it; and I leave off as I began, that live or die, survive or perish, I am for the Declaration. It is my living sentiment, and by the blessing of God it shall be my dying sentiment. Independence now, and Independence forever.[19]

The resolution approving a Declaration of Independence was adopted on July 2, 1776. Adams thought July 2nd would become the great day of celebration. The next day he wrote to Abigail:

> Yesterday the greatest Question was decided, which ever was debated in America, and a greater, perhaps, never was nor will be decided among Men. . . . The Second Day of July, 1776, will be the most memorable Epocha [sic], in the History of America.— I am apt to believe that it will be celebrated, by succeeding Generations, as the great anniversary Festival. It ought to be commemorated, as the Day of Deliverance by solemn Acts of Devotion to God Almighty. It ought to be solemnized with Pomp and Parade, with Shews [sic], Games, Sports, Guns, Bells, Bonfires, and Illuminations from one End of this Continent to the other from this Time forward forever more.[20]

With the resolution approved, now the body had to debate the wording of the Declaration as proposed by the committee and written by Thomas Jefferson. On July 4, the draft was adopted and signed by John Hancock, president of the Congress, and then by Charles Thompson, secretary. Twelve colonies voted in the affirmative, New York being silent. New York finally adopted a resolution approving and supporting the Declaration on July 9. It then became the Unanimous Declaration of the Thirteen United States of America. The remaining 54 members of Congress affixed their signatures on the final handlettered parchment document on August 2,1776.

Diplomat in France and Holland

Independence had been declared, but the war was far from being won. Again, John Adams played a pivotal role in the making of America. In 1778, Congress sent Adams to France to join with

Benjamin Franklin in negotiating for much needed financial aid. Adams remained in Europe or England for the next ten trying years, with only one brief trip home. As an appointed diplomat to France, Adams labored with Benjamin Franklin or Thomas Jefferson, or sometimes both of them, to secure what was in America's best interests.

Shortly after his arrival in France, Adams discovered why Dr. Benjamin Franklin was the center of attention and much adored by the French citizens. Franklin was a man of science and much admired for his scientific discoveries. Franklin had wisely adopted some of the characteristics of the French people. Like them, he was often aloof or indifferent and sometimes even careless about details and money. Because of his advanced age, Franklin had the enviable privilege of embracing the ladies as much as he pleased . . . and to be embraced by them in return. Adams and Franklin favored markedly different lifestyles. After his morning walks of four or five miles, followed by an early breakfast, Adams was eager to get to work. But Franklin seldom rose before ten o'clock. Even though Franklin was suffering from gout and boils, he loved his pleasures and ease. As time passed, and his French improved, Adams began to realize that Franklin spoke and understood the language less than he pretended. In diplomatic matters, Franklin let the French officials set the pace. All of this probably worked to the benefit of the Americans, but it was frustrating to Adams. He wanted to work at a regular pace and to see steady results and success.

In 1780, John was tired of waiting for the French to make any diplomatic decisions. He decided to go to Holland to see if something might be done to render the United States less dependant on France. Through dogged perseverance, he accomplished his goal. Adams was able to convince Holland to join in a treaty of commerce with the United States. He met with private parties and manipulated an introduction into the community of prominent Amsterdam bankers. He reported to Congress that a considerable loan from the Dutch was entirely possible. Congress granted Adams the authority to work on such a loan. His idealism, zeal, determination, and energy—qualities that seemed to hinder him in France—now bore fruit in Holland. He was able to convince the Dutch bankers that America would accept no outcome in the war short of complete independence from Great Britain. A loan would be forthcoming. This was a turning point in the war.

Lacking the financial resources to raise a new army, the British Government appealed to the Americans for peace. On October 19, 1781, Britains' General Cornwallis surrendered in Yorktown. This victory was critical to the American triumph, and effectively ended the Revolutionary War. Six months later, on April 19, 1782, Holland recognized and accepted the independence of the United States of America.

After the surrender of Yorktown, Adams received his next assignment: to negotiate a peace settlement with Great Britain. The British sent their Ministers to France to negotiate with the Americans. In addition to John Adams, the American negotiating team included Benjamin Franklin and John Jay. On November 30, 1782, a preliminary peace treaty was signed in Paris. On September 3, 1783, almost two years after General Cornwallis surrendered, a final peace treaty was signed in Paris. The Revolutionary War was officially over. Adams, Franklin, and Jay had combined bluff with diplomacy and walked out of the negotiations with a treaty much in America's favor.

While in France, John sorely missed Abigail and his homeland. John wrote to Abigail of his desire to be back with her in Braintree:

> I know not the Reason but there is some Strange Attraction between the North Parish in Braintree and my heart. It is a remarkable Spot. It has vomited Forth more Fire than Mount Etna. It has produced three mortals, Hancock and two Adams', who have, with the best Intentions in the World, set the World ablaze . . .
>
> Glorious however as the flame is, I wish I could put it out. Some people say I was born for such times. It is true I was born to be in such times but was not made for them. They affect too tenderly my heart.[21]

In 1784, Abigail and her daughter Nabby traveled to Europe to join John and John Quincy. When John Adams learned of their safe arrival, he said, "I am twenty years younger than I was yesterday."[22] His stay in England lasted another five years, until June 1788.

About the same time Abigail arrived, Jefferson also appeared in France to take the place of Dr. Franklin. While Dr. Franklin and John and Abigail had less expensive rural dwellings, Jefferson took up residence in the heart of the city. He did not seem to practice what he preached in matters of economy. Jefferson told his daughter Patsy to never purchase anything unless she had the money to pay for it, but he himself seemed to purchase anything he wished in the way of material possessions or comforts. He was constantly remodeling his Paris house. The booksellers knew they had an American patron who shopped like no other. Along with shopping he loved architecture, science, music, theater, museums, food, and good wine.

Most afternoons, when the three of them were together in France, Jefferson and Adams would meet at the home of Dr. Franklin. While they were earnestly trying to accomplish that which was in America's best interest, sometimes their methods were at odds with each other. Adams wanted to go full speed ahead with business. Both

Jefferson and Franklin had to slow him down. Franklin may have been a little frustrated by Adams' zealous nature. He wrote to their common friend Robert Livingston: "He means well for his country, is always an honest man, often a wise one, but sometimes and some things, absolutely out of his senses."[23]

Diplomat in Great Britain

Adams' valuable contribution to negotiations in France was recognized immediately. He was then commissioned to negotiate a commercial treaty with Great Britain. So he and Abigail moved to London. John Adams was able to accomplish many of his achievements because he had a clear vision. It was evident to him from the moment the first gunshots were fired at Lexington and Concord in April of 1775. He believed that one day the United States of America would be a strong, independent, resourceful, flourishing nation, able to take its place as an equal at the international board. It was this vision which had sustained him through his years of discouragement and loneliness. It was a position of faith.

John Adams felt that Americans were to be Saints in the same way the members of his Congregationalist Church were known as Saints. To become a Congregationalist Saint, one had to achieve grace through moral and spiritual purity. Adams felt the same principle applied to his country. America had to come into a state of grace through being a free society of free men. Men who were free to think, free to feel, free to speak, act, own, and regulate for the good of all. This state of grace demanded a society in which every man would have a chance to grow. Representatives of the people would protect those whose chances for growth were naturally limited. If successful, this would be the most significant movement and revolution in the history of mankind. It must be done; it would be done. The costs were high, but the results would be magnificently manifest. John compared the United States to a city on a hill. "A city that is set on a hill cannot be hid," as stated in Matthew chapter 5, verse 14.

John Adams grew extremely frustrated as he continued to receive word from the states. Now that the war with Britain was over, America seemed to be at war with herself. Adding to that frustration was his seeming ineffectiveness with the leaders in England. John complained to Abigail about a letter James Warren had written from America. As Warren described it, interest in self-government had vanished. Few attended town meetings any more or even bothered to vote. John considered the Massachusetts Constitution to be one of his offspring, every bit as much as Nabby or Johnny or Charley or Tommy. It must not be allowed to die or be destroyed. The Continental Congress was considered another one of his children. It now seemed to want to disband.

The Articles of Confederation were no longer working. The finances of the central government were a shambles. The Congress was growing more ineffectual every day. Only five states bothered to send delegates. Each state insisted on being a separate sovereignty. Their stubborn dignity would not allow them to tolerate a federal government strong enough to secure life, liberty, and property. There was talk of men of property forming an army to take over the government.

John had made the rounds of British Ministers. They knew of America's condition from their Tory informants. As America grew weaker, the British grew stronger. John was in England for a year and a half, trying to arrange a commercial treaty with the British which would bring prosperity to the states and respect and power to the American central government. It was made clear to John that he need no longer supplicate for a treaty. He felt he had failed. He would be allowed to accomplish nothing for the remaining 16 months of his term as diplomatic Minister to Great Britain. Many people in Boston, New York, and Philadelphia put the lack of a treaty with the British squarely on the shoulders of John Adams.

Massachusetts was on the verge of civil war, with armed bands defying the militia. Congress was in danger of being dissolved or taken over by the large property owners. And John Adams found himself 3,000 miles away from home. But he refused to just sit there in England for a year and a half and do nothing. Every victory he had ever won had come through the word: spoken or printed. Was it possible that his words could help to conquer the chaos in his country? Feeling desperate to accomplish something useful, John Adams made this monumental decision: he would write a book! He wanted to prove through his writing that only a balanced system of government, with a strong, independent executive, two separate legislative bodies, and a judiciary, can keep a republic alive. He planned to demonstrate from the thousands of years of recorded history that, without a balance of the three powers, governments become tyrannies or oligarchies, with human freedoms destroyed.

At first, Abigail seemed incredulous. Then she decided with him, yes, he should write a book. Adams knew it would be a long one, maybe several volumes, and would take a year or more to write. But he was never one to doubt the power of the printed word. He believed the printed word could cut through tissues of falsehood, evasion, and ignorance. This seemed the only way that John could turn his failure into success.

The Annapolis Convention was already meeting to consider a uniform system between the states in their commercial regulations. John knew they simply could not stop with so simple an objective, not with the whole of America falling in on their heads. Some of

America's best men would be there: James Madison, Edmund Randolph of Virginia and Alexander Hamilton of New York. Brilliant men and patriots. Surely they would realize that they needed to call a greater convention for the purpose of writing a new, strong, workable federal constitution.

John wanted to have his book ready in time for their consultations. He would call it *A Defence of the Constitutions of Government of the United States of America.* It was aimed as much at Massachusetts as at the Continental Congress, or at any other body meeting to write a federal constitution.

Unbelievably, almost miraculously, Adams' book about government principles was available in the United States by spring 1787 and was widely circulated. It proved to be an invaluable asset when the Constitutional Convention first met on May 25, 1787. One historical scholar noted: "Even a casual glance at the records of the Federal Convention will show that Adams' book was used as a sort of repertory by many speakers, who found in it a confirmation of their views, [with] historical illustrations and precedents."[24]

A Hero's Welcome

Finally, it was time for John and Abigail to return home. After a rough, 58-day crossing of the Atlantic Ocean, the couple arrived back in Boston on July 17, 1788. The town orchestrated a welcome such as John Adams never imagined. It was nothing short of a hero's welcome. A crowd of several thousand were assembled to greet them. John Hancock made his fine coach readily available at the end of Long Wharf to carry them back to Braintree. The outpouring of admiration was inexpressibly gratifying to John and Abigail, who in the long absence had often felt unappreciated or forgotten.

The Constitution of the United States had been signed on September 17, 1787.[25] It then went to the states for ratification. By

August, 1788, eleven states had ratified it, with a majority of only nine necessary. The State of Virginia ratified upon the provision that a Bill of Rights be adopted. Then, under this new Constitution, on April 6, 1789, the Senate witnessed the counting of 69 ballots unanimously electing George Washington as the first President of the United States, and 34 ballots electing John Adams as the first Vice-President.[26] Adams served two rather uneventful terms as Vice-President. While serving as second in command, Adams described the position as "the most insignificant office that ever the invention of man contrived or his imagination conceived."[27]

The Ablest Man Becomes President

George Washington refused to serve a third term as President. In the 1796 election, neither Adams nor Jefferson actively campaigned for the presidency. However, both men were nominated to represent their parties, Adams as a Federalist, and Jefferson as a Republican. The framers of the Constitution had established that the candidate receiving the most votes would become President, and the one who received the second highest number of votes would be the Vice-President. But they had never anticipated that the President and Vice-President might represent antagonistic points of view. The count of the Electoral College in 1796 gave Adams the Presidency by the narrow margin of three votes, 71 for Adams and 68 for Jefferson. Adams was elected President, Jefferson Vice-President.

Due to the weather, Abigail was unable to travel to Philadelphia for the inauguration. In a letter describing the affair to her, John wrote, "Washington seemed to enjoy a triumph over me. Methought I heard him say, 'Ay! I am fairly out and you fairly in! See which of us will be the happiest!'"[28]

It was a bit daunting to occupy the place of the beloved retiring President George Washington. Adams did not enjoy the favor and acclaim that Washington had received. Washington was a war hero; Adams had not even lifted a musket. Washington was tall and dignified; Adams was short and increasingly round. Washington was known for his patience and reserve; Adams was short-tempered and could be easily provoked.

As with the whole of America, John and Abigail Adams had a high regard for the retiring President. Abigail found the august President Washington a "singular example of modesty and diffidence. . . . He is polite with dignity, affable without familiarity, distant without Haughtiness, Grave without Austerity, Modest, wise, and Good."[29]

Not only were Washington's shoes hard to fill, but from the moment he assumed office, Adams was met with a crisis in relations with France. And it continued for his whole administration. Adams did his best to walk the tightrope of neutrality between France and England. The leaders of France wanted the United States to join them in their war against Great Britain. When America refused to join such a war, France refused to recognize or accept United States diplomats.

Early in 1798, Adams received news from the three commissioners that he had sent to France. The commissioners reported that agents of the French government (referred to only as X, Y, and Z) demanded a bribe before the American envoys would be received by the Foreign Minister Talleyrand. Adams restrained himself from making a declaration of war. Instead, he asked Congress to permit American merchant ships to arm themselves. His request was violently opposed by Congress. Only when Adams felt he had no other choice did he make the dispatches of the XYZ affair public. There was an immediate public outcry against the French agents, "Millions for defense, but not one cent for tribute."[30] Adams then called George Washington to active duty as Commander in Chief of a new United States Army. An aging Washington complied with the request, and a new Department of the Navy was also organized. In the end, the conflict with France was handled diplomatically, and Washington was never called to active duty.

Early in 1799, one year after the XYZ incident, Adams proposed that a new attempt be made to establish diplomatic relations with France. Eventually, three new commissioners were sent to France and the threat of war abated. Fifteen years later, Adams reminisced, "I desire no other inscription over my gravestone than: 'Here lies John Adams, who took upon himself the responsibility of the peace with France in the year 1800.'"[31]

George Washington died December 14, 1799. It shocked the nation when their beloved leader of the past few decades was no longer there for them. Abigail Adams recorded her deep emotions:

> No Man ever lived more deservedly beloved and Respected. . . . If we look through the whole tenor of his Life, History will not produce to us a Parrallel [sic]. Heaven has seen fit to take him from us. Our Mourning is sincere, in the midst of which, we ought not to lose sight of the Blessings we have enjoy'd [sic] and still partake of, that he was spaired [sic] to us, untill he saw a successor filling his place, pursueing [sic] the same system which he had adopted . . .[32]

For six weeks, the country continued to pay honor and homage to their dead hero, until even Abigail Adams had had enough. Out of patience with the issue, she penned these words:

> At no time, did the fate of America rest upon the Breath of even a Washington, and those who assert these things, are Ignorant of the spirit of their countrymen, and whilst they strive to exalt one

> character, degrade that of their Country. . . . Simple Truth is his best his greatest Eulogy. She alone can render his Fame immortal.[33]

John Adams revealed a bit of jealous humor and a bit of prophecy when he predicted what the future historians would record about his time:

> The History of our Revolution will be one continued Lye from one end to the other. . . . The essence of the whole will be that Dr. Franklin's electrical Rod, smote the Earth and out sprung General Washington. . . . That Franklin electrified him with his rod—and thence forward these two conducted all the Policy, Negotiations, Legislatures and War. . . . Mausoleums, Statues, Monuments will never be erected for me, . . . nor flattering orations spoken to transmit me to Posterity in brilliant Colours.[34]

The Final Years

After serving as the second President of the United States for four years, John Adams ran for a second term. But he had two strokes against him. First, the Federalist Party was split over Adams' actions in avoiding war with France. Second, Alexander Hamilton sabotaged Adams' chances for re-election by circulating a letter stating that Adams was unfit for office.[35]

In the presidential election of 1800, the tables were turned, and John Adams was narrowly defeated by the man who had served as his Vice-President, the lanky Thomas Jefferson. Though Jefferson was declared the winner, the system's weakness became apparent during this election. In 1804, Congress adopted the 12th Amendment to the Constitution providing separate ballots for President and Vice-President. This also meant the Vice-President was no longer the second choice for the Presidency. This lessened the prestige of the Vice-Presidency.

Adams was sorry to leave the high office, but welcomed the rest. To keep active after leaving the Presidency, Adams turned to writing. He published a number of articles which upheld the advantages of the structure of the government of the United States as opposed to that established in France after the French Revolution. Thomas Jefferson, being a staunch supporter of the French Revolution, was offended by some of the things Adams wrote in these articles. In addition to this, one of Adams' last acts as President had been to fill a large number of lifetime judgeships with Federalist judges. The appointment of these so-called "midnight judges" especially angered Jefferson because Adams named them after Jefferson had already won the election. Tragically, these two issues led to a break in their friendship.

After his tenure as President, Adams lived in modest circumstances. He spent most of his time alone in his garden or with his books and papers. He became interested in local and family history and began to trace his genealogy.

On April 17, 1804, Jefferson's daughter Mary died, and Abigail Adams sent him sincere letters of condolences. Abigail's letters helped to break the ice that had formed between these two great men, who at one time had also been great friends. Later, their mutual friend, and co-signer of the Declaration of Independence, Dr. Benjamin Rush, was responsible for bringing about the reconciliation between John Adams and Thomas Jefferson. Dr. Rush regularly reminded Adams and Jefferson of their past comradeship. The good doctor repeated to each of them all the kind words they had to say about each other. When Jefferson heard that John Adams had said,

"I always loved Jefferson, and still do,"[36] Jefferson recalled how much they had worked together in 1776, and his feelings softened.

In 1812, after more than a dozen years of non-communication, Adams made the first move towards reconciliation by writing Jefferson a letter. Jefferson immediately responded. They agreed they ought not to die before they had explained themselves to one another. Their correspondence continued over the next 14 years and touched on virtually every subject, from agriculture and architecture to politics and religion. This renewal of friendship with Thomas Jefferson was one of the greatest delights of Adams' old age. Their correspondence has become a classic in American letters.

Forty-four years after their beautiful love story began, Abigail Adams died on October 28, 1818, from the effects of typhus fever. It was only three days after their 44th wedding anniversary. John and Abigail were not only husband and wife for all those years, but were best friends, confidants, and equal companions.

Four years after her death, John wrote about his sweetheart to his granddaughter, Caroline:

> This Lady was far more beautiful than Lady Russell [an admired Englishwoman], had a brighter genius, more information, a more refined taste, and at least her equal in virtues of the heart. [She also had] equal fortitude and firmness of character, equal resignation to the will of Heaven, . . . equal in all the virtues of the Christian life.[37]

In 1825, only one year before his death, John Adams experienced another delight of his old age. It was indeed a satisfying moment when his son John Quincy Adams became the sixth President of the United States.[38]

Throughout his life, John Adams denied being blessed with numerous talents, but was brimful with loyalty and perseverance.

> "I never in my life," he wrote to Mercy Warren, "believed that I had any talents beyond mediocrity. I have always been sensible, to my mortification, that all I have done has been accomplished by the severest and most incessant labor . . . I will open my whole soul to you on this subject. I have great satisfaction believing that I have done more labor, run through more and greater dangers, and made greater sacrifices than any man among my contemporaries, living or dead, in the service of my country; and I should not hesitate to hazard all reputation, if I did not convince the public of it too, if I should undertake it."[39]

A mystifying coincidence took place on July 4, 1826, the 50th anniversary of the Declaration of Independence. On that sacred day, hallowed 50 years earlier by untold sacrifice and dedication and divine guidance, John Adams lay dying in his bed. He was 90 years of age. What thoughts must have been going through his mind as he reflected on the historical importance of the Fourth of July. He himself had written or delivered many powerful words that had incited people to rise to the cause of freedom those many years ago. Perhaps in his last moments on this earth, he heard them once again, delivered as with the trump of an angel, those God-inspired words:

> Sink or swim, live or die, survive or perish, I give my hand and my heart to this vote . . . there's a Divinity that shapes our ends. . . . But whatever may be our fate, be assured . . . that this Declaration will stand. It may cost treasure, and it may cost blood, but it will stand and it will richly compensate for both.

> Through the thick gloom of the present, I see the brightness of the future as the sun in heaven. . . . Before God, I believe the hour is come. My judgment approves this measure, and my whole heart is in it. . . . It is my living sentiment, and by the blessing of God it shall be my dying sentiment. Independence now, and Independence forever.[40]

Independence forever! Perhaps that was one of his last thoughts. For as he died, he struggled to utter one last message that was important to him. His family leaned close as he quietly murmured, "Thomas Jefferson still survives."[41] He didn't know that his great friend and patriot, author of the Declaration itself, Thomas Jefferson, had died just hours earlier on that same extraordinary anniversary.

Yet Adams was correct, just the same. Thomas Jefferson does still survive. And Benjamin Franklin and George Washington and Patrick Henry and James Madison. They survive every time our flag is raised and every time our voices choke with emotion as we sing "Oh say, does that star spangled banner yet wave o'er the land of the free and the home of the brave."[42] They are with us every time we vote and exercise our sacred freedoms, the priceless gift that they bequeathed to us. And, yes, John Adams is there, too. John Adams, who feared that he would never be transmitted to posterity in brilliant colors. He is one of the brightest, most colorful beacons of them all. Our Founding Fathers *do* survive . . . whenever we let them.

Chapter 4

Patrick Henry

May 29, 1736 – June 6, 1799

PATRICK HENRY

Though considered the instigator of the Revolution itself and dubbed by his contemporaries as "America's noble patriot" and America's "first national hero," Patrick Henry is often overlooked as one of our nation's Founding Fathers. He has tragically, silently, faded in history . . . like an old photograph. Yet without Patrick Henry, there might have been no revolutionary fire under Thomas Jefferson. And without Thomas Jefferson—would there have been a Declaration . . . at least as we know it? Though not well remembered, Henry was a crucial thread in the web of the American Revolution.

Early Years

Patrick Henry was born May 29, 1736, to John Henry and Sarah Winston Syme, at Hanover, Virginia. He was the second son of 11 children. Henry was educated mainly by his father and his uncle. As a youth attending a country school, Patrick and education never took kindly to each other. He was dreamy and playful, with a passionate regard for guns and fishing-rods. There was no indication that he possessed any talents that would allow him to amount to anything.

Patrick Henry was raised during the evangelical movement known as the Great Awakening and often attended the Presbyterian Church with his mother. The dramatic preaching of the ministers of that time no doubt had a profound effect on Henry's later style and manner of expression. Perhaps his church affiliation during his youth helped induce him to develop his own noble maxims for living: "To be true and just in all my dealings. To bear no malice nor hatred in my heart. To keep my hands from picking and stealing. Not to covet other men's goods; but to learn and labor truly, to get my own living, and to do my duty in that state of life unto which it shall please God to call me."[1]

In 1751, when Patrick was only 15, his father, Colonel John Henry, set him up as an apprentice clerk in a country store. A year later, in 1752, Colonel Henry set up a store for his sons William and Patrick. His older brother was even lazier than Patrick—who suddenly developed a profound interest in reading. He would scarcely look up from his book or newspaper when a customer walked into the store. Besides that, the brothers were too quick to offer credit. Not surprisingly, the enterprise failed.

In 1754, Patrick married Sarah Shelton, whom the family nicknamed "Sallie." Sallie "had a pretty, round face, dark brown hair, and deep brown eyes." Her family lived only a few miles down the road, and "Patrick had known her all of his life." Naturally, they would have been together at barbeques, picnics, dances, and other social events as they grew up.[2] At 18 years of age, Patrick married four or five years younger than the typical Virginian male of his station. Understandably, the Sheltons had misgivings about this penniless young man who had no bright prospects. However, the intense young couple pressed their desires for marriage in overpowering fashion. They are said to have told their families, with some embarrassment, that "passion had raced ahead of the parson," making an early wedding somewhat of a necessity. In October 1754, in a small ceremony at the Shelton's home, they were married by Patrick's uncle, Patrick Henry.[3]

For his daughter's dowry, Patrick's new father-in-law set the couple up in housekeeping giving them six slaves and a 300-acre tobacco farm. Although he had never farmed before, nor had much experience at directing the labor of slaves, somehow Patrick was expected to make a success of this new venture. He experienced the sad misfortune of taking up farming in a year plagued with a summer drought that was disastrously followed by an early frost. During this trying year, baby Martha, nicknamed "Patsy," arrived early in the summer of 1755. A second child, John, was added to the family in the spring of 1757. When fire destroyed the family's home and most of their possessions, they could not go on. Patrick sold the slaves and invested the proceeds in another mercantile establishment. During this year, the couple lived with Sarah's mother and father. But this venture seemed to do nothing but consume capital and create bad debts, so, after yet another financial disaster, Patrick began to tend bar at the Sheltons' tavern and help his father-in-law with the business.

At the tavern, Patrick had ample opportunity to observe the members of the bar of justice. He listened carefully to their talk about covenants, declarations, and pleadings. He grew intrigued with their discussions of strategies and their boasting about how one had outfoxed the other on some obscure point or technicality. He began to use his spare time to dabble in reading about the law. Coincidentally, the Hanover County Courthouse lay across the street from the tavern. This offered Henry a convenient opportunity to observe the legal proceedings that took place. Henry had proved that he couldn't farm and that he couldn't make a success out of a country store. But he could talk. Why not get a living by his tongue? Why not become a lawyer?

Lawyer and Politician

In 1760, becoming a lawyer was a fairly simple procedure. One had merely to study at the law and be tutored, guided, and apprenticed by a lawyer or two. There followed a lengthy, oral examination by at least three lawyers who were willing to certify that the student was ready to be admitted to the bar. (The "bar" was a gate at the courthouse beyond which only the witness and lawyer could pass).

Patrick Henry wasn't much for studying. He studied for the law for only three months. He told one friend that his study lasted only one month and consisted of reading only *Coke upon Littleton*,[4] and the laws of Virginia! After this short period of self-study, he felt ready to seek his professional license to practice law. His five examiners were George Wythe (a signer of the Declaration of Independence and Thomas Jefferson's mentor), Robert Carter Nicholas (a prominent member of the Virginia bar and future Chief Judge of Chancery), Peyton Randolph (the attorney general and another future appointee to the Continental Congress), John Randolph (who later succeeded his brother Peyton as attorney general, but who sided with the Crown in the Revolution and returned to England to live out an embittered life), and Edmund Pendleton (who spent his entire life in service to the people of Virginia, including serving as the president of the Virginia Supreme Court of Appeals until his death in 1803).

George Wythe signed Henry's professional license to practice law. At first Mr. Nicholas refused to sign it, but on repeated importunities and promises of Henry's future reading, finally gave his approval. Peyton and John Randolph both signed the license with great reluctance. They acknowledged that Henry was ignorant of the law but they perceived him to be a young man of genius and did not doubt that he would soon qualify himself.

John Randolph had an interesting experience while determining whether to sign Patrick Henry's license: "At first he was so shocked with Mr. Henry's ungainly figure and address that he refused to examine him. Understanding, however, that he had already obtained two signatures, he [agreed to listen to him]." Randolph was soon impressed with Patrick's style, boldness, and originality, and the examination stretched to several hours. He found Henry to be wanting in his knowledge of the municipal law, but with a good grasp of the principles of the common law. At one point, Randolf disagreed with one of Patrick's conclusions—even though he was swayed by Henry's argument. When the examiner went to look up the authorities, he found that Henry was correct. "You have never seen these books, nor this principle of the law; yet you are right and I am wrong. And from the lesson you have given me . . . I will never trust to appearances again. Mr. Henry, if your industry be only half equal to your genius . . . you will do well, and become an ornament and an honor to your profession."[5]

Patrick Henry became a very successful lawyer. During the first 3½ years of his practice, the slowest time of his career, Henry listed 1185 lawsuits for which he charged fees. He also prepared numerous other legal documents. His was an extremely busy workload. During a similar time period, Thomas Jefferson charged fees for only 504 cases.

In 1763, a third child, William, was born to the Henrys. It was in December of this year that Patrick Henry gained notoriety by his participation in the "parsons' cause." Under a regulation of the Crown, a Virginia Act of 1748 provided that each clergyman should be paid with tax dollars and have an annual salary of 16,000 pounds of tobacco. Confronted with a crop failure in 1758, the Virginia House of Burgesses passed what were referred to as the Two Penny

Acts: all debts and taxes that were payable in tobacco could instead be paid at the rate of two pence per pound of tobacco owed, a rate of about one-third the price that tobacco was bringing. As could be expected, the clergy objected and brought suit. The dispute was appealed to the King's Privy Council, which promptly annulled the Two Penny law. The case was remanded to trial before a jury to determine the amount of damages to be paid to the ministers. The colonials were angry because the King had overturned an act of their own legislation. Patrick Henry was hired to represent the people. This was a case in which no other lawyer wanted to be involved.[6]

In presenting the case to the court, Patrick Henry at first stumbled and paused, then started over. This time he was strong, clear and penetrating, and seemed to stand taller. He emphasized that the Virginia law had been passed legitimately. What right did the King have to declare it void? Was the King to be their dictator?

"When a king degenerates into a tyrant, he forfeits all right to obedience!" declared Patrick Henry.

The king's attorney was outraged. "Treason!" he interrupted.

But Henry continued on. He challenged the benevolence of the 20 ministers who had filed the lawsuit.

> "Do they manifest their zeal . . . by practicing the mild and benevolent precepts of the gospel of Jesus? Do they feed the hungry and clothe the naked? Oh, no, these rapacious harpies would, were their powers equal to their will, snatch from the hearth of their honest parishioner his last hoe-cake, from the widow and her orphan children their last milch cow! the last bed, nay, the last blanket from the lying-in woman!"
>
> Astounded, the offended clergymen stormed from the courthouse. But Patrick Henry rushed on, speaking

> passionately for nearly an hour. . . . The audience [was] "taken captive. . . ."
>
> As he concluded, Patrick reminded the jury of the court's earlier ruling: the plaintiff was entitled to damages. Let him receive damages, then, Patrick exclaimed. But let it be no more than one farthing!
>
> The awestruck jury left the room and consulted together for all of five minutes. When they returned, they announced their decision: the plaintiff, and thus each of the other clergymen, would indeed receive one farthing. Nothing more. The court adjourned in an uproar. The people hoisted their young lawyer to their shoulders and pushed outside, shouting and cheering. [7]

From that outcome, Patrick Henry became a monumental force in the leadership of Virginia. From that time on, he was the idol of the people. In 1765, shortly after the "parsons' cause" victory, Henry was elected to the House of Burgesses.

Patrick Henry was seven years older than Thomas Jefferson. They met each other for the first time at a party given by a mutual acquaintance. They found that they had some mutual interests. Both Tom and Patrick could play the fiddle, and they both liked to dance. They developed a mutual friendship. When Jefferson had arrived at Williamsburg to begin his schooling, Patrick Henry sought him out for a friendly visit. Henry proudly announced that after studying law for only three months, he had been admitted to the bar in Virginia. Tom already had lots of books, and Patrick often borrowed them . . . though Tom noticed that he mostly returned them unread.

On Thursday morning, May 29, 1765, they walked to the Capitol together. Tom was dressed in the height of fashion, while Patrick wore plain hunting clothes and carried an old copy of *Coke upon Littleton*, which he had borrowed from Tom. When they reached the Capitol, Patrick continued to his seat in the House, while Tom took a place at the door to the Assembly Room.

Patrick Henry appeared out of place in that hall—wearing his shabby hunting clothes while all the burgesses, members of the wealthy planter aristocracy, were dressed in their London best. Shortly after the meeting was called to order, Patrick instinctively chose the right moment to rise from his seat. He began reading, first quietly, but with passion, a series of resolutions against the Stamp Act. He had scribbled his notes in the flyleaf of Tom's book:

> Resolved, That the settlers brought with them to this colony all the privileges, franchises, and immunities held by the people of Great Britain.
>
> Resolved, That the colonists are entitled to all the privileges, liberties, and immunities of citizens and natural born subjects as if they had been born within the realm of England.
>
> Resolved, That taxation of the people by themselves, or by persons chosen by themselves to represent them is the distinguishing characteristic of British freedom.
>
> Resolved, That colonists should be governed by their own Assembly in the article of their taxes and internal police.
>
> Resolved, therefore, That the general assembly of the colony has the sole right and power to lay taxes and impositions upon the inhabitants of this colony. Every attempt to vest such power in any other persons would destroy both British and American freedom.[8]

Patrick continued to speak, at first haltingly. But after a few moments, seemed to gain confidence. He straightened his shoulders and stood erect. His voice picked up, and soon his words rang through the room. People were hearing for the first time words they had only dared to think—but had been too afraid to whisper—even to themselves.

> "Old Coke's" comments on the Magna Carta were suddenly being transformed from dead law into living truths.
>
> Tom stood spellbound [at the door] as he heard Patrick thunder, "Caesar had his Brutus, Charles the First his Cromwell and (pausing) George the Third. . . ."
>
> "Treason," cried Mr. John Robinson, the speaker [of the Assembly,] "Treason! Treason!" echoed from every part of the House.
>
> But with amazing presence of mind, when the rude exclamations were ended, with a look and bearing of proud determination, he closed the sentence, ". . . and George the Third may profit by their example. If this be treason, make the most of it."[9]

All but the last Resolution carried. From that time on, Patrick Henry became the spokesman for the common people. And Jefferson, for the first time, understood that Virginia was on the road of separation from the Mother Country.

Thomas Jefferson said of Patrick Henry's powerful oratory:

> Henry spoke wonderfully. Call it oratory or what you please, but I never heard anything like it. He had more command over the passions than any man I ever knew. . . . It was his profound knowledge of human

> nature and his manner of speaking more than the matter of his orations.[10]

"It has been said that Jefferson later referred to this day as the most important day of his life."[11] It was undoubtedly one of the most important days in the life of a budding America. Copies of Henry's resolutions were published in newspapers throughout the colonies. Without a doubt, they helped start the Revolution. Perhaps, before Concord and Lexington, Patrick Henry's Stamp Act Resolutions were the first shots fired in the War for Independence.

Family Life

In 1767 and 1769, two more baby daughters were born to the Henrys—Anne and Betsey, respectively. By the time Anne was born, their oldest daughter, Patsy, was 12. Her two brothers, Johnny and Billie, seemed to please their father as they ran barefoot around the farm. The children spent hardly any time at book learning, even though by this time, their father, Patrick Henry, had acquired a taste for reading. Henry never became an overly bookish person, but he knew that in books he could find not only information but also entertainment.

Then, in 1771, the Henrys had their sixth and last child, a baby boy named Edward. In that same year, Patrick saw a newspaper ad announcing that Scotchtown Plantation was for sale. He bought the nearly 1000-acre plantation, together with its manor house and working farms, for about 600 pounds. Nearly all his associates considered this a bargain price. Henry moved his family to Scotchtown, but was soon to experience great tragedy in his new home. After the birth of baby Edward, his wife suffered severe mental health problems from which she never recovered.

There was, however, one bright occurrence that year. Robert Carter Nicholas, an important lawyer in Virginia, and one of the five men who had examined Patrick Henry in order that Henry might be admitted to the bar, retired and turned his law practice over to Patrick Henry.

Three years later, on March 31, 1774, the British passed the Boston Port Bill as a way of responding to the Boston Tea Party. On May 24, 1774, the House of Burgesses received the alarming news. As with the Sugar Act, it was obvious to Henry that this British bill would have a negative effect on the commerce of Virginia. As a sort of counter, he presented a bill to the Virginia House of Burgesses. This bill declared the first day of June, the day the Port Bill would take effect, as a day of "fasting, humiliation, and prayer, devoutly to implore the Divine interposition for averting the heavy calamity which threatens destruction to our civil rights."[12]

The declaration was adopted, with full support from Thomas Jefferson and George Washington, who were also members of the House of Burgesses at this time. This action caused Lord Dunmore, the Governor, to dissolve the House of Burgesses. Even after the House was disbanded, the Virginia representatives kept meeting together as elected officials of their respective districts. The meetings were held down the street from the Williamsburg Capitol, at the Raleigh Tavern.

The Continental Congress

In 1774, the colonies called an emergency Continental Congress in Philadelphia to discuss the problems they were now facing with Great Britain. Those chosen to represent Virginia included Peyton Randolph, George Washington, and Patrick Henry. Henry was described as "moderate and mild, and in religious matters a saint; but the very devil in politics; a son of thunder; he will shake the Senate."[13] Patrick Henry, now 38 years of age, was well respected in Virginia.

The Congress almost broke up before it got started. Delegates from the smaller states wanted equal representation with delegates from the larger states. Henry and other representatives from the more populous states, disagreed. Still, Henry was convinced that it was imperative that the colonies unite against Great Britain and so spoke to the delegation, "The distinctions between Virginians, Pennsylvanians, New Yorkers, and New Englanders are no more. I am not a Virginian, but an American!"[14] These words helped turn the delegates from their internal squabbling to the more important task at hand. They had to join together to find solutions to the problem of British tyranny. It was at this meeting that the colonies united in developing a non-importation association. By refusing to import British goods, they put an uncomfortable pressure on the British.

Henry's Immortal Speech

Patrick Henry delivered his most famous and powerful speech the following year, on March 23, 1775. British troops were occupying Boston. The Boston Massacre had taken American lives. The King continued to refuse to hear American petitions. The delegates to the Virginia Committee of Safety decided to meet at St. John's Church in Richmond, Virginia, because it was the only building in that city which would be big enough to accommodate all of them. It was a simple, white, wooden building with about 60 pews. Many people from the city also gathered in and around the church. They were anxious to hear what the delegates would recommend in an attempt to reconcile with Great Britain.

Patrick Henry stood before the huge crowd. Unknowingly, the speech that he was about to make would forever keep alive the name of Patrick Henry and emblazon him—almost as some mythical hero—in our country's glorious history. After listening to the conciliatory resolutions being read, an indignant Patrick Henry jumped to his feet and delivered his famous speech. Included in his elegant, moving message were the following words:

> [British troops] are sent over to bind and rivet upon us those chains which the British ministry have been so long in forging. . . . We have done everything that could be done to avert the storm which is now coming on. . . . An appeal to arms and the God of Hosts is all that is left us! They tell us, sir, that we are weak, unable to cope with so formidable an adversary. But when shall we be stronger? . . . Shall we gather strength by irresolution and inaction? Shall we acquire the means of effectual resistance by lying supinely on our backs, and hugging the delusive phantom of hope, until our enemies shall have bound us hand and foot? Sir, we are not weak, if we make a proper use of those means which the God of nature hath placed in our power. . . . Besides, sir, we shall not fight our battles alone. There is a just God who presides over the destinies of nations, and who will raise up friends to fight our battles for us. . . . The battle, sir, is not to the strong alone; it is to the vigilant, the active, the brave. . . . Gentlemen may cry, peace, peace—but there is no peace. The war is actually begun. . . . Why stand we here idle? . . . Is life so dear, or peace so sweet, as to be purchased at the price of chains and slavery? Forbid it, Almighty God! ***I know not what course others may take; but as for me, give me liberty or give me death!***"[15]

The effect of Henry's speech was electric. The news of those powerful words quickly spread out the chapel doors, throughout the colony of Virginia, and across a country anxious for freedom. Henry was ahead of others in his thinking about the Revolution. Some 50 years later, Thomas Jefferson stated, "After all, it must be allowed that he was our leader in the measures of the Revolution in Virginia, and in that respect more is due to him than to any other person. . . . He left all of us far behind."[16]

Patrick Henry's fame as an orator and statesman overshadowed his importance and service as a soldier during the beginning of the Revolution. But he did experience a brief blaze of glory in that arena also. Only weeks after Henry's powerful "liberty or death" speech, Lord Dunmore, the Virginia Governor, seized the stock of gunpowder stored in Williamsburg. Patrick Henry, commander in chief of the Virginia forces, responded quickly. Raising a force of 150 men, he demanded the return of the gunpowder or payment for it—about 330 pounds. As Henry marched with his little army toward Williamsburg, the number of his troops swelled to 5,000 armed men. This was the first armed resistance to British authority in Virginia. At the last moment, when Henry's men were only 16 miles outside of Williamsburg, Lord Dunmore sent an emissary to the army with a bond for 330 pounds. Henry accepted the bond and sent his forces home.

Because he had done so much to bring on the war, it was logical for himself and others to assume that Henry would be a key figure in the actual fighting. But his military career was short-lived. The Committee of Safety found that he didn't have the experience or gift for military action that he did for civil life. So at their insistence, and being discouraged over not being appointed a full general (he was a colonel), on February 28, 1776, he resigned his commission.

The Death of His First Wife

In the midst of these historically momentous events, in 1775, the wife of his youth, the mother of his six children, his beloved Sarah, passed away. Henry had done whatever he could for her. She had began to suffer despondency and had been unable to adequately care for herself after the birth of her last child. She had never regained her sanity. She had become subject to "fits of lunacy." Patrick had been unable to do much for her. He had hired a black woman to nurse her and guard her against injury. Sarah sometimes had to be put in a "strait-dress" and confined to a ground-level work room. "Word went around the neighborhood that a crazy woman was kept in a dungeon at Scotchtown, talk later embroidered into a tradition that 'Pahtrick' himself passed food to his afflicted wife through a trapdoor in the front hallway."[17]

The Second Continental Congress

But personal tragedy did not stop the Revolution. The Second Continental Congress convened at Philadelphia on May 10, 1775. Then, almost immediately after resigning his commission in the military, Henry was elected by the people of Virginia to represent them at their state convention. The Virginia state convention began their business May 6, 1776. Along with Henry, James Madison, a young political philosopher, was a member of the convention. This was the first time Madison appeared on the public scene.

Before the Virginia legislature, Patrick Henry presented a resolution calling for "an immediate, clear, and full declaration of independence." This resolution passed. Richard Henry Lee was sent as a delegate from Virginia to the Continental Congress, with instructions to propose the resolution.

On June 7, 1776, Lee stood in Congress and made the historic motion that Congress resolve "that these united Colonies are and of right ought to be, free and independent States." John Adams of Massachusetts seconded the motion. But the motion was not put to a vote, as not all the colonies were ready to make such a decision. However, in preparation, a committee was appointed by Congress to write a declaration that might be considered. This committee included the elder statesman, Benjamin Franklin (age 70) of Pennsylvania; John Adams (age 41) of Massachusetts; Roger Sherman (age 55) of Connecticut; Robert Livingston (age 30) of New York, the youngest member of Congress; and Thomas Jefferson (age 33) of Virginia, the author of the document.

Although Patrick Henry didn't attend this Second Continental Congress, he had called for the resolution of "free and independent States" to be presented to the Continental Congress by a Virginia legislator. Without Virginia's backing, it is highly unlikely that a committee would have been chosen at this time to write the Declaration.

Governor Henry

A pamphlet entitled *Thoughts on Government* (written by John Adams, but originally distributed anonymously) was being circulated among the colonies. It advocated that each colony establish its own form of state government. Patrick Henry, George Mason, and James Madison were placed on a committee to consider a state plan for Virginia. On June 24, 1776, the committee submitted to the convention at Williamsburg their proposed constitution for the new state of Virginia. After its third reading, this proposal was unanimously adopted by the convention on the 29th of June. The new state of Virginia was born.

In accordance with the last provision of the new constitution, the convention proceeded to select a Governor for Virginia. Patrick Henry was formally declared to be the new Governor. He would serve until the next session of the Assembly—in March 1777. On Friday, the 5th *of July*, 1776, Patrick Henry took the oath of office and entered into his duties as the new Governor of Virginia.[18] As Governor, he would reside in the Governor's Mansion—the very edifice in which

Lord Dunmore had lived when he disbanded the House of Burgesses and branded Patrick Henry a traitor. He would sit at the same desk at which Lord Dunmore had sat to write out proclamations *against* Patrick Henry!

Henry Marries Again

Patrick Henry served a second term as Governor of Virginia from June 28, 1777, to June 28, 1778. During his second term, Henry remarried. It had been two years since the death of his first wife. On October 9, 1777, he married Dorothea Dandridge (nicknamed "Dolly"), a granddaughter of the old royal Governor, Alexander Spotswood.

Dorothea was 21 years younger than Patrick, a dark eyed, dark haired woman of 22. This made her the same age as Patrick's newly married daughter, Patsy. "Neighborhood gossip held that "Dolly" had fancied an impecunious young sailor named John Paul Jones, then visiting cousins on a nearby plantation, but her father dashed her hopes in favor of the more glorious match with the Governor." Dorothea's companionship proved to be a great solace to him during the remainder of his life. During their 22 years of marriage, Dolly gave birth to 11 children. Patrick's sister Elizabeth once sourly remarked, "The cradle began to rock in his household when Patrick was eighteen, and it was still rocking when he died at sixty-three."[19]

It was around the time of Patrick Henry's marriage to Dorothea that he was able to offer an invaluable service to General George Washington. Henry warned Washington of a plot to replace the Commander in Chief with General Horatio Gates. Henry's warning allowed Washington to prepare for the problem and prevent it. Patrick Henry remained a lifelong, loyal friend to George Washington.

> "When Henry learned in January 1778 of the army's horrible destitution at Valley Forge, he immediately sent 10,000 pounds of meat and 2,000 bushels of salt to the starving troops. According to some [historians], Henry's prompt actions may have prevented the complete dissolution of the army."[20]

In any event, Valley Forge became the turning point of the Revolution.

Also in 1778, as Governor, Patrick Henry showed great vision when he backed an impressive soldier named George Rogers Clark. When the Revolutionary War broke out, Clark wanted to protect the settlers in Kentucky. He convinced Virginia to declare Kentucky a county of Virginia, entitling Kentucky to a government and supplies. Clark proposed a difficult, daring plan to drive the British from the western portions of Virginia. The lands Clark won back would later became the states of Ohio, Indiana, Illinois, Michigan, Wisconsin, and half of Minnesota. "Had it not been for Clark's superhuman march and Patrick Henry's official support, that entire area would most likely have become part of Canada."[21]

Not surprisingly, Patrick Henry was unanimously elected to a third one-year term as Governor of Virginia in May 1778. But a year later, on June 1, 1779, Thomas Jefferson was elected to the office by a majority of only six votes. Shortly after his descent from the Governor's chair, Henry was elected by the General Assembly as a delegate to Congress. However, he declined the position because of ill health.

Henry moved his family from the Governor's Mansion to a country place about 200 miles southwest of Richmond. The existing county was split into two counties—with the new one being named Henry County in honor of Patrick Henry. A year after his move from the Governor's Mansion, in May of 1780, Henry returned to service in the General Assembly. But due to ill health, he was forced to leave again after only two weeks. Henry served off and on for three years, depending on the state of his health.

Patrick Henry was with Thomas Jefferson and other government officials when they were nearly captured near Charlottesville in 1781. They had moved there to be out of the way of the approach of a hostile army, a force of about 800 men under command of the turncoat Benedict Arnold.

Patrick Henry had proven his competence as Governor when he served in the office for three consecutive terms, July 1776 through June 1779. After the Revolutionary War was over, he was once again elected Governor of Virginia on November 30, 1784. After this one-year term, he was elected yet once more. So Henry served as Governor for his fifth term, but this would be his last term. Even though the Virginia state constitution allowed it, he decided against running for a third consecutive term. Patrick Henry retired from service on November 30, 1786.

Henry had always been very abstemious in his diet, using no wine or alcoholic stimulants. He became alarmed at the abuse of alcohol and the increase of drunkenness after the Revolutionary War and did everything in his power to arrest the vice. He even caused a non-alcoholic barley drink to be developed, hoping it would become fashionable. It was something like root beer. To set the example, during his last term as Governor, he had it regularly placed on his table.[22]

In order to keep up appearances while serving as Governor, Henry overspent his Governor's salary and retired from the office in debt. So he took up the practice of law once again and immediately became quite successful. By this time, he had sold his old

"Scotchtown" plantation for a good price. Henry now bought a new place and returned to self-sufficient farming, with a small depreciating reserve of capital, along with ample resources in slaves and livestock. His new farm was called "Leatherwood" and, like Scotchtown, was also considered to have been purchased at a bargain.

The Constitutional Convention

Only five days after Henry left the office of Governor of Virginia, he was chosen to be one of seven delegates to represent Virginia at the Constitutional Convention. The Convention was to be held the following May (1787) in Philadelphia. There, delegates from the 13 states were to revise the Articles of Confederation. Edmund Randolph, the new Governor of Virginia, wrote to Henry at Leatherwood, urging him to accept the appointment and attend the Convention. Randolph advised Henry that matters had grown so perilous that "those who first kindled the Revolution" must now come forward again to create the means to save it.[23]

But Henry refused to attend the Convention. He had been soured by what had transpired before in attempting to correct the Articles. Because of a proposed treaty with Spain, he was concerned that the northern states would require the southern states to give up their control of the Mississippi River. And he was heard to say he "smelt a rat."[24]

Three years earlier, in 1784, general weaknesses in the federal government had already become apparent. Patrick Henry was among the foremost to declare alarm and to provide an appropriate remedy. He counseled his close associate and representative to the House, James Madison, to support a method that would give greater strength to the federal government. Henry recommended doing something to give Congress a compulsory process over delinquent states. But he did not believe that a whole new form of government was necessary. Henry wanted to merely amend the Articles of Confederation—the job the states had originally instructed the delegates to carry out. Henry argued that the delegates had no power to start anew and that they exceeded their granted authority by preparing a new Constitution. He thought they could just make some radical changes to the Articles of Confederation to solve the problems.

The drafting of the new Constitution was a far cry from "rewriting"the Articles of Confederation. On June 2, 1788, when Virginia convened its convention to determine whether or not the state would accept the new Constitution, Patrick Henry was among the many Virginian leaders who were against it. Those siding with Patrick Henry against the new Constitution included Thomas Jefferson, James Monroe, George Mason, and Richard Henry Lee.

The Virginia convention lasted 23 days, and on 18 of those days Patrick Henry spoke at least once. One day he made eight different speeches. One of his speeches lasted seven hours. The transcription of the debates filled a volume of 663 pages. Nearly one-fourth of those pages encompass the fluent arguments of Patrick Henry.[25] Because the delegates to the Constitutional Convention had arrived at a whole new Constitution, Henry argued against it on the grounds that it represented a significant loss of states' rights. The states were giving up their sovereignty to a new federal government, and the individual had been given no shield of protection. There was no Bill of Rights. A Bill of Rights was simply indispensable.

"A general positive provision should be inserted in the new system, securing to the States and the people every right which was not conceded to the general government." declared Henry. Then he added, "Even say it is a natural implication,—why not give us a right . . . in express terms, in language that could not admit of evasions or subterfuges?"[26]

Patrick Henry's objections to the new Constitution all sprang from a single idea. The new government, as it was then presented, seriously endangered the rights and liberties of the people of several states. In spite of Henry's gifted oratory against it, the new Constitution was adopted in Virginia . . . but by only ten votes. Even then, it passed solely because of the adoption of a preamble that solemnly affirmed that by signing the new Constitution, "Virginia . . . retained every power not expressly granted to the general government." There was also a subsidiary resolution that promised to recommend to Congress "whatsoever amendments may be deemed necessary." Sensing beforehand what the outcome would be, Patrick Henry gave a remarkable conciliatory speech, promising to be a "Peaceable citizen."[27]

The great effect of the words and measures of Patrick Henry became apparent after the organization of the first Congress of the United States in May of 1789. Virginia had elected James Madison to the House of Representatives. Many state leaders were still advocating another convention in which radical changes would be made to the new Constitution. But such a process would have undoubtedly reconstructed the work done by the Convention of 1787.

James Madison knew the extensive damage that would cause. He appreciated the great minds that had met at the first Convention. Yet even those brilliant men had experienced great difficulty in arriving at a final agreement; so James did all in his power to avoid a new convention. Patrick Henry and others had pointed out the shortcomings of the Constitution. James Madison worked behind the scenes, in the House and the Senate, to get a fair hearing of proposed amendments which would satisfy those shortcomings. Under the direction of James Madison, 17 amendments were sent from the

House to the Senate for consideration. Of these, 12 were approved and sent back to the states for ratification. Ten were adopted by the states and attached to our Constitution as the "Bill of Rights."

Much credit for America's Bill of Rights must go to Patrick Henry and James Madison. Henry strenuously argued for protection of individual rights. Madison refused defeat and pushed the bill through Congress, thus avoiding the need of a new convention (where the whole Constitution would undoubtedly have been reworked). The Constitution was finally ratified by all 13 states in 1790.

His Later Years

For many years in his later life, it was Henry's practice to spend "one hour every day . . . in private devotion. His hour of prayer was the close of the day, including sunset . . . and during that sacred hour, none of his family intruded upon his privacy."[28] He studied the Bible and several commentaries. He remarked that his studies had "removed all his doubts of the truth of Christianity."[29] Every Sunday, he read to his family out of the best books. After reading together, they all joined in singing sacred music while he accompanied them on the violin.

Both Patrick and Dolly had considered Leatherwood to be too remote and desired to move to a more densely populated area. In 1794, he purchased Red Hill and moved his family to the 700-acre estate on the Staunton River in Charlotte County. He referred to it as "one of the garden spots of the world."

Even in his last years, Patrick Henry continued to practice law. And he was good at it. He was also sought after to hold several important government offices. In 1793, he declined an appointment by Governor Henry Lee of Virginia to fill an unexpired term as U.S. Senator. In October of 1795, George Washington asked him to become the Secretary of State. Henry declined. Then, in December of 1795, he was selected by George Washington to become the Chief Justice of the Supreme Court. When he also declined this great compliment, he was then considered for the Vice-Presidency.

In 1796, under the political influence of Thomas Jefferson, Patrick Henry was once again elected Governor of Virginia. But the man who had refused to accept the attraction of some of the highest offices in the land did not succumb to the opportunity to become (for the sixth time) the Governor of Virginia. On April 16, 1799, after a passionate request from John Adams to help avert war with France, Henry declined the appointment as Minister to France. But he did listen to one more impassioned appeal from George Washington. At the time, Virginia was leading the states down a path towards civil war. Washington implored Henry to consider how much the Virginia House of Delegates needed Henry's powerful leadership at this precarious time. As a good friend, George convinced Henry to make himself a candidate for the office.

Word went out that Patrick Henry would once more address the people at the courthouse in Charlottesville. By all accounts, Patrick Henry gave another memorable and convincing speech.

> If I am asked what is to be done when a people feel themselves intolerably oppressed, my answer is ready—overturn the government!
>
> But do not, I beseech you, carry matters to this length without provocation. Wait at least until some infringement is made upon your rights, and which cannot otherwise be redressed. For if you ever recur to another change, you may bid adieu forever to representative government. You can never exchange the present government but for a monarchy.[30]

Henry was then elected, by a great majority, to the Virginia House of Delegates. But his failing health required him to return home to his family. He never again made another public appearance. He never again even left his home. He would not live to see the legislature, to which he had been elected, convene in the autumn.

Early in June, his eldest and favorite daughter, Martha Fontaine,[31] received a letter from her father, saying that he was very unwell and the doctor was with him. He was dying of some kind of growth, or infection, in the intestines. On June 6, 1799, other remedies having failed, the doctor was to administer a dose of liquid mercury. Henry was told, "it will give you immediate relief, or . . . " It was too painful for the doctor to finish the sentence.

Henry replied, "Excuse me, doctor, for a few minutes." He drew down his silk cap and prayed in clear words a simple prayer for his family, for his country, for his own soul, and then for the presence of death. After administering the liquid, Henry's doctor left the house, threw himself down on the lawn, and wept bitterly for his dear friend. The doctor returned to the bedside to find Patrick watching the congealing of blood under his fingernails and speaking words of love and peace to his family, who were weeping around him.[32] Among other things, Henry told them that he was thankful for the goodness of God, which, having blessed him through all his life, was then permitting him to die without any pain. Henry turned to his friend the doctor and expressed to him how great a reality and benefit religion was to a man about to die. He breathed a short while longer and then departed this life. He was 63.

In his own, handwritten Last Will and Testament, bearing the date of November 20, 1798, Patrick Henry distributed his estate among his descendants. Then he concluded with these inspiring words: "This is all the inheritance I can give to my dear family. The religion of Christ can give them one which will make them rich indeed."[33]

With his will was found a note advising future generations to "practice Virtue thyself, and encourage it in others." And among his effects was this urgent message which had been appended to his copy of his Stamp Act Resolutions: "Whether this will prove a blessing or a curse will depend on the use our people will make of the blessings which a gracious God hath bestowed on us. . . . Righteousness alone can exalt them as a nation."[34]

> As he requested, Henry was buried with simple ceremony at the foot of his sloping garden at Red Hill. Later, a large marble slab was laid on the ground to mark the grave. This gravestone, still there, bears this inscription carved long ago: "His fame is his best epitaph."
>
> There is deep irony here. His fame has gone into almost total eclipse. Henry has been relegated to limbo, where he does not belong.
>
> Everyone knows his "give me liberty or give me death" phrase, but little else is known about Henry, what he accomplished and what he failed to accomplish, his strength and his faults, and the many forces, both personal and general, that enabled him to emerge unheralded from the back country to play such an important role in founding the nation and shaping its beginnings.
>
> As one of the greatest of the Founding Fathers, as the one who "gave the first impulse to the ball of Revolution" and almost overnight became the "Noble Patriot," our first national hero, "the idol of the

> country" in his day, Patrick Henry deserves to be better remembered and more highly honored by his countrymen than he has been for generations.[35]

Perhaps a more fitting epitaph for this amazing man is the one paid to him by his grandson who described Henry as always setting "a good example of honesty, benevolence, hospitality, and every social virtue. He assisted in the education of his . . . children and especially devoted much time to earnest efforts to establish true Christianity in our country."[36] And one could list many other noble virtues and accomplishments of "America's first patriot." It was Patrick Henry who first proposed the resolution that we make a complete declaration of independence from Great Britain. It was his initiative, his fire for independence, his skillful oratory, his undeniable inspiration in the cause for freedom that first awoke our nation to its magnificent destiny. It was Patrick Henry who ignited within Jefferson the spark of patriotism, literally breathing the zeal for independence into Jefferson's soul with his "Brutus Speech," while inadvertently guiding Jefferson to the path that would seal Jefferson's own immortal fame. It was Patrick Henry who sent critically needed supplies to Washington's army at Valley Forge, supplies that literally kept the army alive . . . that probably kept the nation alive. It was Patrick Henry who stirred a young country to attempt the virtually impossible: to challenge the greatest, most powerful nation on the face of the earth.

An intricate web was carefully woven in the bringing forth of our great nation. Like pieces of a puzzle painstakingly fitted together to form the perfect picture, Benjamin Franklin, George Washington, John Adams, Thomas Jefferson, James Madison, and many other Founding Fathers all had their critical role to play. Patrick Henry was an important piece of that inspired design. For it was his words that lit the match to the Revolutionary fires . . . his inspired, deathless words:

> Is life so dear, or peace so sweet, as to be purchased at the price of chains and slavery? Forbid it, Almighty God! ***I know not what course others may take; but as for me, give me liberty or give me death!***"[37]

Chapter 5

Thomas Jefferson

April 13, 1743 – July 4, 1826

THOMAS JEFFERSON

Like George Washington, Thomas Jefferson was large for his time. In a day when the average man measured only 5 feet 7 inches, Thomas Jefferson stood an imposing 6 feet 2½ inches tall. His very height seemed to bespeak the greatness of the man. He was a walking example of self-discipline—both physically and spiritually. He always arose at or before daybreak. He abstained from the use of tobacco in any form. He refused to use profane words. He didn't play cards. He didn't eat much meat, but loved vegetables and fruit, and raised a variety of them. He was a creative genius—designing buildings and inventing numerous objects to enhance daily life. His intellectual prowess was met by few, and he wrote perhaps the most inspired document ever penned by the hand of man.

Jefferson's Birth and Youth

Virginia lays proud claim as the birthplace of Thomas Jefferson. Born on April 13, 1743, he was the third child, the first son born into his family. He would later be joined by seven more siblings. Thomas' father, Peter Jefferson, was neither rich nor well-born. Peter loved the outdoors and was an excellent horseman and hunter. He also loved to swim. Peter was one of the earliest settlers of the Piedmont Section of Virginia. While still young, he learned the art of surveying, which he considered a suitable profession in a new county.

When Peter Jefferson was 30 years old, his good friend William Randolph introduced his cousin Jane Randolph to Peter. Peter fell in love with 17-year-old Jane. They were married two years later, on October 19, 1739. He was 32, she was 19. With this union into the Randolph family, Peter Jefferson became identified with one of the wealthiest, most prestigious families in Virginia.

Only six years later, William Randolph died. His wife had died three years earlier, so now their three young children were orphans. William's dying wish was that his dear friend, Peter, would move into William's home to care for his orphaned children and manage his estate. Peter Jefferson complied with his friend's last request. Thomas Jefferson was about two years old at the time his family moved to the Randolph estate.

Peter Jefferson hired a tutor to teach two of Tom's cousins, along withTom's two older sisters, Jane and Mary. When Tom was five, he was allowed to join the older children in the tree-shaded white-frame building that had become their school. Tom was inquisitive and impatient in the classroom. Once, in his early childhood, he sneaked out of the classroom, knelt behind the school building, and repeated the Lord's Prayer, hoping to hasten the hour of dismissal.[1]

During the summers, Peter was able to spend much time with his son Tom. He taught Tom mathematics. He taught him to shoot deer and wild turkey. He taught him how to get along outdoors. He taught him how to mend canoes and carry them overland from one navigable river to another. "Never ask another to do for you what you can do for yourself" was a principle by which his father lived, a principle that Tom never forgot.[2]

When Tom was ten, his father wanted to further encourage self-reliance in his promising young son. He gave Tom a rifle and sent him on an outdoor hunting expedition. But Tom never learned to enjoy hunting. Instead, he preferred to leave wild animals in their natural habitat. Peter Jefferson also taught his son to ride horses. Tom became an excellent horseman and came to know the forest as few ever did. He learned the names and habits of all the birds and insects in the fields.

Peter's library was small but select. His Bible and his works of Shakespeare were well-worn from much use. He instilled in his son a passion for books and a love for language that would remain a part of Tom all of his life. A strong bond of love and respect continued to grow between father and son. As Tom grew older, the physical resemblance between the two was astonishing.

In June of 1757, when Tom was just 14 years of age, Peter suddenly became ill. His good friend Dr. Thomas Walker could do nothing for him. Peter Jefferson died on August 17, at the age of 50. Tom felt helpless and alone. Peter's dying instructions were that his son Tom should receive a "thorough classical education . . . [and] not to neglect the exercise requisite for his bodie's [sic] development."[3]

Jefferson Goes to College and Marries

When Tom was nearly 17, he decided that he should apply for entrance into the College of William and Mary at Williamsburg. On March 25, 1760, just a few weeks before his 17th birthday, the results of his entrance examinations were reviewed. His outstanding results allowed Tom to be admitted into an advanced class in the school of philosophy. Tom would reside at Williamsburg for the next seven years.

Before Tom left for college, he had become acquainted with Patrick Henry. They had met at a party given by a mutual acquaintance, and they found that they had some mutual interests. Tom's sister Jane became an accomplished musician. When Tom became interested in her music, his father bought him a violin, which at that time was called a fiddle. Both Tom and Patrick could fiddle. Patrick didn't know the classical music that Tom played, but he had a keen ear and could follow any tune. They developed a warm friendship. Soon after arriving at Williamsburg, Tom had an unexpected visit from Patrick, who proudly informed him that after studying law for only three months, he had been admitted to the bar in Virginia. Perhaps it was Patrick Henry's example that inspired Tom to later "read" law under the established lawyer George Wythe, the first law professor at William and Mary. In a day when most law students studied less than one year, Jefferson continued his intensive study of the law for five years.

Thomas came of age on April 13, 1764. At age 21, he officially came into the inheritance left to him by his father. He was now the sole owner of a fine estate covering more than 5,000 acres of land (2,500 acres of which would not become his outright until the death of his mother). These holdings included a little mountain where he had determined to live. Tom decided to call this beautiful spot Monticello, the Italian word for "little mountain." He especially enjoyed the romantic sound of the word when it was pronounced in the Italian fashion: Montichel'lo.[4]

One short year later, May 29, 1765, Jefferson experienced what he subsequently described as the most important day of his life. On this historic day, he accompanied his friend Patrick Henry to a session of the House of Burgesses, of which Patrick Henry was now a member. The House of Burgesses was the first representative legislative assembly in America and the first in any English colony. It first met at Jamestown, which was then the capital of Virginia, on July 30, 1619. The House of Burgesses was moved to Williamsburg when it became the capital of Virginia in 1699. England neither approved nor disapproved of the House. The English government was occupied with its own internal affairs and simply allowed the House of Burgesses to make legislation respecting the colony, reserving a veto power in the Governor appointed by the Crown. Tom could not know the inspired course his life would take as he sat listening to Henry's impassioned speech. It involved a little issue of taxation without representation. During that speech, a flame was kindled in Thomas Jefferson that became a guiding influence throughout his life.[5] It obviously affected the rest of the legislature as well. At the instigation of Patrick Henry, the Virginia Assembly passed a set of resolutions denouncing taxation without representation. They thought it a dangerous and unprecedented innovation and a threat to colonial liberties.

Early in 1767, two years after his visit to the legislature with Henry and shortly before his 24th birthday, Tom was examined for admission to the bar. He was found to be superbly prepared. He began to practice law and was to spend the next seven years as a Virginia lawyer. He was laborious and painstaking in his work. His success as a lawyer surprised some of his more seasoned colleagues in the surrounding county. His law practice produced a sizable sum in addition to his income from the lands he owned. Records show that Jefferson handled nearly 1,000 cases between 1767 and 1774. Many years later, one of Jefferson's grandsons met an elderly gentleman who had often heard Jefferson present legal argument at the court in Williamsburg. The curious grandson inquired about his famous grandfather's performance as a courtroom lawyer. The gentleman replied, "Well, it is hard to tell, because he always took the right side."[6]

Jefferson learned there were drawbacks to the practice of law. He was able to collect only about one-third of the fees which he earned. He soon required at least partial payments in advance for legal representation. Although he loved the law, lawsuits over land and property rights must have become tiresome to Jefferson's brilliant mind. He said, "I was bred to the law and that gave me a view to the dark side of humanity. Then I read poetry to qualify it with a gaze upon its bright side."[7]

Jefferson's comments on an item he drafted and sent to the Virginia legislature give us an insight into his attitude toward the cryptic language of the legal profession:

> I should apologize, perhaps, for the style of this bill. I dislike the verbose and intricate style of the English statutes. . . . You, however, can easily correct this bill to the taste of my brother lawyers by making every other word a "said" or "aforesaid," and saying everything over two or three times, so that nobody but we of the craft can untwist the dictation and find out what it means; and that, too, not so plainly but that we may conscientiously divide, one half on each side.[8]

In 1769 Tom was elected to represent Albemarle County in the House of Burgesses. Here he joined his friend Patrick Henry. He took his oath of office the same day as a fellow Virginian, George Washington. Jefferson was re-elected for the next four years. Then, in September of 1774, he was chosen to represent Virginia at the association of colonies meeting in Philadelphia. This association became known as the Continental Congress.

Probably sometime in 1771, Tom began courting his future wife, Martha Wayles Skelton, according to the formal style of the times. At this point in his life, Tom had matured from a shy, bashful student, to become a successful lawyer and a member of the House of Burgesses. Martha was the daughter of John Wayles, who was also a successful lawyer.

She is described as having been very beautiful. A little above middle height, with a lithe and exquisitely formed figure, she was a model of graceful and queen-like carriage. . . . She was well educated for her day, and a constant reader. . . . Her well-cultivated talent for music served to enhance her charms not a little in the eyes of such a musical devotee as Jefferson.[9]

Though still very young when Thomas started courting her, Martha was a widow. She had married Bathurst Skelton when she was only 18 years old. She became a mother at the age of 19 and a widow before she turned 20. After a suitable period of mourning, Martha found she had several suitors. Many were more handsome than Thomas Jefferson, but she took delight in Tom's intelligence and his interest in music. Nothing appealed to Tom more than Martha's love of music. In Williamsburg, Tom had taken violin lessons from an Italian, Francis Alberti. The same man had taught Martha to play the harpsichord. Often, when Tom visited Martha at her father's home, the two played music together. Sometimes Tom sang to Martha's accompaniment. Besides being musically gifted, Martha was a well-read woman who could discuss books with intelligence and converse about many subjects that interested Tom. They seemed to be unusually well matched. Their courtship became a serious romance, and it ushered in the happiest period of Thomas Jefferson's life.

Tom enjoyed conversations with Martha's father, John Wayles. Tom also loved to play with Martha's son, John, and looked forward to being the child's stepfather. However, this was not to be. Tragically, little John died suddenly on June 10, 1771, not quite four years of age. He had developed one of the infections that was common in the 1700's, an infection which the doctors were helpless to diagnose or to treat.

On November 11, 1771, John Wayles finally consented to the marriage of his daughter to the budding politician who had recently been re-elected to the House of Burgesses. Tom began to prepare for his marriage. He sent a letter to his British agent requesting that his agent send him "a Forte-piano . . . worthy of the acceptance of a lady for whom I intend it."[10]

Thomas and Martha were married at her father's plantation on New Year's Day, 1772. He was 29 and she was 24. The house was filled with guests, and the festivities lasted for days. It was not until January 18th that Tom and Martha set out for Monticello, more than 100 miles away. After a rough trip, they finally arrived at their destination on January 26th. Through a blustery snowstorm, Martha had her first view of her partially completed new home. Dark and deserted, the little brick home clung to the slope of a hill. There was no light to greet them, no voice to welcome them, no fire to warm them. Tom stabled the horses and took his new bride into the home. It was bitterly cold, dark, and dismal. He built a fire and pulled out a hidden bottle of wine to warm them. And in spite of the darkness, their laughter of sheer happiness seemed to light the cottage.

The honeymoon lasted until April. Tom did not attend the meeting of the House of Burgesses in February, nor did he take care of any legal business in Williamsburg until spring. Martha had her new husband completely to herself. She immediately set out to be a good housewife. Tom kept busy building his mountaintop mansion. Work on the main house was well under way. The foundations and the basement were finished, but the house itself was not yet liveable. So Tom continued building and laying out the grounds. He kept exact records of whatever was happening to the construction.

On September 27, 1772, at one o'clock in the morning, Martha gave birth to their first child, a daughter that they named Martha. She was a sickly baby, and for the first six months, they worried that she might not live. But she grew to adulthood and outlived her father.

Jefferson's Early Career

Tom continued with his law practice and his work in the House of Burgesses. One biographer of Jefferson observed that Tom would have a lot of trouble running for a political office today as he probably would not have been very successful on television. There is no record of his ever making a political speech. John Adams even remarked that Jefferson's comments on any of the political proceedings at the Continental Congress never included more than two complete sentences at a time.[11] Tom shied away from public speaking because his vocal chords were weak. When speaking, he became hoarse and inaudible. He was, however, very adept at writing and was one of the most widely read men in America. Because of this, he gained a prestigious reputation in the colonies.

One of his most impressive works was entitled *A Summary View of the Rights of British America*. This was referred to as Jefferson's Bill of Rights. In this booklet, Tom made this statement: "The God who gave us life, gave us liberty at the same time; the hand of force may destroy but cannot disjoin them."[12] This work also caused him to be branded an "Arch-Rebel" by the British Parliament.

Beginning in 1773, an interesting series of events occurred that would bring Thomas Jefferson his greatest fame—the writing of the Declaration of Independence. First, the British Parliament passed the Tea Act on May 10, 1773, and the colonists became furious. Then, on December 16th of that year, as a protest against the hated tax on tea, the Boston Tea Party took its proud place in history. As a result of this insurrection, the British closed the Boston Harbor. In response, in the House of Burgesses, Thomas Jefferson proposed a day of fasting, humiliation [humility], and prayer to focus attention on the closure. The proposal passed, but that angered Lord Dunmore (the new Royal Governor of Virginia) and he consequently dissolved the House of Burgesses on May 27, 1774. Reacting to the dissolution of the House, members of the House met together at the Raleigh Tavern, just down the street from the Capitol building, and began to form a new association. This group instructed the Committee of Correspondence[13] to propose that similar groups from the other colonies appoint a representative to meet on September 5, 1774, in Philadelphia. This Philadelphia meeting would be known as the Continental Congress, and Thomas Jefferson was chosen to represent Virginia. At the age of 32, he was the second-youngest member of that meeting of mighty men. Only John Jay from New York was his junior.

It is interesting that even after the hostilities at Lexington and Concord in April of 1775, most Americans were not anxious to separate from Great Britain. Jefferson himself supported and hoped for reconciliation with England, but he considered the suppression of his countrymen's liberty a gross infringement upon their rights.

Congress adjourned in August 1775, and Jefferson was happy to return to his family at Monticello. But his happiness soon turned to grief. A month after he arrived home, his second child, one-year-old Jane Randolph Jefferson, died. Jane had been born April 3, 1774, only 3½ months after the Boston Tea Party had occurred.

Jefferson was reappointed to Congress and returned to Philadelphia again by the end of September. His mother, Jane Randolph, after whom his deceased baby daughter had been named, became seriously ill. Tom received permission to return to Virginia to be with her. She passed away on March 31, 1776. This doubled the sorrow of losing his daughter a few months earlier and left Jefferson incapacitated by severe migraine headaches for at least the next five weeks. Because of these tragedies, Jefferson nearly missed his appointment with destiny. It is a sad twist of fate that Jefferson's mother died in March of 1776. Had she lived only four months longer, she could have witnessed her son create the inspired, immortal document that gave birth to the United States of America.

Jefferson's Declaration of Independence

By May, Tom had recovered enough from his grief to return to Philadelphia and resume his position in Congress. On June 7, Richard Henry Lee, a fellow Virginian, introduced a resolution calling for a complete separation from Great Britain. Jefferson kept detailed notes on the arguments that took place after Lee's resolution was pronounced:

> It appearing in the course of these debates, that the colonies of New York, New Jersey, Pennsylvania, Delaware, Maryland, and South Carolina were not yet matured for falling from the parent stem, but that they were fast advancing to that state, it was thought most prudent to wait a while for them, and to postpone a final decision to July 1st; but, that this might occasion as little delay as possible, a committee was appointed to prepare a Declaration of Independence. The committee were John Adams, Dr. Franklin, Roger Sherman, Robert R. Livingston, and myself.[14]

The first step of the committee that was to write this immortal document was to appoint one of its members to prepare a draft. Franklin, though the oldest and most experienced, was ill. (It is thought by some that he wasn't chosen to prepare the draft because his son William remained loyal to the crown.) Both Adams and Jefferson had achieved recognition as writers, so it seemed likely that one of them would be selected. Jefferson noted only, the committee "desired me to do it."[15] John Adams left a more interesting account:

> [The sub-committee met.] Jefferson proposed me to make the draft. I said, "I will not. You should do it."
>
> [Jefferson] "Oh, no! Why will you not? You ought to do it."
>
> "I will not."
>
> [Jefferson] "Why?"
>
> "Reasons enough."
>
> [Jefferson]"What can be your reasons?"
>
> "Reasons are: first—you are a Virginian, and a Virginian ought to appear at the head of this business. Reason second—I am obnoxious, suspected, and unpopular. You are very much otherwise. Reason third—You can write ten times better than I can."
>
> "Well," said Jefferson, "if you are decided, I will do as well as I can."[16]

While attending congress in Philadelphia, Tom rented the second-floor suite of the Graff house. This was a two-story home built by a bricklayer named Jacob Graff. Here, Jefferson worked 17 days preparing the draft of the Declaration of Independence. He did so without the use of any reference materials. By this time, Jefferson had extensive experience in the drafting of legal documents as well as political experience in the Virginia legislature.

Jefferson was a creature of habit. He wrote between the hours of six o'clock in the evening and midnight. He arose with the sun. Each morning he plunged his feet into a basin of cold water. He claimed this morning ritual was the reason he rarely had a cold.

After his work on the draft was completed, he presented it to Benjamin Franklin and John Adams, who made only a few changes. The draft was submitted to Congress on Friday, June 28th. It was tabled until a vote could be taken on the resolution to break with Great Britain. This resolution was finally adopted by Congress on July 2, 1776.

Jefferson appreciated the support he received—mainly from John Adams—relative to the adoption of the Declaration of Independence. Jefferson sat, silently, anxiously, as Congress edited his draft. Dr. Franklin, sitting beside Jefferson, noticed he was writhing a little under the criticism and shortening of his document. Franklin offered some words of consolation, "I have made it a rule, whenever in my power to avoid becoming the draftsman of papers to be reviewed by a public body." Franklin then shared a story from his printer days.

> One of [my] friends, an apprentice hatter, had decided to open a shop for himself. His first concern was to have a handsome signboard with a proper inscription. He composed it in these words: *John Thompson, hatter, makes and sells hats for ready money,* with a figure of a hat subjoined. But he thought he would submit it to his friends for their amendments.
>
> The first man he showed it to thought the word "hatter" was superfluous because it was followed by the words "makes hats". Thompson agreed and struck it out.
>
> The next friend observed that the word "makes" might as well be omitted, because the customers would not care who made the hats, as long as they were good ones. Thompson agreed and struck it out.

> A third friend suggested eliminating "for ready money" because none of the local merchants sold on credit. Again Thompson bowed to the will of the majority, and now he had a sign which said: "John Thompson sells hats."
>
> "Sells hats," said his next friend, "why nobody will expect you to give them away. What then is the use of that word?" Again poor Thompson conceded.
>
> Moments later, the word "hats" went into oblivion when another friend pointed out that there was one painted on the board. And so he was left with a sign that said: "John Thompson" beneath the painted hat.[17]

John Adams, speaking on behalf of the Committee, took up the defense of the paper. He supported the Declaration with zeal and ability, fighting fearlessly for every word of it. Jefferson gratefully nicknamed Adams the "Colossus" of the important debate. The revised edition of the Declaration of Independence was approved in the late afternoon of July 4, 1776. Only John Hancock, as president of the Congress, and Charles Thompson, who attested as Secretary, actually signed it on that date. The other delegates affixed their signatures to an engrossed copy on August 2, 1776.

Jefferson explained the object of the Declaration was:

> Not to find out new principles or new arguments never before thought of, not merely to say things which had never been said before; but to place before mankind the common sense of the subject, in terms so plain and firm as to command their assent, and to justify ourselves in the independent stand we [are] compelled to take.[18]

The Declaration was intended to be an expression of the American mind. Jefferson wrote of his completed project: "Whether I had gathered my ideas from reading or reflection I do not know. I know only that I turned to neither book nor pamphlet while writing it."[19]

The Declaration of Independence is one of the greatest and truly inspired documents of all time. Ezra Taft Benson, Secretary of Agriculture under President Dwight D. Eisenhower, uttered these profound thoughts:

> If we accept the premise that human rights are granted by government, then we must be willing to accept the corollary that they can be denied by government. If Americans should ever come to believe that their rights and freedoms are instituted among men by politicians and bureaucrats, then they will no longer carry the proud inheritance of their forefathers, but will grovel before their masters seeking favors and dispensations. . . . We must ever keep in mind the inspired words of Thomas Jefferson, as found in the Declaration of Independence:
>
> "We hold these truths to be self-evident, that all men are created equal; that they are endowed by their Creator with certain unalienable Rights, that among these are Life, Liberty and the pursuit of Happiness. That to secure these rights, Governments are instituted among Men, deriving their just powers from the consent of the governed."
>
> Since God created man with certain inalienable rights, and man, in turn, created government to help secure and safeguard those rights, it follows that man is superior to government and should remain master over it, not the other way around.[20]

In the Declaration, there is an appeal to the "Supreme Judge of the world" and to "the laws of nature and nature's God." It concludes with these words: "And for support of this Declaration, with a firm reliance on the Protection of Divine Providence, we mutually pledge to each other our Lives, our Fortunes, and our Sacred Honor." Jefferson's position on the existence of Deity and the importance of relying on Deity is made perfectly clear in his immortal Declaration. And every man who signed that world-changing document likewise expressed himself to the affirmative.

Every man who signed the Declaration also clearly declared his severing of personal allegiance to the King of England. Every signer knew he was putting his safety, his very life on the line by declaring independence.

After he had signed, Hancock looked at the enormous signature on the parchment and grinned: "There! His Majesty can now read my name without spectacles, and can now double his reward of five hundred pounds for my head. That is my defiance!"

Then, as he backed away from the table, Hancock said, "We must be unanimous. There must be no pulling different ways; we must all hang together."

Old Benjamin Franklin's eyes twinkled. The man who had started out as a printer's devil and was now the most widely known man in America, said: "Yes. We must all hang together, or most assuredly we shall all hang separately."[21]

Every signer knew that the English would regard this as a treasonous act. Every signer knew the personal repercussions would be extensive . . . could be devastating. And they were right:

> Of those 56 who signed the Declaration of Independence, nine died of wounds or hardships during the war. Five were captured and imprisoned, in

> each case with brutal treatment. Several lost wives, sons or entire families. One lost his 13 children. Two wives were brutally treated. All were at one time or another the victims of manhunts and driven from their homes. Twelve signers had their homes completely burned. Seventeen lost everything they owned. Yet not one defected or went back on his pledged word. Their Honor, and the nation they sacrificed so much to create is still intact.[22]

Thomas Jefferson considered writing the Declaration the greatest achievement of his career. But there were many other distinguished accomplishments in the life of Thomas Jefferson. He succeeded Patrick Henry as the Governor of Virginia in 1779. And in that same year, Jefferson was proud of introducing a bill for "Establishing Religious Freedom in Virginia." This bill affirmed that no church would be supported by taxes . . . the real meaning of the phrase "the separation of church and state." This bill did not imply that religion was unimportant in the affairs of men. It meant only that the government could not interfere with religious activity.

Jefferson's Beloved Martha Dies

On September 6, 1782, Martha Wayles Skelton Jefferson, Tom's beloved wife of only ten years, passed away. Their life together brought Tom "ten years of uncheckered happiness."[23] Tom wrote only these words in his daily account book: "My dear wife died this day at 11:45 a.m." But Tom's daughter wrote this description of her father's emotional struggles after the death of her mother:

> A moment before the closing scene, he was led from the room in a state of insensibility by his sister, Mrs. Carr, who, with great difficulty, got him into the library where he fainted, and remained so long insensible that they feared he never would revive. The

> scene that followed I did not witness, but the violence of his emotion when, almost by stealth, I entered his room by night, to this day I dare not describe to myself.
>
> He kept his room three weeks, and I was never a moment from his side. He walked almost incessantly night and day, only lying down occasionally, when nature was completely exhausted, on a pallet that had been brought in during his long fainting fit. My aunts remained constantly with him for some weeks—I do not remember how many.
>
> When at last he left his room, he rode out, and from that time he was incessantly on horseback, rambling about the mountain in the least frequented roads, and just as often through the woods. In those melancholy rambles I was his constant companion—a solitary witness to many a burst of grief.[24]

In the preceding seven years Jefferson had buried two young daughters, an infant son, and his mother, but he still seemed ill prepared for the devastating death of the cherished companion of his life. Martha was only 33 at the time of her death. Jefferson never married again.

Jefferson's Service as Diplomat

In 1785, Jefferson replaced Benjamin Franklin as the Minister to France. Jefferson often stated that it was not easy to fill the shoes of Dr. Franklin.

> There appeared to me more respect and veneration attached to the character of Dr. Franklin in France than to that of any other person in the same country, foreign or native . . . [this succession] was an excellent school of humility. On being presented to

> anyone as the minister from America, the commonplace question used in such cases was, "it is you, sir, who replaced Dr. Franklin?" I generally answered no one can replace him, sir; I am only his successor.[25]

Jefferson was still serving as a diplomat in France on May 14, 1787, when the Constitutional Convention convened in Philadelphia. Originally, this meeting was planned in order to revise the Articles of Confederation. Later, the delegates realized that the government under the Articles had to be replaced. The central government simply had to have more power to be successful. James Madison, known as the Father of the Constitution, was closer to Thomas Jefferson than any other delegate. Madison obtained much of his learning at the feet of Thomas Jefferson. Jefferson fought long distance for a Bill of Rights to be added to the Constitution while Madison fought the battle at the Convention itself. After it was adopted and ratified, Jefferson referred to the Constitution as "unquestionably the wisest ever yet presented to man."[26] Although Tom wasn't there, he undoubtably had a great impact on the language adopted because of his correspondence and friendship with Madison.

Jefferson Serves with Washington and Adams

Almost 2½ years later, September 26, 1789, Jefferson left Paris to return to the United States. He was unaware that on that very date Congress had confirmed his appointment as Secretary of State in the first administration of George Washington. Jefferson was reluctant to accept the position but was influenced by Washington's insistence.

In his new appointment, Jefferson had two particular concerns. Too many regal forms and ceremonies seemed to beset the executive office. It was only his confidence in the unquestionable character of George Washington that quelled his fears. However, Jefferson's distrust of Alexander Hamilton's proposals and motives as Secretary of the Treasury could not be quelled. Jefferson was concerned that Hamilton's financial programs were both unwise and unconstitutional. Washington often sided with Hamilton, which resulted in Jefferson's becoming dissatisfied with his minority position within the cabinet. Twice he had determined to resign, but was dissuaded. Then, on December 31, 1793, he finally did so.

In 1796, Washington decided against running for a third term as President. John Adams became the candidate for the Federalist party and Jefferson the candidate for the Democratic-Republican party. Under the system in effect at that time, Adams won the Electoral College vote by a narrow margin, and Jefferson, as the runner-up, became the Vice-President. Because both men held a common bias against Hamilton, Jefferson hoped he and his old friend Adams could work well together. But their tenure as a team was disappointingly rocky.

Jefferson is Elected President

Jefferson's principles and clever strategies helped him win the election of 1801 against Aaron Burr. Since there had been a tie in the Electoral College, the election was shifted to the House of Representatives. Even then, it took 36 different votes to settle upon Jefferson. When he gave his inaugural speech, Jefferson advocated that any political problems of the past decade be buried in order for Americans to unite. He also clearly detailed his definition of a *good government:*

> A wise and frugal government, which shall restrain men from injuring one another, which shall leave them otherwise free to regulate their own pursuits of industry and improvement, and shall not take from the mouth of labor the bread it has earned—this is the sum of good government. [27]

Sadly, due to Jefferson's weak voice, no one could hear his important message. In spite of his appeal to unite as a nation, the Federalist leaders remained adamantly opposed to Jefferson. The people, however, approved his policies:

> Internal taxes were reduced; the military budget was cut; the Alien and Sedition Acts were permitted to lapse; and plans were made to extinguish the public debt. Simplicity and frugality became the hallmarks of Jefferson's administration. The Louisiana Purchase (1803) capped his achievements. . . . The purchase was received with popular enthusiasm. In the election of 1804, Jefferson swept every state except two—Connecticut and Delaware. . . . The following year, the Lewis and Clark Expedition, which the president had dispatched to explore the Louisiana Territory, returned triumphantly after crossing the continent.[28]

Thomas Jefferson was the first President to preside in the new Capital at Washington, D.C. As he promised his wife, Jefferson never remarried and so was a widower in the White House. He invited Dolley Madison, the wife of James Madison, to become a hostess on many social occasions. Also, his daughter Martha often served as hostess. The White House became famous for entertaining.

When John Adams had been President, under the encouragement of his wife, Abigail, he had reserved Tuesday evenings for receptions. These receptions had become a special social gathering, much anticipated by the female society. Thomas Jefferson decided to eliminate these receptions. That decision was not well received. Many of the ladies of Washington were indignant and determined that they would not be cut off from these functions. On the traditional reception day, many ladies appeared at the White House for their habitual social gathering. Jefferson was out on his usual horseback ride. Upon his return, the President was told that the public rooms were filled with ladies.

He understood their true motives, and without changing from his dusty boots and riding clothes, he went in to receive his guests. He had never been more graceful or courteous. The ladies, charmed with the ease and grace of his manners and conversation, forgot their indignation. At the end of the evening, the ladies went away feeling guilty of being impolite because they had visited the White House when not expected. They never again attempted to infringe on the rules of Jefferson's household.

Even though Jefferson eliminated the Tuesday social gatherings, nearly every day Jefferson invited ten or twelve guests to an informal dinner, with Dolley Madison or his daughter Martha acting as the hostess. The President's table became famous for fascinating conversation and extraordinary menus. It was at these meals that such European treats as macaroni, waffles, and ice cream were introduced.[29]

Jefferson never used public funds to entertain his guests, even when they came as official representatives of foreign governments. He owed about $8,000 to $10,000 by the time he left the presidency. One consolation he claimed upon leaving the office of President was: "Having added nothing to my private fortune during my public service, and of retiring with hands as clean as they are empty."[30]

After two years in office he said:

> The path we have to pursue is so quiet that we have nothing scarcely to propose to [our legislature]. A noiseless course, not meddling with the affairs of others, unattractive of notice, is a mark that society is going on in happiness. If we can prevent the government from wasting the labors of the people

> under the pretense of taking care of them, they must become happy.[31]

Jefferson was elected to serve a second term as President, giving his inauguration speech on March 4, 1805. He reviewed his efforts of the previous four years to maintain peace with foreign powers. He spoke of domestic achievements. He then said:

> At home, fellow citizens, you best know whether we have done well or ill. The suppression of unnecessary offices, of useless establishments and expenses, enabled us to discontinue our internal taxes. . . . The remaining revenue, on the consumption of foreign articles, is paid cheerfully by those who can afford to add foreign luxuries to domestic comforts. . . . It may be the pleasure and pride of an American to ask, what farmer, what mechanic, what laborer ever sees a tax-gatherer of the United States?[32]

Jefferson was a popular President. He governed well, but didn't take himself too seriously. A little insight into the humorous personality of Thomas Jefferson is revealed in the following story that occurred while he was living in the White House:

> One day, as President Jefferson was riding along one of the highways leading into Washington, he overtook a stranger who was making his way toward the city on foot. He drew up his horse and greeted the man, as was his custom. The traveler returned his greeting, and they immediately launched into a political discussion. (People talked as freely about politics back then as we do about the weather now.)
>
> Not realizing whom he was addressing, the man indulged in some unkind remarks about the President, referring to several indecent and slanderous

accusations which his political opponents had recently printed in the newspapers. Jefferson's first impulse was to bid the fellow a good day and ride on, but he was held by his amusement at the situation. After listening a few more minutes, he asked the stranger whether he knew the President personally.

"No" said the man, "nor do I wish to."

"But do you think it fair," Jefferson asked, "to repeat such stories about a man whom you dare not face?"

"I will never shrink from meeting Mr. Jefferson should he ever come my way."

"Will you go to his house tomorrow at ten o'clock and be introduced to him, if I promise to meet you there at that hour?"

"Yes, I will," he decided after a moment's thought. Jefferson then excused himself, touched his hat to the traveler, and rode away toward Washington.

When the man appeared at the Executive Mansion the next morning, a servant answered the door and escorted him down a hall to President Jefferson's office. As he came face to face with the President, he suddenly realized what had happened. Greatly embarrassed, but with gentlemanly bearing, he managed to say, "I have called, Mr. Jefferson, to apologize for having said to a stranger"—

"Hard things of an imaginary being who is no relation of mine," interrupted Jefferson. He gave the man his hand and a warm, good-natured smile.

> The red-faced visitor turned out to be a merchant of high standing from Kentucky, and Jefferson insisted that he stay for dinner so they could become better acquainted. He did stay, and was quickly won over to the President he had unknowingly insulted the day before.
>
> From that day forward the merchant and his family were "fiery Jeffersonians." Like so many other Americans, they quickly acquired a sincere affection for this tall, soft-spoken statesman from Virginia—and a deep commitment to the principles of freedom that he advocated.[33]

Given his own description of service in the presidency as a financial drain and social discomfort, it is not surprising that at the end of his second term, in 1809, Jefferson referred to the presidency as "A splendid misery . . . [brings] nothing but unceasing drudgery and daily loss of friends."[34]

Jefferson as Architect and Inventor

Besides being a distinguished statesman, Jefferson was also known as a great architect. He designed Monticello, the Virginia State Capitol Building, and numerous other mansions and public buildings. But one of his great dreams, one of which he was most proud, was the building of the University of Virginia in Charlottesville. He conceived it, planned it, and designed it. He supervised its construction and even the hiring of the faculty. Although work on the university did not begin in earnest until after his two terms as President of the United States, Jefferson had long been contemplating its establishment. Some 40 years earlier, in 1778, he had introduced a bill for the general diffusion of knowledge.

His ideas for the designing and building of the college were quite unique. He envisioned something entirely different from the typical large building commonly constructed. He planned to build small buildings in which each professor would live and give his lessons. These buildings would be connected by covered walkways. This design would help avoid fires and the spreading of infection.

The cornerstone ceremony took place October 6, 1817. The message of the opening prayer that was given at the laying of the stone effectively pronounced Jefferson's feelings about the school:

> May almighty God, without invocation to whom, no work of importance should be begun, bless this undertaking and enable us to carry it on with success—protect this College, the object of which institution, is to instill into the minds of Youth principles of sound knowledge. To inspire them with the love of religion & virtue, and prepare them for filling the various situations in society with credit to themselves and benefit to their country.[35]

Besides being an accomplished architect, Jefferson was a ingenious inventor. He once commented, "Science is my passion, politics my duty."[36] His field of knowledge and experience was extremely broad. A visit to his home, Monticello, would impress anyone with its practicality of design, as well as the creative instruments found within. Among his inventions which can still be seen at Monticello are his revolving chair, a walking stick which could be turned into a folding chair, musical stands, a writing box which could serve as a reading stand as well as a writing surface, and a "polygraph" to copy every letter he wrote. Jefferson invented the polygraph to avoid the tragedy that had beset his father—whose correspondence had all been destroyed in a fire. This contraption would hold two pens together by a connection of pulleys and frames, so that when one letter was written, a duplicate was created by the second pen. Jefferson also designed many other gadgets and conveniences for his home.

The entry hall to Monticello did not house the popular grand stairways of the day. Jefferson felt they took up too much otherwise usable space. The upstairs was reached by narrow stairways. Monticello's entry served both as a reception hall and as a museum. It held one of the largest private collections of natural history and Indian artifacts. It was crowded with maps; fossils; natural history specimens; mastodon bones; antlers of moose, elk, and deer; paintings of religious subjects; five works of sculpture; curios brought back from the expeditions of Lewis and Clark; and even a model of the pyramids of Egypt. Jefferson's seven-day calendar clock, which operated by weights along the wall, hung above the entrance door. The weights indicated the day of the week as they descended past markers on the south wall. The distance necessary to allow the weights to fall was misjudged, however, and holes had to be cut into the floor to permit the weights to descend into the basement, where the marker for Saturday was located.

Straight ahead from the entry hall was the parlor, the most formal room at Monticello, sometimes referred to as the ballroom. It was the scene of many fine occasions, including weddings, christenings, musical evenings, and balls. The double doors located between the ballroom and the museum were designed by Jefferson to be unique to Monticello. The two doors were joined together under the floor through the basement. A series of weights caused both doors to open together, even if only one of them were pushed. Entering the parlor through these unusual doors revealed Martha's harpsichord standing directly to the right. The parlor floor was a magnificent parquet, fashioned after those Jefferson had loved in France. It was the first of its kind in America. More than 48 paintings, mostly portraits and religious and mythological subjects, hung on the walls of this room. Jefferson often read in the parlor, and here, one granddaughter noted, "in the shady twilight I was wont to see him resting."[37]

From the parlor, one could enter the dining room. Here, Jefferson had designed a revolving serving door with shelves. By using this device, servants could deliver food from the kitchen without even entering the dining room. This allowed Jefferson the luxury of private conversations with his guests without the worry of servants who might eavesdrop and gossip. The mantel over the fireplace concealed two dumbwaiters that were directly connected to the wine cellar below.

A tearoom adjoined the dining room at the coldest corner of the house, so Jefferson installed double doors between them, allowing the tearoom to be closed off during the winter months. Jefferson called the tea room, or breakfast room, his "most honorable suite." It was in this room that he displayed the busts of Benjamin Franklin, George Washington, John Paul Jones, and Lafayette. Sculpted by Jean-Antoine Houdon, the pre-eminent French artist of his time, Jefferson had purchased them in Paris. Also in this room, Jefferson had another one of his reading and writing arrangements under the niche of the north wall to avail himself of the late afternoon light.[38]

Jefferson called the most private part of the house the "sanctum sanctorum" (holy of holies.) This included his library, his study, and his bedroom with the bed alcove. While he lived at Monticello, he rarely admitted anyone other than close family into these rooms. To allow for ventilation, he located his bed in an alcove between his bedroom and his study. When the windows to both the study and bedroom were open, a draft would flow over Jefferson's bed to cool him while sleeping. This placement also allowed him to arise directly into his study or his bedroom as he desired. A door at the right of his bed opened on a stairway that led to a closet above his bed, where his clothes were stored in the off season.

Jefferson's study, or cabinet room, contained several of his inventions and contraptions. These included his polygraph for copying letters and his telescope and surveying equipment. For extra illumination, his chaise lounge had candle holders on both arms. There was also a table with a revolving surface that allowed him easy access to several books at once. This table was designed to fit over his lounge chair so that he might use it whenever he desired to study in comfort. Also kept in this room was his portable writing desk, on which he had written the Declaration of Independence.

Many thousands of books were stored in Jefferson's library and elsewhere throughout his house. During the War of 1812, British troops had burned the City of Washington. Because of this, Jefferson offered to sell his personal collection of books to the federal government to serve as a nucleus for the new Library of Congress. His was the finest collection in America at that time, containing thousands of volumes that had been gathered over a 50-year period. His collection was more than twice the size of the Library which had burned. In 1815, the government accepted his offer, and Jefferson sold more than 6,700 books to the Library of Congress. Unfortunately, he was paid less than half their value—only $23,950. It took ten wagons to transfer the books to Washington. Within weeks of the sale, Jefferson spent over $700 for the beginnings of another library. His new library grew to over a thousand volumes. "I cannot live without books," he confessed to John Adams.[39]

Adjoining the library was the south piazza, a glassed-in space which served as a greenhouse and in which Jefferson also kept his workbench and tools. Monticello's vegetable garden had first been laid out in 1774. A fresh and abundant supply of vegetables was essential to the welfare and health of those living at the mansion. Jefferson studied gardening and grew many new hybrid varieties. Peas were his favorite vegetable.

At Monticello, Jefferson constructed buildings for weaving, nail-making, and carpentry. The outside kitchen, the cook's room, the house servants' rooms, a smokehouse, and a dairy were concealed in the south hillside terrace, out of sight from the house and lawns. These rooms were connected to the cellar of the house by an all-weather passage. Concealed beneath the north terrace were the stables, carriage bays, ice house, and laundry. In the south pavilion, the first building to be erected on the mountaintop, Jefferson and his new bride spent the early months of their marriage.

As one who could not live without books, Jefferson was an extraordinarily learned man, as evidenced in the following story:

> This breadth of learning is illustrated by an anecdote involving a highly educated man from New England who chanced to meet Jefferson at a country inn one evening, not knowing who he was. The man repeatedly introduced new topics into the conversation, and he was so astounded at his dinner companion's knowledge that he later inquired of the landlord regarding Jefferson's identity.
>
> "When he spoke of law, I thought he was a lawyer; when he talked about mechanics, I was sure he was an engineer; when he got into medicine, it was evident that he was a physician; when he discussed theology, I was convinced that he must be a clergyman; when he talked of literature, I made up my mind that I had run against a college professor who knew everything."[40]

But his books were not his only source of education. Jefferson learned much from his associations with other brilliant Founding Fathers such as Benjamin Franklin and George Washington. Like both of them, he was not prone to argue or be disagreeable. He was usually quiet in political situations. He tried to be a peacemaker. Of his experience in Congress, he wrote in his autobiography the following words, which are overflowing with solid, sound advice and stand as a witness to the genius of the man:

> Our body was little numerous, but very contentious. Day after day was wasted on the most unimportant questions. A member, one of those afflicted with the morbid rage of debate, of an ardent mind, prompt imagination, and copious flow of words, who heard with impatience any logic which was not his own, sitting near me on some occasion of a trifling but wordy debate, asked me how I could sit in silence, hearing so much false reasoning, which a word would refute? I observed to him, that to refute indeed was easy, but to silence was impossible.[41]

Jefferson continues to explain his procedure to listen carefully to points being made, and to interrupt only when he thought it was necessary or justified. He believed that procedure would be beneficial to all legislative bodies or committees in order to save time and actually accomplish something. He then went on to describe how he learned such a principle:

> I served with General Washington in the legislature of Virginia, before the revolution, and, during it, with Dr. Franklin in Congress. I never heard either of them speak ten minutes at a time, nor to any but the main point, which was to decide the question. They laid their shoulders to the great points, knowing

> that the little ones would follow of themselves. If the present Congress errs in too much talking, how can it be otherwise, in a body to which the people send one hundred and fifty lawyers, whose trade it is to question everything, yield nothing, and talk by the hour? That one hundred and fifty lawyers should do business together, ought not to be expected.[42]

Jefferson's Private Religious Projects

One of Jefferson's projects in his later years was a compilation of all of the *New Testament* passages which he understood to be the true words or actual statements made by Jesus Christ.

> I too have made a wee-little book . . . which I call the "Philosophy of Jesus." It is . . . made by cutting the texts out of the book, and arranging them on the pages of a blank book, in a certain order of time and subject. A more beautiful or precious morsel of ethics I have never seen. It is a document in proof that *I am a real Christian*, that is to say, a disciple of the doctrines of Jesus, very different from the Platonists, who call *me* infidel and *themselves* Christians and preachers of the gospel, while they draw all their characteristic dogmas from what its Author never said or saw. They have compounded from the heathen mysteries a system beyond the comprehension of man, of which . . . were He to return on earth would not recognize one feature.[43]

His wee-little book has since been published as the *Jefferson Bible.* Jefferson also compiled another book which he called *The Life and Morals of Jesus*. This project was probably compiled in the summer of 1820. (Although, in 1803, Jefferson ordered two Greek copies of the *New Testament* from a bookseller, so perhaps he started working on it as early as 1803.) *The Life and Morals of Jesus* is a collection of verses from the *New Testament* in Greek, Latin, French, and English. It was a result of Jefferson's private search for religious truth. His grandson, Thomas Jefferson Randolph, noted that this book of morals was not known to the family before Jefferson's death. But after he died, the family read a letter that Jefferson had written to a friend in which the great man had mentioned that he was in the habit of reading nightly from his book of morals before going to bed.

After Jefferson's death, copies of several *New Testaments* were discovered in his rooms in which the scriptures that referred to Christ had been cut out. Perhaps these "mutilated copies" helped give rise to the claim that some historians have made that Jefferson was an atheist, that he did not believe in Christ. However, Jefferson's writings belie this supposition. The Declaration of Independence, *Jefferson's Bible*, and Jefferson's compilation, *The Life and Morals of Jesus*, give ample evidence of his religious beliefs. Moreover, there are constant references in his private letters to "Our Savior." On one occasion, a distinguished gentleman commented to Jefferson about his own disbelief in the truths of the Bible. Tom's reply was as simple as it was profound, "Then sir, you have studied it to little purpose."[44]

In spite of his ardent religious convictions, Jefferson seldom spoke about his beliefs with anyone, even those who were closest to him. His deep commitment to religious freedom led him to respect the right of others to hold religious opinions different from his. In addition, Jefferson asserted ". . . it is in our lives, and not from our words that our religion must be read."[45]

While Jefferson's family may not have been entirely familiar with all of his religious beliefs, they had no doubt about his personal commitment to religion and morality. Thomas Jefferson Randolph (Jefferson's grandson) said:

> I never heard from him the expression of one thought, feeling, or sentiment inconsistent with the highest moral standard, or the purest Christian charity in its most enlarged sense. His moral character was of the highest order. . . . He had seen and read much of the abuses and perversions of Christianity; he abhorred those abuses and their authors, and denounced them without reserve.[46]

Jefferson regularly attended church, taking his prayer book with him. He drew the architectural plans of the Episcopal Church in Charlottesville and was one of the largest contributors to its erection. He contributed regularly to the support of its minister. After his death, his subscription of $200 was paid to the Presbyterian Church in the same village.

Jefferson's Last Days

Declining in health at age 83, Jefferson hoped he would live to see the 50th anniversary of the Declaration of Independence which he had drafted and of which he said, "I pray to God that these principles may be eternal."[47] He was invited to speak at the celebration of this anniversary in Washington, D.C., but he had to refuse because of his deteriorating health and the danger of a long trip.

In a letter to the mayor, he offered the following word of inspiration:

> I should, indeed, with peculiar delight, have met and exchanged there congratulations personally with the small band, the remnant of that host of worthies, who joined with us on that day . . .
>
> May it be to the world what I believe it will be (to some parts sooner, to others later, but finally to all), the

> signal of arousing men to burst the chains under which monkish ignorance and superstition had persuaded them to bind themselves, and to assume the blessings and security of self-government. That form which we have substituted restores the free right to the unbounded exercise of reason and freedom of opinion.
>
> All eyes are opened, or opening, to the rights of man. The general spread of the light of science has already laid open to every view the palpable truth that the mass of mankind has not been born with saddles on their backs, nor a favored few booted and spurred, ready to ride them legitimately by the grace of God. These are grounds of hope for others. For ourselves, let the annual return of this day forever refresh our recollections of these rights, and an undiminished devotion to them.[48]

This remarkable letter was Jefferson's last. He died peacefully in his bed at Monticello on July 4, 1826, the 50th anniversary of the signing of the Declaration of Independence. Coincidentally, his dear friend and fellow patriot, John Adams, died only a few hours later on that same day.[49]

After Tom's death, a secret drawer was found in a private cabinet. The drawer contained locks of Martha's hair and other little mementos of his wife. It also held a remembrance of each of his children, including those who had died. All these precious objects were labeled in Tom's handwriting and gave evidence of having been frequently—and lovingly—handled. A touching finale to the magnificent life of a sensitive soul.[50]

Thomas Jefferson filled a critical role in our American history. He can stand tall, next to the best of the Founding Fathers. His was a life of amazing achievements: A gifted statesman—serving as

Secretary of State, Governor, Minister to France, Vice-President, President. An inspired writer. An original architect. An ingenious inventor. A cutting-edge horticulturalist. A naturalist. A linguist. In spite of his many and mighty achievements, his modesty becomes evident when one reads the inscription that he wrote for his own tombstone: "Author of the Declaration of American Independence, of the Statute of Virginia for religious freedom, and Father of the University of Virginia." Those are the three things for which he wanted to be remembered, the three things he wanted inscribed on his tombstone, and "not a word more." His death became a memorial to freedom: freedom from English rule, freedom to worship God, and freedom of education.[51]

Chapter 6

James Madison

March 16, 1751 – June 28, 1836

James Madison

James Madison Jr. was born March 16, 1751—25 years before the Declaration of Independence would be written by his close friend, Thomas Jefferson. His parents, James and Nelly Conway Madison, were well-to-do members of the landed gentry, a slave-owning family who lived in Orange County, Virginia. James was the first of twelve children, two of which were stillborn, and he himself was small and sickly. Even as an adult, he was slight of build, never weighing much more than 100 pounds and reaching a height of only 5 feet 6 inches.

James Madison's early schooling began at his grandmother's knee. It probably amounted to little more than instruction in reading, writing, and arithmetic. But if he followed the bookish inclination always evident in his adult life, we may imagine that as he learned to read, he devoured almost every scrap of printed matter on the family farm. And there were many books available at the farm, through inheritances and purchases. His grandfather left the family at least 28 volumes on religion and various other subjects.

Although he was frail and experienced poor health, James Madison was an excellent student. He attended his first school in 1762, when he was 11 years old. It was run by a Presbyterian minister named Donald Robertson. The school, located in King and Queen

County, was so far from home that he lived there until the age of 16. At that time, he returned to his home, Montpelier, and continued his education for the next two years with his tutor, Thomas Martin.[1]

Madison was only 14 years old when the Stamp Act was passed. He listened carefully as his father and others discussed the injustice of the situation. His interest in public affairs became irrepressible. He chose to study government and public law to deepen his understanding of public affairs, not to master technical courtroom law. He never intended to practice law and never qualified as a counselor-at-law. Madison's general health, his weak speaking voice, and perhaps some moral reservations, deterred him from such a career.

Madison Goes to College

Madison and his father had heard high praise for The College of New Jersey at Princeton from graduates of that institution. It had been founded primarily to train Presbyterian ministers, but also produced many lawyers and politicians, with effective training in expression and speaking. Madison set his sights northward and enrolled at Princeton College, where he received a solid education and graduated in only 2½ years.

The daily schedule of the college was itself a prime source of the discipline he so earnestly sought. A bell at five o'clock in the morning awoke the students, and another, at six o'clock, summoned them to morning prayer. Here, the college president expounded a passage of scripture. Pupils then studied (by candlelight in the winter) for an hour before breakfast. At nine o'clock, they had recitation, which was followed by study until dinner at one o'clock. The time between dinner and three o'clock was free, followed by recitation and study until five o'clock. Then bells pealed for evening prayers, where the students took turns singing psalms. Supper was served at seven o'clock. By nine o'clock, a room check required all pupils to be in their rooms, either studying or sleeping. At recitation periods, each class sat together with its tutor, reciting for him, listening to his explanations, and responding to his questions.[2]

If James Madison had followed the most common path to higher education in Virginia, he would have gone to the College of William and Mary in Williamsburg, like his good friend and mentor, Thomas Jefferson. However, James tells us in his autobiography that the climate at Williamsburg was "unfavorable to the health of persons from the mountainous region." And Madison was not a very physically stalwart person. Also, Jefferson's brilliant and beloved teacher, William Small, had departed, leaving the college in the hands of less accomplished and not very capable administrators and teachers. At the time Madison might have gone there, the college was in "a dissolute and unenviable state."[3]

Madison graduated from the College of New Jersey in the spring of 1771, a paragon of the well-educated scholar who had acquired a great thirst for knowledge. The college president often stated that "during the whole time [Madison] was under [my] tuition, [I] never knew him to do, or to say, an improper thing."[4] Upon graduating from college and considering his profession, he contemplated both divinity and law, but neither excited him. It was the American Revolution that drew James Madison into politics, but he would not realize his great calling until the beginning of the Revolutionary War. A political vocation would dominate his life.

For the rest of his life, Madison retained his reputation as a scholar. His college friends came to him regularly for discussions. Jefferson turned to him repeatedly for help in research and in compiling bibliographies. Even his political foes admitted that on nearly every question before any legislative body in which he sat, he was likely to be the best informed member.

Two years after his graduation from college, on December 16, 1773, a group of men disguised as Indians boarded British tea ships in the Boston Harbor and dumped all the tea into the water. Madison approved the principle, if not the violence, of the Boston Tea Party and denounced the "obduracy and ministerialism" of the Governor of Massachusetts.[5]

One year later, in December of 1774, he took a seat—along with his father—on a local "Committee of Safety" to which he had been appointed. These committees, consisting of patriots, oversaw the local militia and were springing up all over the colonies to carry on the necessary functions of government during the Revolutionary War. As he was a good marksman, Madison desired to be a soldier during the Revolution: "I should not often miss the bigness of a man's face at 100 yards."[6] He was likely one of the "orange militia men" led by Patrick Henry to retake the large quantity of gunpowder which had been confiscated by Lord Dunmore after the bloodshed at Lexington and Concord. On the march to Williamsburg, Henry demanded and received payment from the Governor for the value of the powder, and the militia was sent home.

Madison Chooses His Vocation

It was pitiable that Madison's health (he sometimes had sudden attacks that resembled epilepsy, among other problems) and the feebleness of his constitution forced him to resign from the fight for independence on the battlefield. But his zeal for the patriot cause equaled that of men twice his size! In fact, he was so supportive of the Revolution that if anyone showed, or even seemed to show, the slightest backwardness or caution toward the cause, Madison was immediately suspicious of them. Rumors were rife in Philadelphia that Benjamin Franklin, just returned from ten years' residence in England, "came back rather as a spy than as a friend, and that he means to discover our weak side and make his peace with the minister Lord North by discovering it to him."[7] Sadly, Madison believed this rumor. He wrote:

> Little did I ever expect to hear that Jeremiah's Doctrine that "the heart of man is deceitful above all things and desperately wicked" was exemplified in the celebrated Dr. Franklin. . . . It appears to me that the bare suspicion of his guilt amounts very nearly to a proof of its reality. If he were the man he formerly was . . . his conduct . . . on this critical occasion could have left no room for surmise or distrust. . . . His behavior would have been explicit and his Zeal warm and conspicious [sic].[8]

Actually, Franklin had already withstood severe temptation from the Ministry in London. And when he arrived home to America in May 1775, he purposely remained inconspicuous in certain efforts to further the Revolutionary cause. He tried for a month to convince two influential American Loyalists, his son, Governor William Franklin of New Jersey, and his long time friend Joseph Galloway, to support the patriot cause. Much to his chagrin, his efforts were in vain. But Franklin soon proved himself to be at least as vigorous a foe of Great Britain as was Madison.

While he had previously considered both divinity and law, Madison had never been driven to either profession. Madison's inability to serve as a soldier propelled him to his critically important destiny: he became a Nation Builder. By the time the battles of Lexington and Concord had been fought, he adopted the ideals that were to motivate and guide him through 40 years of public service and then 20 years as his country's authentic sage.

Madison was elected as a delegate to that Virginia Convention where Virginia was transformed from a colony to a state in July of 1776. "There he strengthened the conventional clause guaranteeing religious 'toleration' to proclaim 'liberty of conscience for all.'"[9] The state constitution was submitted to the Convention and adopted on June 24, 1776. Patrick Henry took the oath of office as the first Governor of the new state of Virginia on the 5th of July, 1776. James Madison continued to serve with Governor Henry as a member of his executive council through 1779. Then, in 1780, at the age of 28, Madison was elected to the Continental Congress and became the youngest member of that body.

After the war was over, Madison returned home to Virginia. Like others, he was concerned with how the new republic could be made stronger and more stable. He studied fervently the fields of law, history of nations, and governments. At Madison's request, Thomas Jefferson sent him two trunks of "literary cargo" from France.[10] The trunks contained more than 100 carefully selected books—in Jefferson's opinion, the most useful reference books available. Madison made himself into a walking encyclopedia about the history and political philosophy of governments of the past.

Madison's systematic study led him to complete an important treatise called *Ancient and Modern Confederacies*. He outlined the kind of constitution which he thought would remedy the situation then existing in the several states. During this time, he continued to serve in the Virginia House of Delegates.

The Constitutional Convention

At the end of 1785, in an effort to bring about change and reform in America's system of government, Madison proposed a convention of all the states to discuss interstate commerce problems. Only five states were represented at this "Annapolis Convention." But, as

Madison had hoped, they called for all states to convene again the following May for the purpose of revising the Articles of Confederation.[11]

Madison knew they must move quickly, or it might be too late to save the infant nation. He said in his writings:

> The crisis is arrived at which the good people of America are to decide the solemn question, whether they will by wise and magnanimous efforts reap the just fruits of that independence which they have so gloriously acquired . . . or whether by giving way to unmanly jealousies and prejudices, or to partial and transitory interests, they will renounce the auspicious blessings prepared for them by the Revolution.[12]

This federal Convention was to convene on May 25, 1787. Madison wrote letters to Washington and to Governor Edmund Randolph of Virginia outlining a plan of government. This plan embodied his insights from his serious studies of the "literary cargo" which Thomas Jefferson had sent him from France. Madison had come up with a master stroke of genius for the proposed new government. He could support Governor Randolph's insistence that state prerogatives be protected and Washington's insistence on a thorough reform giving dignity and authority to the national councils. He wrote:

> Conceiving that an individual independence of the States is utterly irreconcilable with their aggregate sovereignty, and that a consolidation of the whole into one simple republic would be as inexpedient as it is unattainable, I have sought for middle ground, which may at once support a due supremacy of the national authority, and not exclude the local authorities wherever they can be subordinately useful. [In this,

> Madison was proposing what he later called a] "mixed government," a unique blend of the federal principle (a government whose constituents were states, not people) and of national government designed to preserve at once freedom, national dignity, and local self-government. Madison believed that a plan suitable to Randolph's local biases and to Washington's sense of national needs might just have a chance of adoption [by the convention].[13]

George Washington did not wish to be a part of this new Convention. He considered that his service to his country had been completed when he resigned his commission as Commander in Chief of the Revolutionary Army on December 23, 1783. He had resolved to retire to Mount Vernon. He specifically told Madison that he did not intend to be present at this Convention. However, Madison believed that Washington's appearance was vital to provide the Convention the strength necessary to create a new government and the stature to make that government acceptable to all Americans. Madison was clever enough, and determined enough, to successfully coax the nation's most popular man, George Washington, into attending this Convention as a powerful and badly needed symbol of legitimacy. Madison was persistent in his continued invitations.

At 55, Washington was almost a generation older than Madison. Yet the two had known each other for years, as Madison had been in the Virginia government since 1776. It is hard to say which man was the more serious by nature. Their writings on politics, with their forceful arguments and stately rhythms, show an underlying intensity of concern for the country. Perhaps we should rejoice that these men felt no embarrassment at being persistently and sometimes even awkwardly serious.

Washington could have found reasons to absent himself from the Convention that was to be held in May 1787. In January, his favorite brother, Augustine, a companion of his youth, died "by a fit of gout in the head."[14] In March, Washington was attacked by rheumatism so severe he could scarcely move in bed, or raise his hand to his head. In addition to his own physical problems, his letters to Madison revealed another concern. It was clear that Washington had little wish to risk his reputation in a movement that might fail.

Because of Washington's critical importance to the Convention, Madison took a calculated risk and announced that the General was going to attend the Convention—before Washington himself had agreed to do so. Eventually, the expectation of his fellow countrymen, and the pressure of Madison, forced Washington to appear in Philadelphia. On Sunday, May 13, Washington arrived amid chiming bells, booming cannon, and cheering citizens. Months of patient, skillful encouragement by Madison had ended as he had hoped.

While waiting for a quorum to arrive, Madison met together with Washington, George Mason, and a few others to create a proposal to present to the Convention. Because of Madison's intense study and preparation, he was able to offer well-conceived and inspired suggestions. Based largely on Madison's recommendations, this handful of men worked together to skillfully hammer out what became known as the Virginia Plan of Union. This plan called for the three branches of government and the checks and balances that became the basis for much of the discussions at the Convention.

James Madison often displayed a clever use of strategy in his connection with the Constitutional Convention. He was obviously aware of the importance of timing and conditioning. Knowing that the Convention had been called to amend the Articles of Confederation, he didn't want to immediately propose a different purpose for the meeting. So Madison convinced Governor Edmund Randolph[15] to introduce the Virginia Plan to the Convention merely as a way to correct and enlarge the Articles of Confederation.

Madison determined that he would perform the vital task of preserving for posterity a record of "the processes, the principles, the reasons, and the anticipations"[16] of the Founders in creating the new Constitution. He selected a seat in front of the newly elected presiding officer, George Washington. From this position he could hear what was said by all the members to the president, or what was read by the president to the Convention. Madison gave us the most complete picture of what transpired during those three amazing months.

Many of the most important men in the nation were present at the Convention, including George Washington, Benjamin Franklin, Alexander Hamilton, and Gouverneur Morris. Notably absent were Thomas Jefferson, John Adams, and Patrick Henry. Thomas Jefferson was in Europe, serving as Minister to France. But as Madison's close friend and mentor, he corresponded frequently with Madison and gave his impressions on Madison's reports of the proceedings. In this manner, Jefferson exercised a great influence on the outcome of the Constitution.

John Adams was also in Europe, serving as minister to Great Britain. Madison had read Adam's treatise, *A Defence of the Constitutions of Government of the United States of America*, as had many other delegates at the Convention. Like most other thinking Americans, Adams was afraid the United States would die an early and ugly death because of the weak Articles of Confederation. In January of 1787 he published the first volume of his *A Defence of the Constitutions of Government of the United States of America*. In this, he reminded Americans of the true principle on which free America must be established. This book was available in the United States by spring and was widely circulated. One historical scholar noted: "even a casual glance at the records of the Federal Convention will show that Adam's book was used as a sort of repertory by many speakers, who found in it a confirmation of their views, [with] historical illustrations and precedents."[17]

In spite of his physical absence, John Adams' voice was a mighty presence at the Constitutional Convention. Doctor Benjamin Rush, a signer of the Declaration of Independence from Philadelphia, reported that the fortunate arrival of copies of the first volumes of John Adams' *A Defence of the Constitutions of Government of the United States of America* had "diffused such excellent principles among us, that there is little doubt of our adopting a vigorous and compounded [bicameral] federal legislature."[18]

Patrick Henry had been chosen as a delegate but refused to attend. He refused because of his disdain for what he thought would end in a loss of control by Virginia and the southern states of the Mississippi river commerce. John Marshall wrote to Arthur Lee: "Mr. Henry, whose opinions have their usual influence, has been heard to say that he would rather part with the Confederation than relinquish the navigation of the Mississippi."[19]

Madison himself took an active part in the debates at the Convention, speaking on nearly every important principle. He stood and spoke a reported 161 times. Madison recorded that he made lengthy speeches on nearly every subject of importance. He was also largely responsible for the preparation and presentation of the Virginia Plan, which became the basis for the Constitution.

Thomas Jefferson wrote:

> [Madison] acquired a habit of self-possession, which placed at ready command the rich resources of

> his luminous and discriminating mind, and of his extensive information, and rendered him the first of every assembly afterwards, of which he became a member. Never wandering from his subject into vain declamation, but pursuing it closely, in language pure, classical, and copious, soothing always the feelings of his adversaries by civilities and softness of expression, he rose to the eminent station which he held in the great National Convention of 1787.[20]

Madison was unwavering in his belief that members of both Houses of Congress should be elected by population. This was, of course, a bone of contention with the smaller states, who desired equal representation in at least one House. This led to many bitter and heated discussions.

One evening, Washington took Madison to listen to some music and dine together. He told Madison that there was a need for a consensus among the delegates. There was a need for harmony in the Convention, just as in music, where there was harmony between the string instruments and the flute. "History will not forgive us," Madison said, asserting the firm opinion that both Houses must represent the people.

Washington replied, "You persuaded me to come to this Convention, Mr. Madison. Here I am. I will not see this Convention crumble around me because the brightest and stubbornest of us will not yield the Senate to the smaller states."[21] An amazing compliment for James Madison, a man of only 36 years. Washington's statement inadvertently exemplified his own humility. Washington, who was 55 years of age, who had been asked to be King, who would be elected the first President—referred to Madison as "the brightest." Eventually even Madison relented and accepted compromise.

There was an amazing, even hallowed, web that drew the men at the Constitutional Convention together. The key players each had an indisputable, vital role to perform. The oldest, and perhaps wisest, of the Founding Fathers to attend was Benjamin Franklin. He came, in spite of the fact that his health was so poor that most of the time he had to be carried from his home to Independence Hall in a sedan chair. His role was often subtle. There was much argument, rancor, and debate during the Convention about such things as slavery, elections, powers of the different branches of government, tenure, and especially the manner of the election of Representatives and Senators. As the quarreling continued, Franklin submitted his famous motion for daily prayer:

> Mr. President, The small progress we have made . . . is, methinks, a melancholy proof of the imperfection of the human understanding. . . . In this situation of this assembly, groping, as it were, in the dark to find political truth, and scarce able to distinguish it when presented to us, how has it happened, Sir, that we have not hitherto once thought of humbly applying to the Father of Lights to illuminate our understandings? In the beginning of the contest with Britain, when we were sensible of danger, we had daily prayers in this room for the divine protection. Our prayers, Sir, were heard—and they were graciously answered. . . .
>
> I have lived, Sir, a long time; and the longer I live, the more convincing proofs I see of this truth, that *God governs in the affairs of men*. And if a sparrow cannot fall to the ground without his notice, is it probable that an empire can rise without his aid? We have been assured, Sir, in the sacred writings that "except the Lord build the house, they labor in vain that build it." I firmly believe this; and I also believe that, without his

> concurring aid, we shall succeed in this political building no better than the builders of Babel…
>
> I therefore beg leave to move that, henceforth, prayers imploring the assistance of heaven and its blessings on our deliberations be held in this assembly every morning before we proceed to business, and that one or more of the clergy of this city be requested to officiate in that service.[22]

As it turned out, the motion was not carried because the Convention had no fund to hire a clergyman, and many of the delegates feared that introducing such a change at that point would spark rumors of dissension. But this sobering proposal did manage to settle that atmosphere considerably, and a new spirit of cooperation began to emerge.

When a final consensus seemed to be evolving, some of the delegates were still not completely satisfied. Benjamin Franklin made one more carefully drafted speech:

> I confess that I do not entirely approve of this constitution at present. But, Sir, I am not sure I shall never approve it; for, having lived long, I have experienced many instances of being obliged, by better information or fuller consideration, to change my opinions even on important subjects, which I thought right but found to be otherwise. It is therefore that, the older I grow, the more apt I am to doubt my own judgment. . . .
>
> Thus I consent, Sir, to this Constitution, because I expect no better and because I am not sure that it is not the best. The opinions I have had of its errors I sacrifice to the public good. I have never whispered a

> syllable of them abroad. Within these walls they were born, and here they shall die. If every one of us, in returning to our constituents, were to report the objections he has had to it and endeavor to gain partisans in support of them, we might prevent its being generally received. . . . I hope, therefore, for our own sakes as a part of the people, and for the sake of our posterity, that we shall act heartily and unanimously in recommending this Constitution, wherever our influence may extend, and turn our future thoughts and endeavors to the means of having it well administered.
>
> On the whole, Sir, I cannot help expressing a wish that every member of the convention who may still have objections to it would, with me, on this occasion doubt a little of his own infallibility and, to make manifest our unanimity, put his name to the instrument.[23]

Perhaps, without Benjamin Franklin's inspired speech, agreement would never have been reached. Perhaps, without Washington's commanding presence, his very attendance, the meeting would never have transpired. Perhaps, without Adam's vision, the groundwork would never have been laid. Perhaps, without Madison's dedication to study and careful planning, the Constitution would never have been written. An intricate web. An inspired document.

A committee of style was chosen to put into a final, written form the principles to which the Congress had agreed. This committee consisted of James Madison, Alexander Hamilton, William Samuel Johnson, Gouverneur Morris, and Rufus King. Gouverneur Morris was selected as the one who would actually write it in its final form and language. Madison is the best witness to the part Gouverneur Morris played. "The finish given to the style and arrangement fairly belongs to the pen of Mr. Morris. . . . For my part, I think the whole of it is expressed in the plain, common language of mankind."[24]

After 16 weeks of unrelenting work, the finished Constitution was signed on September 17, 1787. George Washington signed first, followed by 37 others, state by state. James Madison recorded that at the climactic moment when the delegates came forward to sign the document:

> Dr. Franklin, looking towards the president's chair, at the back of which a rising sun happened to be painted, observed to a few members near him, that painters had often found it difficult to distinguish in their art a rising from a setting sun. I have, said he, often and often in the course of the session, and the vicissitudes of my hopes and fears as to its issue, looked at that [sun] behind the president, without being able to tell whether it was rising or setting: But now at length I have the happiness to know that it is a rising and not a setting sun.[25]

One historian tells us that when Franklin's turn came to add his signature to the Constitution, he "was helped forward from his place; afterward it was said the old man wept when he signed."[26]

When John Adams, still in England, received his copy of the new document, he went to the British Secretary, threw a copy of the new Constitution on his desk, and said, "There. You have a copy of the most important document in the world. America is now an equal in the family of nations. We've done it. We are a Nation!"[27]

James Madison was hailed as the prime creator of the Constitution, but he rejected all such praise. "You give me credit to which I have no claim, in calling me THE writer of the Constitution of the U.S. This was not, like the fabled Goddess of Wisdom, the offspring of a single brain. It ought to be regarded as the work of many heads and many hands."[28] This was not a case of false modesty. Madison knew the vital influences of such great men as Thomas Jefferson, his friend and mentor, through the writings and discussions they had together, and the experiences they shared in the Virginia government; of the great authors of the many books he had so carefully studied, including that of John Adams; of the patient and gently persuasive leadership of the universally respected George Washington; of the influence of the wisdom of Benjamin Franklin and the many others who had participated in that miracle at Philadelphia. Madison wrote: "There was never an assembly of men . . . who were more pure in their motives." And when their work was done he added: "It is impossible for the man of pious reflection not to perceive in it a finger of that Almighty hand which has been so frequently and signally extended to our relief in the critical stages of the revolution." [29]

One member of the Convention reported that after the delegates filed out of Independence Hall, an anxious woman approached Dr. Franklin and asked, "Well, Doctor, what have we got—a republic or a monarchy?"

"A republic," said Franklin, "if you can keep it."[30]

The woman asked that question because the Constitution, history-changing document that it was, had been produced in strictest secrecy in that little room in Philadelphia. It was in the ratifying conventions in each state that the public would learn of the provisions of the proposed new government. The Constitution had been signed by the delegates to the Convention. Now, as designated in the Constitution itself, it was up to the states to adopt it.

Fight For A Bill of Rights

The signers of the Constitution were not sure that it ever would be ratified; many people opposed the new Constitution. Patrick Henry was one of them. However, Madison's thoughtful reasoning could not be denied, and it eventually won out over Henry's markedly superior oratory. Even though not as polished as Patrick Henry, Madison was a very good and knowledgeable speaker in his own right. He sometimes got so excited when speaking about the Constitution that he finally asked a friend to tug at his coat tails if he became too wrought up. Once, after talking himself to the point of exhaustion, Madison reproved his friend, "Why didn't you pull me when you heard me going on like that?" The friend replied, "I would rather have laid a finger on the lightening!"[31]

Beginning in October 1787, in an effort to sway the vote for ratification in the hesitant state of New York, James Madison, Alexander Hamilton, and John Jay collaborated on essays that were printed in New York newspapers. These essays were later collected into two volumes titled *The Federalist Papers*. By January 9, 1788, Delaware, Pennsylvania, New Jersey, Georgia, and Connecticut had ratified the new Constitution. But, as stated in Article VII, nine states had to accept it before the Constitution could become the principle document that united them. Four additional votes were needed for ratification, and those votes would not be cast without a promise of some amendments guaranteeing individual rights.

Jefferson had fought long distance from Europe for a Bill of Rights to be added to the Constitution. The Anti-Federalists—those opposed to the adoption of the Constitution—firmly believed in the need for amendments guaranteeing individual rights. The debate between them and the Federalists—those who advocated the adoption of the Constitution and the establishment of a strong central government—was intense.

Madison's efforts to inspire the states to ratify the Constitution paid off. Massachusetts, Maryland, South Carolina, and the ninth state, New Hampshire, ratified. The new nation had begun. Shortly thereafter, Virginia and then New York also ratified.

In 1789, a Bill of Rights was proposed in Congress, and Madison drafted 12 amendments to the Constitution. At that point, North Carolina ratified the Constitution. The tiny state of Rhode Island held out for a full three years before it ratified the Constitution on May 29, 1790. Ten of Madison's proposed amendments were ratified by the required number of states and became known as the Bill of Rights on December 15, 1791.[32] Creating a Bill of Rights avoided another Constitutional Convention, which would have started the whole process over again.

In spite of the number of great men and brilliant minds involved in writing the Constitution and the Bill of Rights, Madison remains preeminent in the realization of the documents. He was the primary author of the Virginia Plan. He was one of the most active participants in the debates. He was the prime mover in getting the participants together, including putting pressure on George Washington to even appear. He gave us the most complete record of the Convention. He was a co-author of the dynamically written argument for the Constitution, *The Federalist Papers*. He was the most influential supporter in fighting for ratification within the states, especially his powerful home state of Virginia. While there were many men who contributed to the concepts and writing of the inspired document that has proved itself for over 200 years, it is James Madison who has been dubbed "the Father of the Constitution."[33]

James Madison and Dolley

While still in the struggle to get the Constitution ratified, Madison served in Congress. He represented Virginia from 1789 to 1797, the years that George Washington was President. In 1794, the 43-year-old Congressman gave up his long-held bachelorhood when he married a lovely, 26-year-old widow, Dorothy Payne.[34] History is better acquainted with her as Dolley Madison.

It is entirely possible that James may have been first introduced to Dolley at an afternoon tea, which was so popular at that time in Philadelphia. At age 21, Dorothy (Dolley) Payne, an eligible "belle," would have been a welcome guest at a tea hosted by one of Madison's fellow congressmen, Colonel Isaac Coles. Dolley would have been pleased to meet the congenial Virginian James Madison, as she had grown up in Virginia herself. Dolley, however, would be married within a year to John Todd.

Dolley was born May 20, 1768, to John and Mary Payne. John Payne had converted to Mary's Quaker faith. They moved from Virginia to North Carolina to live in an isolated Quaker farming community. It was here that Dolley was born, the third of five children. But it wasn't long before the Payne family moved back to Virginia. They lived for a time at Scotchtown, a plantation once owned by Mary's cousin Patrick Henry.

In 1782, when the manumission, or freeing of slaves, became legal in Virginia, John and Mary Payne freed the many Negro slaves who worked their farm. At age 14, Dolley understood the great sacrifice her parents had made for the sake of their beliefs. John left their farm and moved his family to Philadelphia in 1783 so that their children could be educated in their religion. They were welcomed by the Quaker community. But John, skilled only in farm management, found it impossible to earn a living as a starch-maker and went bankrupt in 1789. He was then rejected by the Quaker congregation for failing to pay his debts. He died two years later, broken and dispirited.

Dolley, who had been brought up in strict Quaker fashion, found life in America's largest city most exciting. She enjoyed Quaker outings, blossomed into a beautiful young woman, and soon had young men competing for her attention. Shortly after her father's bankruptcy, she married a young Quaker lawyer, John Todd. In spite of her father's financial problems, this match pleased the Quakers, and 80 of them came to the ceremony to solemnize the union and sign the marriage certificate. The conscientious lawyer gained many clients, and John and Dolley were able to move into a fine house.[35]

By 1793, the Todds had two sons, an 18-month-old and a newborn baby. That year, a terrible yellow fever epidemic struck, which nearly drove the government from Philadelphia. Dolley retreated to the suburbs with her two children, her mother, and three of her siblings. John stayed in the stricken city, caring for his parents, ministering to the sick, and writing dozens of wills.

John pressed his luck too far. After two months among the sick and dying, he contracted the fever and died in his wife's arms. That same day, her infant son died. Dolley, now desperately ill herself, in the suburbs without any close friends nearby, and with only $19 to her name, struggled to survive. However, through the bequests of her husband and his father, Dolley was not long in great need.

In the spring of 1794, Dolley became the center of attention. She was now in comfortable circumstances, vivacious, handsome, bright-eyed, and winsome—one of the eligible women of Philadelphia. Congressman James Madison, 43 years old, was also highly eligible, in spite of the fact that some friends feared he was a confirmed bachelor. In May 1794, the 26-year-old Quaker widow wrote excitedly to her best friend: "Thou must come to me. Aaron Burr says that the great little Madison has asked to be brought to see me this evening."[36]

By mid-June, when Congress adjourned and Madison left for Virginia, he had said nothing to his friends Jefferson or Monroe of any romantic plans. However, Dolley had made arrangements to visit her relatives in Virginia and obviously to be near James, her husband-to-be . . . in case she should decide on marriage.

Catherine Coles, the wife of Dolley's uncle, Congressman Isaac Coles, wrote to Dolley:

> Now for Madison. He told me I might say what I pleased to you about him. To begin, he thinks so much of you in the day that he has lost his Tongue; at Night he Dreames [sic] of you and starts in his sleep a Calling on you to relieve his Flame for he Burns to such an excess that he will be shortly consumed and he hopes that your Heart will be calous [sic] to every other swain but himself. He has consented to everything that I have wrote about him with sparkling Eyes. Monroe goes to France as Minister Plenipotentiary. Madison has taken his House. Do you like it?[37]

On September 15, 1794, the reverend Alexander Balmain pronounced the solemn words that began 42 years of devotion in marriage for James Madison and Dolley Payne Todd. Three months later, in a Quaker meeting on December 12, 1794, the strict Quakers disowned Dolley for marrying a non-Quaker "before a hireling priest."[38] This virtually wiped the family name from the Quaker rolls.

There is a poignant irony in that neither George Washington, the "Father of our Country," nor James Madison, the "Father of the Constitution," ever had any children of their own. However, they both married widows and raised stepchildren.

Seven years after they were married, James Madison began his service as Secretary of State under President Thomas Jefferson. He served in this capacity from 1801 to 1809. This put Madison right in the thick of things. Since President Jefferson was a widower in the White House, he asked his good friend James Madison if Dolley could serve as the White House hostess. Nearly every day, Jefferson invited ten or twelve guests to a luncheon where Dolley charmed them all.

Madison Becomes President

In 1809, James Madison followed Thomas Jefferson as President of the United States. At his inauguration, Madison wore a suit of black American-made cloth, much like the retiring President Jefferson's. Dolley's finery, on the other hand, had been imported from Paris. As the crowd continued to press, Madison's discomfort grew. Nodding toward the new President, Jefferson remarked that he himself was "much happier at this moment than my friend. . . . All eyes were on Dolley, who 'looked like a queen,' and displayed such manners as 'would disarm envy itself, and conciliate even enemies.' "[39]

As the First Lady, Dolley engaged in her own daily routine: She rose early, dressed in plain clothes, and spent the morning shopping and attending to other domestic duties. Then, donning finer dresses, she graced the sitting rooms of the White House, where her husband often visited her, sure "of a bright story and a good laugh . . . as refreshing as a long walk." Otherwise, James labored incessantly, sleeping "very little, going to bed late and getting up frequently during the night to write or read; for which purpose a candle was always burning in the chamber. Despite committing White House social life as much as possible to his wife, Madison still found it made "sad inroads on his time." He was therefore somewhat cold and stiff, taciturn in general society and preoccupied. After dinner, however, at which he usually took a liberal portion of wine, he became free and even facetious, telling . . . many anecdotes."[40]

In June of 1812, at President Madison's request, Congress declared war against Great Britain. There were several reasons for this drastic declaration. The British had incited the Indians to fight against the U.S., had interfered with the American merchants, and had forced American sailors into service for the British. The war had its ups and downs. In August of 1814, President Madison received notice that the British had landed in Maryland and were advancing toward the American Capitol at Washington, D.C. The U.S. militia were fighting valiantly, but he feared that the British would break through their lines. President Madison felt it necessary to go to the soldiers and encourage them in their weakened state.

He told Dolley to act as if everything were fine and to continue with her preparations for the evening's dinner party, planned for 40 guests. He promised that if all were well, he would return by dinnertime, and if he didn't return, then she should flee to the countryside. He warned her to carefully watch and be ready in the event that the British should enter the city, cautioning her that the British must not capture the nation's documents. Just before galloping away, he told her that these documents were in the Great Room. His only hesitation in leaving her was his concern for her safety.

Dolley stayed in the White House, and even though she feared for the President's safety, she continued her preparations for the dinner party. When she heard the sound of cannons in the distance, she realized that it was time to act quickly to save the documents. She picked up the Declaration of Independence and gently wrapped it, placing it in one of her trunks. She resolved that the British would not set their hands to that precious paper. Her eyes filled with tears as she remembered the great sacrifice the signers had made in the name of freedom.

The cannon and muskets grew louder, and Dolley was urged by the servants to flee. She returned to the Great Room and rescued boxes of James' original notes about the Constitutional Convention, some books, a small clock, and some velvet curtains. She headed for the already heavily loaded carriage and then thought of the portrait of George Washington. She could not abide the thought of the British burning his effigy like so much garbage. She ran back into the house and, with the help of two servants, broke the frame which had been bolted to the wall. She carefully cut the portrait from the wall and removed the "Landsdowne Portrait of George Washington," by Gilbert Stuart.[41] She rolled it up and took it with her as she evacuated the White House. She did not return for her jewelry or any other personal items. She was able to escape at the last moment by using a back road. A kind farmer graciously took her in.[42]

The British burned the President's Mansion, the War Building, the Treasury Building, and all other government buildings, including the Congressional Library.[43] But the British plunder of the Capital was mysteriously cut short. Storm clouds that had formed over the city suddenly burst. The rain came in torrents. Hurricane-strength winds blew in from the ocean. Thunder seemed to shake the city. The courage of the British soldiers faltered as the fires, combined with the winds, caused the ravaged buildings to crumble. Many soldiers were trapped under the devastation. Lightning lit the sky, and a rumor went through the lines that the American soldiers were now surrounding the city. Overcome by fear, the British soldiers retreated from the city just one day after their huge victory.

In early January 1815, the tide of the war changed when General Andrew Jackson defeated the British army at New Orleans. Ten days after receiving news of this victory, Madison received some even more welcome news: the previous December, at Ghent, Belgium, a peace treaty had been signed. The war was over.

Madison's presidency ended with the inauguration of James Monroe, another stalwart from Virginia, on March 4, 1817. Madison's work as President was highly lauded by John Adams: "Notwithstanding a thousand faults and blunders, Madison's administration has acquired more glory, and established more union, than all his three predecessors put together."[44]

Madison in Retirement

Madison lived nearly 20 years after he retired from the Presidency. During that time, he helped Thomas Jefferson found the University of Virginia. After Jefferson's death, Madison became the rector of this University. He served longer as the rector while the University had students in attendance than did Jefferson.

Madison also served as president of The American Colonization Society, an organization dedicated to freeing the slaves and helping them return to Africa. Madison challenged those with objections to this plan to come up with a better solution. He reminded them of the "transcendent need to do something about the looming evil that mocked the moral integrity of the nation and even threatened the Union itself."[45]

On June 28, 1836, at the age of 85, James Madison died quietly at his home, Montpelier. It was located near the mountaintop home of his beloved friend, Thomas Jefferson. Madison had rejected the suggestion that he take stimulants to extend his life a few days in order that he might die on July 4, 1836—the 60th birthday of the signing of the Declaration of Independence. It seems beyond merely coincidental that John Adams and Thomas Jefferson had both died on the 50th anniversary and James Monroe on the 55th.

As the Father of the Constitution, it is curiously fitting that James Madison was the last remaining signer of that inspired document. His own words about the ends of government are deeply profound and well worth remembering:

> The aim of every political constitution is, or ought to be, first to obtain for rulers men who possess most wisdom to discern, and most virtue to pursue, the common good of the society; and in the next place, to take the most effectual precautions for keeping them virtuous whilst they continue to hold their public trust.[46]

Thomas Jefferson, a highly respected man himself, and one to whom Madison looked for advice, offered the following two complimentary characterizations of his friend James Madison: "To the purest principles of republican patriotism, Madison adds a wisdom and foresight second to no man on earth." And "I do not know in the world a man of purer integrity, more dispassionate, disinterested, and devoted to genuine Republicanism; nor could I in the whole scope of America and Europe point out an abler head."[47] Those comments are a fitting conclusion to a noble life.

As with all the Founding Fathers, James Madison had strong convictions about his Creator. When questioned about his feelings regarding the nature of Deity, Madison replied, "Belief in a God All Powerful wise and good is so essential to the moral order of the World and to the happiness of man, that arguments which enforce it cannot be drawn from too many sources."[48]

James Madison was undoubtedly the smallest of the Founding Fathers, yet he stands as nobly tall as any of them. On September 28, 1809, about six months after he was elected President of the United States, *The American Mercury*, a newspaper published in Hartford,

Connecticut, printed the following: "Mr. Madison has been in public life more than 32 years. He is 53 years of age. During his whole life it is believed, there is not a single act for which he can be reproached as a man or a citizen." For this, he is worthy of every American's admiration. Indeed . . . he stands tall!

Timeline

TIMELINE

While compiling this book, the almost endless number of important dates became difficult to remember. It was soon obvious to me that a time line of some kind was necessary to help myself—and the reader—to put events into their proper place in time. While I found several different time lines, each with their own unique perspective, none seemed to include much personal information about these great men who are our Founding Fathers. Yet often, the personal information—the marriages, the births, the deaths, etc.—colors the story in a different light. For instance, to realize that Thomas Jefferson wrote the Declaration of Independence just months after the death of his baby daughter and beloved mother makes that marvelous document even more precious. To appreciate that Patrick Henry's wife died only one short month before his dramatic proclamation "give me liberty or give me death," brings a new level of meaning to his decree. Seen in date-by-date perspective, the story of the American Revolution becomes a fascinating experience. I encourage you to take the time to read it.

	1700	1710	1720	1730	1740	1750	1760	1770
Benjamin Franklin	1706 Franklin is born; 1708 Deborah Reed is born		1728 Buys PA Gazette	1730 Marries Deborah	1744 Invents Franklin stove	1752 Experiments with electricity; 1753 Appointed Deputy Postmaster General; 1757 Appointed by PA assembly as agent to England. In London for most of next 18 years		1774 Deborah dies at age 66; 1775 Home from England
George Washington				1731 Martha Dandridge is born; 1732 George Washington is born		1752 Lawrence Washington dies G.W. inherits Mt. Vernon; 1754 French-Indian War; 1759 Marries Martha		1775 Appointed Commander-in-Chief
John Adams				1735 John Adams is born	1744 Abigail Smith is born		1764 Marries Abigail	1770 Boston Massacre; 1775 Bunker Hill
Patrick Henry				1736 Patrick Henry is born; 1738 Sarah Shelton is born		1754 Marries Sarah; 1757 Dorthea Dandridge is born; 1758 Parson's cause		1775 Sarah Henry dies age 37; 1775 "Liberty" Speech
Thomas Jefferson					1743 Thomas Jefferson is born; 1748 Martha Wayles is born			1772 Marries Martha; 1775 T.J.'s daughter and mother dies
James Madison						1751 James Madison is born; 1758 Dolley Payne is born		

1776	1780	1787-1788	1790	1800	1810	1820	1830	1840
Attends Congress. On Committee for Declaration ◆ December 3, 1776 - Sent to France by Congress	◆ **1778** Treaty of Alliance with France ◆ **1783** Negotiates Peace Treaty	◆ **1787** Attends Constitutional Convention ◆ **1785** Returns from France	◆ **1790** Dies age 84					
Fights at Dorchester Heights, Boston, NY. ◆ Reads Declaration to troops	◆ **1777** Valley Forge ◆ **1781** Cornwallis surrenders at Yorktown	◆ **1787** Attends Convention, serves as President	◆ **1793** 2nd Term as President ◆ **1789** Elected as 1st U.S. President	◆ **1802** Martha dies age 71 ◆ **1797** Retires to Mt. Vernon ◆ **1799** Dies age 67				
Attends Continental Congress on Committee for Declaration	◆ **1779** Adams sent to join Franklin in France ◆ **1783** Negotiates Peace Treaty ◆ **1780** Treaty with Netherlands	◆ **1787** Writes Book on Constitution ◆ **1788** Returns from England	◆ **1789** Vice President	◆ **1797** Elected President		◆ **1818** Abigail dies age 74	◆ **1826** Dies age 91 on 50th Anniversary of Declaration of Independence	
Motion for Declaration of Independence ◆ Elected 1st Governor of New State of Virginia	◆ **1777** Marries Dorothea	◆ **1788** Opposes Constitution without Bill of Rights		◆ **1799** Dies age 63			◆ **1831** Dorthea Henry dies age 74	
Attends Continental Congress ◆ Writes Declaration of Independence	◆ **1779** Elected Governor of Virginia ◆ **1782** Martha dies age 34	◆ **1785** Minister to France ◆ Corresponds with Madison	◆ **1789** Returns from France.	◆ **1797** Vice President ◆ **1800** Elected President. ◆ **1803** Negotiates Louisiana Purchase	◆ **1804** 2nd Term as President	◆ **1815** Congress purchases T.J.'s Library	◆ **1826** Dies age 83 on 50th Anniversary of Declaration of Independence	
Serves in Virginia House	◆ **1780** Elected to Continental Congress	◆ **1787** Serves as Secretary to Constitutional Convention	◆ **1794** Marries Dolley		◆ **1809** Elected as 4th U.S. President ◆ **1812** Declares war with Great Britain			◆ **1836** Dies age 85 ◆ **1849** Dolley dies age 91

July 30, 1619: The House of Burgesses is established; it is the first representative legislative assembly in America and the first in any English colony. It first meets at Jamestown, the capital of Virginia at the time.

January 17, 1706: Benjamin Franklin is born in Boston to Josiah Franklin and Abiah Folger.

1708: Deborah Read (future wife of Benjamin Franklin) is born to John and Sarah Read.

October, 1723: Benjamin Franklin arrives in Philadelpia

1728 (about): Benjamin Franklin conceives his plan for arriving at moral perfection.

1729: Benjamin Franklin buys the Pennsylvania Gazette.

September 1, 1730: Benjamin Franklin and Deborah Read are married.

Spring of 1731: William Franklin is born to Benjamin Franklin.

June 21, 1731: Martha (future wife of George Washington) is born to John Dandridge and Frances Jones.

1731: Benjamin Franklin begins what is considered the first public library.

February 22, 1732: George Washington is born to Augustine Washington and Mary Ball.

October 20, 1732: Frances Folger (second child) is born to Benjamin and Deborah Franklin. He dies at four years of age.

1733: Benjamin Franklin begins publishing *Poor Richard's Almanac.* He continues to do so through 1757.

October 30, 1735: John Adams Jr. is born to John Adams and Susannah Boylston.

May 29, 1736: Patrick Henry is born to John Henry and Sarah Winston Syme.

1738: Sarah Shelton (future wife of Patrick Henry) is born to John Shelton and Eleanor Parks.

April 12, 1743: George Washington's father, Augustine, dies. George is only 11 years old.

April 13, 1743: Thomas Jefferson is born in Virginia to Peter Jefferson and Jane Randolph.

September 22, 1743: Sarah (third and last child) is born to Benjamin and Deborah Franklin.

November 22, 1744: Abigail Smith (future wife of John Adams) is born to William Smith and Elizabeth Quincy.

1744 (about): Benjamin Franklin invents the "Franklin stove," which is still in use today.

March 1748: George Washington begins his career as a surveyor when Lord Fairfax, a prominent Virginia landowner, invites him on a venture to the Shenandoah Valley.

October 30, 1748: Martha Wayles (future wife of Thomas Jefferson) is born to John Wayles and Martha Eppes.

March 16, 1751: James Madison, Jr. is born to Col. James Madison and Eleanor Conway.

November 2, 1751: George Washington accompanies his brother Lawrence (who is suffering from tuberculosis) to Barbados. George contracts smallpox.

July 1752: Lawrence Washington dies. George Washington inherits rights to Mount Vernon plantation.

1752: Benjamin Franklin experiments with electricity and flies a kite in a lightning storm.

1752: Thomas Jefferson begins attending school.

November 1753: George Washington leads a Virginia expedition to challenge French claims to the Allegheny River Valley.

1753: Benjamin Franklin is appointed deputy postmaster general.

Early 1754 - 1763: The French and Indian War. George Washington serves as an officer for the British army.

October 1754: Patrick Henry and Sarah Sheldon are married.

Summer 1755: Martha ("Patsy," first child) is born to Patrick and Sarah Henry.

January 1757: Benjamin Franklin is appointed by the Pennsylvania Assembly as agent to the Government in England. Franklin spends most of the next 18 years in London.

Spring 1757: John (second child) is born to Patrick and Sarah Henry.

August 17, 1757: Thomas Jefferson's father, Peter, dies. Thomas is only 14 years old.

September 25, 1757: Dorothea ("Dolly") Dandridge (second wife of Patrick Henry) is born to Nathaniel Dandridge and Dorothea Spottswood.

1758: The Virginia House of Burgesses passes the Two Penny Acts: Instead of paying the clergy with tobacco, the farmers can now pay a much smaller amount—two pence per pound of tobacco owed. This results in the parsons' cause and great esteem for Patrick Henry.

January 6, 1759: George Washington marries Martha Dandridge Custis, a widow with two children.

1759: While fighting in the French and Indian War, George Washington is elected to the House of Burgesses, where he serves for 15 years.

1760: Patrick Henry passes the bar exam.

March 25, 1760: Thomas Jefferson is admitted to the college of William and Mary (studying there for two years); he begins the study of law under George Wythe.

1762: James Madison attends his first school at age 11.

1763: William (third child) is born to Patrick and Sarah Henry.

April 13, 1764: Thomas Jefferson comes of age and inherits his father's large estate.

April 1764: Sugar Act. Duties are increased on non-British goods imported into the colonies. It is the first law Parliament passes that is specifically aimed at raising colonial money for the Crown.

September 1, 1764: Currency Act. Angering many colonists, this act keeps American colonies from making their own currency.

October 25, 1764: John Adams marries Abigail Smith.

1764: Beginnings of Colonial Opposition. American colonists respond with protest to the Sugar Act and the Currency Act. In Massachusetts, participants in a town meeting cry out against taxation without proper representation in Parliament, and suggest some form of united protest throughout the colonies. By the end of the year, many colonies are practicing nonimportation, a refusal to use imported English goods.

March 22, 1765: Stamp Act. Taxing newspapers, almanacs, pamphlets, broadsides, legal documents, writing paper, bills of sale, dice, and playing cards, this is Parliament's first direct tax on the American colonies. It is enacted to help pay for maintaining British armies in America. Issued by Britain, the stamps are affixed to documents or packages to show that the tax has been paid.

March 24, 1765: Quartering Act. The British further anger American colonists with the Quartering Act, which requires the colonies to provide barracks and supplies to British troops.

May 16, 1765: Patrick Henry, a member of the House of Burgesses, offers a series of resolutions declaring the exclusive right of colonists, as Englishmen, to tax themselves. He pronounces the Stamp Act unconstitutional and subversive of British and American liberty. At once, Henry becomes the leader in his colony.

May 29, 1765: During Patrick Henry's impassioned speech about taxation without representation at the House of Burgesses, Thomas Jefferson's life changes as he is inspired to become deeply involved with the revolutionary movement.

May 29, 1765: The "Sons of Liberty" are founded.

July 14, 1765: Abigail (first child) is born to John and Abigail Adams.

1765: Organized Colonial Protest. American colonists respond to Parliament's acts with organized protest. Throughout the colonies, a network of secret organizations, known as the Sons of Liberty, are created. They aim to intimidate the stamp agents who collect Parliament's taxes. Before the Stamp Act can even take effect, all the appointed stamp agents in the colonies have resigned. The Massachusetts Assembly suggests a meeting of all the colonies to work for the repeal of the Stamp Act. All but four colonies are represented. The Stamp Act Congress passes a "Declaration of Rights and Grievances," which claims that American colonists are equal to all other British citizens, protests taxation without representation, and states that, without colonial representation in Parliament, Parliament cannot tax colonists. In addition, the colonists increase their nonimportation efforts.

March 18, 1766: Declaratory Act. It states that Parliament can make laws binding the American colonies "in all cases whatsoever."

May 1, 1766: Repeal of the Stamp Act. Although some in Parliament think the British army should be used to enforce the Stamp Act, others commend the colonists for resisting a tax passed by a legislative body in which they are not represented. Benjamin Franklin is instrumental in getting this act repealed, and the colonies abandon their ban on imported British goods.

1766: Resistance to the Quartering Act in New York. Since New York serves as the headquarters for British troops in America, the Quartering Act has a great impact on New York City. When the New York Assembly refuses to assist in quartering troops, a skirmish occurs in which one colonist is wounded. Parliament suspends the Assembly's powers, but never carries out the suspension, since the Assembly soon agrees to contribute money toward the quartering of troops.

Early 1767 (before April 13th): Thomas Jefferson passes his bar exam.

June 26, 1767: Townshend Acts. To help pay the expenses involved in governing the American colonies, Parliament passes the Townshend Acts. One act places taxes on glass, lead, paint, paper, wine, and tea. Another act establishes a customs agency in Boston to collect them efficiently. When these acts are passed, Samuel Adams writes a statement, approved by the Massachusetts House of Representatives, which attacks Parliament's persistence in taxing the colonies without proper representation. It calls for unified resistance by all the colonies. Many colonies issue similar statements. In response, the British Governor of Massachusetts dissolves the state's legislature. British Troops arrive in Boston.

July 11, 1767: John Quincy (second child) is born to John and Abigail Adams.

July 17, 1767: Anne (fourth child) is born to Patrick and Sarah Henry.

1767: Nonimportation. In response to new taxes, the colonies again decide to discourage the purchase of British imports.

May 20, 1768: Dorothea ("Dolley"—future wife of James Madison) is born to John and Mary Payne.

December 28, 1768: Susanna (third child) is born to John and Abigail Adams. (The baby dies February 4, 1770.)

April 23, 1769: Betsy (fifth child) is born to Patrick and Sarah Henry.

May 18, 1769: Virginia's Resolutions. The Virginia House of Burgesses passes resolutions condemning Britain's actions against Massachusetts, and declares that only Virginia's Governor and legislature can tax its citizens. The members also draft a formal letter to the King, completing it just before the legislature is dissolved by Virginia's Royal Governor.

May 1769: Thomas Jefferson is elected to represent Albemarle County in the House of Burgesses (serving through 1774), joining Patrick Henry and George Washington.

March 5, 1770: Boston Massacre. Although British troops have been in Boston for two years, this day a riot begins and British soldiers fire into the crowd, killing five Americans. The soldiers are tried for murder, but convicted only of lesser crimes; noted patriot John Adams is their principal lawyer.

April 12, 1770: Townshend Acts Cut Back. Because of the colonial boycott of British goods, the British experience a reduction in profits. British merchants petition Parliament to withdraw all of the

Townshend Acts. Parliament agrees, repealing all taxes except that on tea.

May 29, 1770: Charles (fourth child) is born to John and Abigail Adams.

1770: An End to Nonimportation. In response to Parliament's relaxation of its taxation laws, the colonies relax their boycott of British imported goods.

Spring 1771: James Madison graduates from the College of New Jersey.

September 1771: Committees of Correspondence. In a Boston town meeting, Samuel Adams proposes that a network of corresponding societies be established. These committees can communicate to the other colonies the happenings of their town. In response to his suggestion, the Boston Committee of Correspondence is created. Soon, other colonies create similar committees. Patrick Henry becomes a member of Virginia's Committee of Correspondence.

1771: Edward ("Neddy," sixth and last child) born to Patrick and Sarah Henry.

January 1, 1772: Thomas Jefferson marries Martha Wayles at her father's plantation.

June 10, 1772: Attack on the "Gaspee." Several boatloads of men attack and burn a grounded British customs schooner near Providence, Rhode Island. The Royal Governor offers a reward for the discovery of the men whom he plans to send back to England for trial. The removal of the "Gaspee" trial to England outrages American colonists.

September 15, 1772: Thomas Boylston (fifth and last child) is born to John and Abigail Adams.

September 27, 1772: Martha ("Patsy,"first child) is born to Thomas and Martha Jefferson.

May 10, 1773: Tea Act. As an incentive for the Americans to buy tea exclusively from British merchants, the British reduce the tax on imported British tea. American colonists condemn the act, and many plan to boycott tea.

May 1773: Patrick Henry, Thomas Jefferson, Richard Henry Lee, and Dabney Carr carry through the Virginia House of Burgesses a resolution establishing committees of correspondence between the colonies. This gives unity to the Revolutionary agitation.

June 19, 1773: George Washington's only stepdaughter dies of epilepsy.

December 16, 1773: Boston Tea Party. When British tea ships arrive in Boston harbor, many citizens want the tea sent back to England without the payment of any taxes. The Royal Governor insists on payment of all taxes. A group of men disguised as Indians board the ships and dump all the tea in the harbor.

April 3, 1774: Jane Randolph (second child) is born to Thomas and Martha Jefferson. She dies at the age of one.

May 20, 1774: The Administration of Justice Act. One of the Coercive Acts, it offers protection to Royal officials in Massachusetts, allowing them to transfer to England all court cases against them involving riot suppression or revenue collection.

May 20, 1774: The Massachusetts Government Act. One of the Coercive Acts, it puts the election of most government officials under the control of the Crown, essentially eliminating the Massachusetts charter of government.

May 27, 1774: (In response to the Boston Tea Party, Parliament passes the Coercive—or Intolerable—Acts to punish Massachusetts.)

On this day, Lord Dunmore (the new Royal Governor of Virginia) dissolves the House of Burgesses in response to Thomas Jefferson's proposal for a day of fasting, humiliation, and prayer to focus attention on the closure of the Boston harbor.

June 1, 1774: The Boston Port Bill. This bans the loading or unloading of any ships in Boston harbor. The port of Boston is to remain closed until the colonists pay for the destroyed tea.

June 2, 1774: Quartering Act. Parliament broadens its previous Quartering Act of 1765. British troops can now be quartered in any occupied dwelling.

July 6 - 18, 1774: Fairfax County Resolves. Meetings in Alexandria, Virginia, address the growing conflict between the colonies and Parliament. Washington and George Mason co-author these resolves, which protest the British Coercive Acts. The Fairfax Resolves call for non-importation of British goods, support for Boston, and the meeting of a Continental Congress.

September 5, 1774: The First Continental Congress. The Massachusetts House of Burgesses is dissolved by the British Governor; the colonials form a new association and meet in Philadelphia for what will be known as the Continental Congress. Massachusetts sends John Adams; Virginia sends Thomas Jefferson and George Washington. Twelve of the 13 colonies send a total of fifty-six delegates to the First Continental Congress. Only Georgia is not represented. The Congress organizes the Association of 1774, which urges all colonists to avoid using British goods and to form committees to enforce this ban. (Adjourns October 26, 1774)

December 19, 1774: Deborah Read Franklin, wife of Benjamin Franklin, dies of paralysis.

December 22, 1774: James Madison takes a seat—along with his father—on a local "Committee of Safety."

1774: Special groups of militia, known as Minute Men, are organized to be ready for instant action.

February 1775: Sarah Henry, wife of Patrick Henry, dies.

March 20, 1775: Congress Makes Treaty with the Indians. Congress creates a peace treaty with the Indians. Acting as an independent government.

March 23, 1775: Patrick Henry delivers his most famous speech to the Virginia Committee of Safety: ". . . give me liberty or give me death."

March 27, 1775: Thomas Jefferson is elected to represent Virginia in the second Continental Congress.

March 30, 1775: New England Restraining Act. Parliament passes an act banning trade between the New England colonies and any other country besides Great Britain. Royal authorities decide that force should be used to enforce recent acts of Parliament; war seems unavoidable.

April 19, 1775: Lexington and Concord. When British troops plan to destroy American ammunition at Concord, the Boston Committee of Safety learns of this plan. It sends Paul Revere and William Dawes to alert the countryside and gather the Minute Men. On this date, Minute Men and British troops meet at Lexington, where a shot from a stray British gun leads to more British firing. The Americans fire only a few shots; several Americans are killed. The British march on to Concord and destroy some ammunition, but soon find the countryside swarming with militia. At the end of the day, many are dead on both sides. The Revolutionary War has heard its first gunshots.

April 20, 1775: Governor Dunmore orders British officers to seize the stock of gunpowder and disable the muskets stored in the arsenal at Williamsburg. This ignites the spark of revolution in Virginia.

Patrick Henry, commander in chief of the Virginia forces, responds quickly and demands and receives fair payment for the powder from Lord Dunmore.

May 5, 1775: Benjamin Franklin arrives home from his diplomatic service in London. Twenty-four hours later, he is elected to represent Pennsylvania in the Continental Congress.

May 10, 1775: The Second Continental Congress. Convening in Philadelphia, John Hancock from Massachusetts is elected president of Congress. George Washington and Patrick Henry represent Virginia. Massachusetts again sends John Adams and Sam Adams. Benjamin Franklin represents Pennsylvania. (Adjournes in August 1775)

May 26, 1775: Olive Branch Petition. Congress resolves to begin preparations for military defense but also issues a petition declaring its loyalty to King George III. Congress hopes the King will help arrange a reconciliation and prevent further hostilities against the colonies. Four months later, King George III rejects the petition and declares the colonies in rebellion.

June 15, 1775: George Washington is named Commander in Chief. John Adams argues that Congress and all America consider the forces in Boston a Continental Army and recommends George Washington as Commander in Chief. Both ideas are passed.

June 15 - 16, 1775: Bunker Hill. On June 12, British General Gage puts martial law in effect and states that any person helping the Americans will be considered a traitor and rebel. When Americans begin to fortify a hill against British forces, British ships in the harbor discover the activity and open fire. Shortly after, 2,400 British troops arrive and eventually take the fortification from the 1,000 Americans.

June 16, 1775: George Washington makes his acceptance speech as Commander in Chief in Congress. As a gesture of civic virtue, he declines a salary but requests that Congress pay his expenses at the close of the war.

June-July 1775: Thomas Jefferson makes copies of and annotates Benjamin Franklin's draft of the Articles of Confederation, the governing document of the Continental Congress.

July 8, 1775: Congress issues a declaration setting forth the need to take up arms and the reasons for doing so.

July 10, 1775: Congress makes a final, futile appeal to the King in an effort to right matters without any additional fighting.

July 18, 1775: Congress Creates a Navy. The Continental Congress resolves that each colony provide armed vessels. It authorizes building four armed ships and begins to formulate rules for a navy. Eventually, Congress authorizes privateering and issues rules for dealing with enemy vessels and plunder.

August 23, 1775: King George III declares all the colonies to be in a state of rebellion.

August 1775: Congress adjourns.

September 1775: One-year-old Jane Randolph Jefferson, daughter of Thomas and Martha, dies.

1775: Congress Searches for Foreign Aid. When a congressional committee begins to investigate the possibility of foreign aid in the war against Great Britain, France expresses interest.

January 9, 1776: An anonymous pamphlet called *Common Sense* is published in Philadelphia. Later, it is discovered to be written by Thomas Paine.

February 28, 1776: Patrick Henry resigns his commission.

March 2-3, 1776: The Battle of Dorchester Heights. During this battle, the Americans obtain and retain the strong possession of Dorchester Heights, Massachusetts, overlooking Boston Harbor.

March 26, 1776: The British Evacuate Boston. The British fleet leaves Boston Harbor.

March 31, 1776: Jane Randolph, the mother of Thomas Jefferson, dies.

April 1776: John Adams writes *Thoughts on Government.*

May 6, 1776: The Virginia convention meets. James Madison and Patrick Henry have been elected members. Patrick introduces resolutions directing the delegates to move for independence and to immediately frame a bill of rights (including guarantee of religious liberty) and a constitution as an independent state.

May 10, 1776: Congress passes John Adams' resolution charging the states to write constitutions and create new, independent state governments. Years later, John Adams describes this action as Congress' substantive declaration of independence, of greater political significance at the time than the drafting of the Declaration of Independence.

June 7, 1776: Richard Henry Lee of Virginia, acting on a resolution of the delegation meeting at Williamsburg, and proposed by Patrick Henry, stands before the Continental Congress to make the momentous Resolution that "these United Colonies are, and of right ought to be, free and independent States." A committee is appointed to draft a declaration should Lee's resolution pass.

June 12, 1776: The Virginia convention declares Virginia independent of Great Britain and adopts its first state constitution, which includes the Virginia Declaration of Rights—an important forerunner of the Bill of Rights.

June 25, 1776: General William Howe arrives in the New York area to take command of all British forces in the colonies.

June 28, 1776: The draft of the Declaration is submitted to Congress.

June 28, 1776: Thomas Hickey is hanged. One of General George Washington's bodyguards, he was one of the conspirators in a plot to assassinate Washington and other American officers, and to destroy American munitions.

June 29, 1776: Patrick Henry is elected the first Governor of the independent commonwealth of Virginia. (Henry took the oath of office on July 5, 1776.) He serves three consecutive one-year terms as Governor of the largest of the American states, and two additional terms in the 1780s.

July 2, 1776: Congress Declares Independence. The resolution approving the Declaration of Independence is adopted by Congress.

July 4, 1776: The revised edition of the Declaration of Independence is approved in the late afternoon. Only John Hancock, as president of the Congress, and Charles Thompson, who attested as secretary, actually sign it on this date. Copies are sent throughout the colonies to be read publicly.

July 9, 1776: General George Washington reads his copy of the Declaration to his troops in New York, as well as the citizens in the New York area.

July 20, 1776: General Howe sends an officer to offer pardon to General Washington and all American patriots who will cease their rebellion and pledge their allegiance to the Crown. The offer is refused.

August 2, 1776: Other members of Congress affix their signatures on the final, hand-lettered parchment document of the Declaration.

August 27, 1776: Battle of Long Island. After leaving Boston, British General Howe plans to use New York as a base. The British armada of over 400 ships and 32,000 troops arrive in the New York area. In this first battle for New York, the British capture Staten Island and begin a military build-up on Long Island in preparation for an advance on Brooklyn. Under cover of night, Washington succeeds in saving his troops by moving his entire army from Long Island across the East River to Manhattan Island. Washington eventually retreats from Manhattan, fearing the prospect of being trapped on the island, and the British occupy New York City.

September 9, 1776: Congress designates "United States" as the nation's official name.

September 11, 1776: British General Lord William Howe requests a conference, and John Adams, Benjamin Franklin, and Edward Rutledge are sent by Congress to meet with him at Staten Island. Having beaten the Americans and taken the key city, Howe thinks he is entitled to a peace settlement. The Americans, having declared independence in July, consider separation from England as non-negotiable. The conference of Sept. 11, 1776, ends . . . and the war continues for seven years.

September 15, 1776: The Battle of Kip's Bay on Manhattan Island. A disaster for the Americans as the British troops capture New York and push General Washington's troops to the north end of Manhattan Island, called Harlem Heights.

September 16, 1776: The Battle of Harlem Heights. The American forces prevail.

September 21, 1776: While it is unknown who started it, a fire burns about one-fourth of New York City.

September 22, 1776: Shortly after Nathan Hale volunteers to spy behind British lines, he is captured and sentenced to hang. On this day, as he stands before the scaffold, his last words propel him as a hero into history, "I regret that I have but one life to give for my country." Nathan Hale was 21 years old.

October 11, 1776: General Benedict Arnold (who is a hero before he becomes a traitor) leads a tiny fleet of 15, hastily-constructed ships to stall the British fleet of 25 ships on Lake Champlain. This heroic action delays the movement of 13,000 British troops, saving General George Washington's Continental Army from certain defeat.

October 28, 1776: The Battle of White Plains. British and American forces meet at White Plains, New York, where the British capture an important fortification. Washington once again retreats, still attempting to save his army from the full force of the British army. This is the fourth and final battle for New York.

October 1776: Thomas Jefferson and James Madison, serving in the Virginia House in Williamsburg, become friends and begin a lifelong political partnership in which they exchange approximately 1,200 letters.

November 16, 1776: The Battle of Fort Washington. This New York catastrophe causes the Americans to abandon Fort Washington and Fort Lee, which is opposite Fort Washington on the New Jersey side of the Hudson River.

December 2, 1776: Fleeing from the British, Washington's bedraggled army grows smaller daily from disease, desertion, and death. When they reach Trenton, New Jersey, on the banks of the Delaware River, the army gathers every boat they can find, so that the British will be unable to follow. Washington's army crosses the Delaware into Pennsylvania and makes camp. When the river freezes, Washington expects the British to advance across the river, squash his army, and move on to victory in Philadelphia. Washington counts only 6,000 men "almost naked, dying of cold, without blankets, and very ill supplied with provisions." To make things worse, enlistments are about to expire. On January 1, Washington will be left with fewer than 2,000 ill-equipped men.

December 3, 1776: Benjamin Franklin, America's first diplomat, arrives in France. He hopes to persuade the French government to support the American Revolution. Successful in his negotiations, he stays in France for nine years.

December 23, 1776: In Philadelphia, Thomas Paine publishes another stirring pamphlet, *The Crisis*, to inspire men to the cause of liberty. In a direct, simple style, he cries out against King George III and the monarchical form of government.

December 25 - 26, 1776: Battle of Trenton. During the night of December 25, General Washington crosses the Delaware in freezing weather and launches a surprise attack against British and Hessian mercenaries camped at Trenton, New Jersey. After one hour of confused fighting, the Hessians surrender.

January 23, 1777: Battle of Princeton. British General Howe reacts to the Battle of Trenton by sending a large force of men to New Jersey. At Princeton, Washington once again launches a surprise attack and succeeds in defeating the British. His efforts clear most of New Jersey of enemy forces and greatly boost American morale.

May 28, 1777: An unnamed baby boy (third child) is born to Thomas and Martha Jefferson. He lives only three weeks.

June 14, 1777: America Has a Flag. Congress declares that the flag of the United States will consist of thirteen alternating red and white stripes and a blue field with thirteen white stars.

June 27, 1777: The Marquis de Lafayette arrives in Philadelphia from France to offer his services to the American cause. He is nineteen years old. He is commissioned a major general by Congress and meets Washington on August 1. He and Washington form a close friendship.

June 28, 1777: Patrick Henry is elected to his second consecutive term as Governor of Virginia.

October 9, 1777: Patrick Henry marries Dorothea Dandridge, granddaughter of Alexander Spotswood, who had been Governor of Virginia in the 1720s.

October 17, 1777: American troops trap General John Burgoyne's 9,000 British troops at Saratoga, New York. The surrender of Burgoyne's entire army convince the French that they can enter the war against Britain.

October 19, 1777: The British Attack Philadelphia. Howe enters and occupies Philadelphia. Congress flees to York, Pennsylvania.

October 1777: As Governor, Patrick Henry supports General George Rogers Clark's efforts to conquer the vast territory northwest of the Ohio and protect the people and land of Kentucky from the British. This forces England to yield the Kentucky territory at the time the peace treaty is signed.

November 15, 1777: Articles of Confederation. When Richard Henry Lee makes a motion for independence in 1776, he also proposes a formal plan of union among the states. After a discussion lasting more than a year, the Articles of Confederation are adopted by Congress on this date. However, the states do not ratify the Articles until 1781.

November 27, 1777: Congress names John Adams a Commissioner to work with Benjamin Franklin and Arthur Lee to negotiate a French alliance.

December 19, 1777: General Washington settles his army in Valley Forge. Location wise, it is a good choice—a high plateau. One side is protected by the river. Two shallow creeks provide natural barriers that will present problems for attacking cavalry and artillery. Any attackers will have to charge uphill. But the soldiers endure a horrible winter; men are both freezing and starving. However, it is here that a vigorous, systematic training regimen transforms ragged amateur troops into a confident military organization capable of beating the Redcoats in the open field of battle. On June 19, 1778, Washington leads his troops out of Valley Forge.

December 24, 1777 (approximately): George Washington receives a marvelous personal vision as he beholds the birth, progress, and destiny of the United States.

1777: It is this year that Thomas Jefferson originally drafts the Virginia Statute for Religious Freedom, but it is not passed by the General Assembly until 1786.

January 1778: Governor Patrick Henry sends much-needed supplies to the army at Valley Forge.

February 6, 1778: The Franco-American Treaty of Amity and Commerce. In Paris, Benjamin Franklin negotiates and signs the alliance between France and America, which states that each considers the other a "most favored nation" for trade and friendship. France is obligated to fight for American independence, and America is obligated to stand by France if war should occur between France and Great Britain. (The French government has been secretly providing Congress with military supplies and financial aid since 1776.)

February 17, 1778: John Adams sails to France. Adams is sent by Congress to join with Benjamin Franklin and Arthur Lee in negotiating an alliance with France.

February 23, 1778: Lieutenant General Friedrich Wilhelm Ludolf Gerhard Augustin Baron von Steuben, a volunteer from Germany, arrives at Valley Forge with a letter of introduction from the president of Congress. His military training manual is published by Congress, and he plays an important role in training the American army. Congress commissions von Steuben a major general and makes him an inspector general of the Continental Army. Von Steuben becomes an American citizen after the war.

March 13, 1778: The French Minister in London informs King George III that France recognizes the United States.

March 16, 1778: In one last attempt at peace, the British send peace commissioners to America to announce the repeal of all British Acts passed since 1763. But the commissioners fail because most Americans are now determined to be recognized as independent.

May 4, 1778: Congress ratifies the Treaty of Alliance with France, and further military and financial assistance follows. By June, France and England are at war. The American Revolution has become an international war.

May 1778: Patrick Henry is elected to his third consecutive term as Governor of Virginia.

August 1, 1778: Mary ("Polly," fourth child) is born to Thomas and Martha Jefferson.

August 2, 1778: Dorothea (first child) is born to Patrick and Dorothea Henry.

June 1, 1779: Thomas Jefferson is elected Governor of Virginia for a one-year term.

June 21, 1779: Spain Joins the War. Spain asks Britain for Gibraltar as a reward for joining the war on the British side. When Britain refuses, Spain joins with France in its war against Britain. However, Spain refuses to recognize American independence.

August 2, 1779: John Adams arrives back in Boston after 1½ years in France. After less than one week he is chosen as a delegate to the State of Massachusetts Constitutional Convention.

September 23, 1779: John Paul Jones Wins Victory. Captain John Paul Jones is battling with a British ship. His own ship is obviously sinking. The British captain asks Captain Jones if the American ship will strike its colors—lower its flag and surrender. Captain John Paul Jones rallies his men with, "I have not yet begun to fight." Captain Jones wins the battle, taking over the British ship.

October 30, 1779: John Adam's 44th birthday. On or about this date he submits a Constitution for the Commonwealth of Massachusetts. It is adopted with minor changes.

October 1779: John Adams is chosen by Congress to return to France as a Minister Plenipotentiary to negotiate a peace treaty with Great Britain, a position he neither expected nor solicited. The choice was unanimous.

November 15, 1779: Adams sails back to France after only 3½ months at home.

1779: The British Attack in North and South. Fighting continues in both the northern and southern states. In the frontier settlements of Pennsylvania, Loyalists and Indians attack American settlers. The Loyalists are soon defeated, and Americans destroy many Native American villages whose residents are fighting on the side of the British.

January 4, 1780: Sarah Butler (second child) is born to Patrick and Dorothea Henry.

March 1780: James Madison (age 28) takes his seat in the Continental Congress, becoming the youngest member of that body.

May 12, 1780: The British Take Charleston, South Carolina. After a brief fight, the British take Charleston, capturing 5,400 men and four American ships in the harbor. It is the worst American defeat of the war.

Spring 1780: James Monroe begins legal studies with Thomas Jefferson.

June 2, 1780: Thomas Jefferson is reelected Governor of Virginia.

September 25, 1780: The Treason of Benedict Arnold. Commander of West Point, Arnold flees to the British ship Vulture in the Hudson River. He has been planning to defect to the British and has learned that his British contact, Major John André, has been captured and that Washington is due to arrive at West Point to review the fort and its garrison.

November 3, 1780: Martha (fifth child) is born to Thomas and Martha Jefferson. She dies at five months.

December 29, 1780: John Adams is commissioned by Congress to conclude a commercial treaty with the Netherlands. This is a turning point in the war.

January 5, 1781: Benedict Arnold invades and burns Richmond, Virginia. Governor Thomas Jefferson and other government officials are forced to flee the capitol.

March 7, 1781: The Articles of Confederation go into effect as Maryland ratifies—the last state to do so. (The Articles had been sent to the states for ratification in 1777.)

June 3, 1781: Virginia legislators meeting in Charlottesville are warned of the approaching British cavalry. Among those who escape are Thomas Jefferson, Patrick Henry, Benjamin Harrison, John Tyler, and Richard Henry Lee.

October 14, 1781: French and American forces join at Yorktown, on land and at sea, and attack British fortifications.

October 19, 1781: Surrender at Yorktown. After a futile counterattack, British General Cornwallis officially surrenders, giving up almost 8,000 men. Washington asks Benjamin Lincoln to receive the surrender; Lincoln had been forced to surrender to British General Henry Clinton at Charleston. This is the final major battle of the Revolutionary War.

October 19, 1781: A British fleet leaves New York harbor to come to the aid of Cornwallis in Virginia. Arriving too late, the fleet hovers about the area for a few days and returns home October 28-30.

November 3, 1781: Martha Cathrina (third child) is born to Patrick and Dorothea Henry.

November 5, 1781: At age 25, John Parke ("Jacky"), Washington's stepson, dies of "camp fever" (probably typhoid fever) at Yorktown. George and Martha Washington raise two of their grandchildren, Eleanor Parke Custis and George Washington Parke Custis at Mount Vernon.

1781: Congress Creates a Department of Finance. American finances are in such dire straits that Congress sees the need for a separate department of finance.

April 19, 1782: Holland recognizes the independence of The United States of America.

May 8, 1782: Lucy Elizabeth (sixth and last child) is born to Thomas and Martha Jefferson. She dies at five months.

August 19, 1782: In the Battle of Blue Licks, in the Appalachian west, the British and their Indian allies inflict heavy casualties and force the retreat of Daniel Boone and the Kentucky militia. In response, George Rogers Clark leads Kentucky militia on an expedition against the British into Ohio country. These are often considered the last formal engagements of the Revolutionary War.

September 6, 1782: Martha Jefferson (wife of Thomas Jefferson) dies after an illness of several months following the birth (May 8) of her sixth child, Lucy Elizabeth.

November 30, 1782: Preliminary Peace Treaty Signed in Paris. British, French, and American commissioners meet in Paris to discuss peace. Its terms call for Great Britain to recognize American independence and provide for the evacuation of all British troops. Great Britain also gives up its territory between the Mississippi River and the Allegheny Mountains, doubling the size of the new nation. John Adams, Benjamin Franklin (the signer), and John Jay negotiate the peace settlement much in America's favor.

1782: Freeing of slaves becomes legal in Virginia.

March 18, 1783: The Army Complains. A delegation of army officers complain to Congress about their unpaid salaries and pensions, but Congress has no quick solution. Washington addresses the army at its headquarters in Newburgh, New York, convincing them to be patient and not to dishonor themselves after their glorious victory. Visibly moved, the officers adopt resolutions to present to Congress and pledge not to threaten violence or rebellion.

April 15, 1783: Congress Ratifies the Articles of Peace. After Spain, France, and Britain successfully come to terms, the treaty between France, Britain, and America is put into effect, and warfare formally ceases.

April 1783: The Loyalists and British Evacuate New York. New York City is the last Loyalist refuge in America. Knowing that the British will soon leave New York, nearly 30,000 Loyalists begin sailing to Canada and England. On November 25, the British evacuate New York.

June 6, 1783: Virginia elects Thomas Jefferson as a delegate to Congress.

June 1783: The American Army Disbands. Most of Washington's army disbands and heads for home.

August 15, 1783: Patrick Henry Jr., (fourth child) is born to Patrick and Dorothea Henry.

September 3, 1783: Final Peace Treaty is Signed in Paris. The war with the British officially ends.

December 23, 1783: Before Congress in Annapolis, George Washington resigns his commission as Commander in Chief of the Revolutionary Army.

March 1784: Jefferson drafts a report for reform of coinage replacing the English system of pounds with a fraction or decimal system. The reform does not pass Congress at this time, but it is adopted with some changes in 1786 and becomes effective several years later.

July 5, 1784: Jefferson sails for Europe from Boston, accompanied by his twelve-year-old daughter Martha (Patsy).

August 1784: Abigail Adams arrives in Paris to join her husband and son. She is accompanied by daughter Abigail (Nabby).

October 1, 1784: Fayette (fifth child) is born to Patrick and Sarah Henry.

November 30, 1784: Patrick Henry begins his fourth term as Governor of Virginia.

March 1785: Thomas Jefferson replaces Benjamin Franklin as the Minister to France.

April - May 1785: John Adams and Thomas Jefferson successfully negotiate a loan from Dutch bankers to consolidate U. S. debts and pay long overdue salaries to French officer veterans of the American Revolution.

July 27, 1785: Franklin sails home to America.

November 30, 1785: Patrick Henry begins his fifth term as Governor of Virginia.

January 16, 1786: The Virginia Statute for Religious Freedom. After much debate, the Virginia House of Burgesses passes a statute (written by Thomas Jefferson in 1779 and sponsored by James Madison) dealing with the separation of church and state. It declares that no person shall be discriminated against because of religious belief, or compelled to join or support any church. This statute helps shape the First Amendment of the United States Constitution.

September 11, 1786: Annapolis Convention Convenes. Nine states agree to send delegates to this convention, but only five state delegations arrive. A new convention is scheduled in Philadelphia in 1787 to discuss all matters necessary to improve the federal government and to revise the Articles of Confederation.

Fall 1786: Shays' Rebellion. Mob violence temporarily reigns in some Massachusetts hills. Angry men run lawyers out of town and break up courthouse meetings. On October 20, 1786, Congress calls several states to raise an army. In late January 1787, Daniel Shays leads an attack on the government arsenal in Springfield. His group is stopped by militiamen, but the incident helps persuade Americans that a stronger central government is necessary.

January 1787: John Adams publishes the first volume of his *Defence of the Constitutions Of Government of the United States of America,* upon which much of the Constitution is based.

May 25, 1787: The Constitutional Convention. Delegates from twelve states (Rhode Island is not represented) meet in the Constitutional Convention in Philadelphia for the purpose of revising the Articles of Confederation. The gathering includes some of the most respected and talented men in America. George Washington is elected President. Benjamin Franklin is a member. Thomas Jefferson is serving as diplomat in France, but James Madison keeps him informed of the developments, and Jefferson generally supports the effort. Under the Articles of Confederation, the government has the power to negotiate treaties but cannot regulate trade, and this has hampered Jefferson's efforts to negotiate commercial treaties with France. Edmund Randolph proposes the "Virginia Plan." This plan, drafted by James Madison, recommends an entirely new form of government, including an executive, a judiciary, and a legislature composed of two houses and including a number of representatives from each state based on their population. In November, Jefferson receives a copy of a draft of the Constitution and generally approves it, but urges Madison and others to add a bill of rights and to limit the number of terms that a President can serve.

September 17, 1787: The Convention approves the Constitution, signs it, sends it to Congress, and then adjourns.

September 28, 1787: Congress Approves the Constitution. Although some congressmen are displeased with the Convention for doing far more than revising the Articles of Confederation, Congress passes the Constitution on to the states, so that each can debate it in separate ratifying conventions. Nine states have to agree to the new Constitution for it to go into effect.

October 27, 1787: First of *The Federalist Papers* published in New York. In an effort to sway the vote for ratification in the hesitant state of New York, James Madison, Alexander Hamilton, and John Jay collaborate on essays that are printed in New York newspapers. These essays are later collected into two volumes titled *The Federalist Papers.*

December 7, 1787: Deleware becomes the first state to ratify the Constitution.

1787: Benjamin Franklin is elected president of America's first anti-slavery society.

March 1788: Patrick Henry is elected to the Virginia House of Delegates and to the Virginia Convention of 1788.

June 2, 1788: Alexander Spotswood (sixth child) is born to Patrick and Dorothea Henry.

June 2, 1788: Delegates convene in Richmond, Virginia, to decide on ratification of the Constitution. Those against it include Patrick Henry, Thomas Jefferson, James Monroe, George Mason, and Richard Henry Lee.

June 21, 1788: The Constitution Is Ratified by Nine States. On June 21, New Hampshire becomes the ninth state to ratify the new Constitution, making its adoption official. Preceding New Hampshire are Delaware, Pennsylvania, New Jersey, Georgia, Connecticut, Massachusetts, Maryland, and South Carolina. Virginia and New York ratify shortly after New Hampshire, followed by North Carolina in November 1789. Rhode Island is last to ratify, not joining the Union until May 1790.

July 2, 1788: Congress Steps Aside for a New Government. Congress announces that the Constitution has been adopted. By September, a committee has prepared for the change in government, naming New York City as the temporary official capital, and setting dates for elections and for the meeting of the first Congress under the new Constitution.

July 17, 1788: John and Abigail Adams arrive home from England.

April 6, 1789: George Washington is unanimously elected President. John Adams is elected Vice-President.

April 30, 1789: George Washington is inaugurated in New York City as the first President of the United States of America.

May 1789: The first Congress of the United States is organized.

June 8, 1789: A bill of rights is proposed in Congress, and James Madison drafts twelve amendments to the Constitution.

1789 to 1797: While still struggling to get the Constitution ratified, Madison serves in Congress, representing Virginia.

July 14, 1789: The fall of the Bastille marks the beginning of the French Revolution.

September 25, 1789: Congress passes twelve amendments to the Constitution, ten of which are eventually ratified by the states to become the federal Bill of Rights.

September 26, 1789: The U.S. Senate confirms Thomas Jefferson's appointment as Secretary of State under George Washington.

October 8, 1789: Not yet knowing of his appointment as Secretary of State, Thomas Jefferson leaves France.

November 23, 1789: Thomas Jefferson arrives safely at Norfolk, Virginia, ending his return voyage from France.

February 1790: Franklin signs a petition to the U.S. Congress, urging abolition of slavery.

April 7, 1790: Nathaniel West (seventh child) is born to Patrick and Dorothea Henry.

April 17, 1790: Benjamin Franklin dies at the age of 84.

May 29, 1790: Holding out for three years, the tiny state of Rhode Island is the last state to ratify the Constitution.

December 15, 1791: Ten amendments to the Constitution are ratified, forming the Bill of Rights.

March 27, 1792: Richard (eighth child) is born to Patrick and Dorothea Henry. The baby dies at 1½ years.

November 16, 1793: Thomas Jefferson writes to Eli Whitney, telling him that he approves of his efforts to win a patent for his cotton gin.

December 31, 1793: Thomas Jefferson resigns as Secretary of State.

January 21, 1794: Edward Winston (ninth child) is born to Patrick and Dorothea Henry.

September 15, 1794: James Madison and Dolley Payne Todd are married.

May 1796: Jean Antoine Houdon's statue of George Washington is shipped from France to Virginia.

1796: John (tenth child) is born to Patrick and Dorothea Henry.

March 4, 1797: John Adams delivers his inaugural address as President of the United States. (With the second highest number of electoral votes, Thomas Jefferson is his Vice-President.)

January 21, 1798: Jane Robertson (eleventh and last child) is born to Patrick and Dorothea Henry. The baby dies four days later.

Spring 1798: President Adams receives news of the French XYZ affair. The French Foreign Minister Talleyrand is attempting to extort money from American envoys sent to negotiate a reduction in hostilities between the United States and the French government.

July 1798: In the wake of the XYZ affair and deteriorating relations with the new government of France, George Washington accepts nominal command of American armies preparing for the impending conflict. War, however, is averted by the Adams administration.

July 14, 1798: The Alien and Sedition Acts. Prohibiting criticism of government officials, Federalists use these new laws to imprison newspaper editors or politicians who disagree with them. The Kentucky and Virginia Resolutions, secretly written by Thomas Jefferson and James Madison, assert a state's right to declare the Alien and Sedition Acts unconstitutional.

Early 1799: President Adams establishes better diplomatic relationship with France.

March 4, 1799: Although his health is failing, Patrick Henry makes his last public speech to the voters at Charlotte County Courthouse. George Washington has convinced Henry to run in the election for the Virginia legislature. He wins the election, but dies before the legislature convenes that autumn.

June 6, 1799: Patrick Henry dies at his home, Red Hill. He is 63 years old.

December 14, 1799: In his home at Mount Vernon, George Washington dies of a severe cold. In his will, he frees his slaves.

June 1800: The U.S. capital is moved from Philadelphia to Washington, D.C.

1800: Thomas Jefferson wins the Presidential race against John Adams and serves two terms.

March 4, 1801: Jefferson is the first President inaugurated in the new capital city.

1801-1809: James Madison serves as Secretary of State under President Thomas Jefferson.

May 22, 1802: Martha Washington (wife of George Washington) dies.

April 30, 1803: Thomas Jefferson negotiates the Louisiana Purchase through Robert Livingston, Ambassador to France, and James Monroe, special envoy.

May 1804: Moving up the Missouri River, Meriwether Lewis and William Clark lead an expedition across America.

July 12, 1804: Alexander Hamilton dies after being shot the previous day by Vice-President Aaron Burr in a duel at Weehawken, New Jersey.

November 1804: Thomas Jefferson is elected President for a second term.

January 17, 1807: Aaron Burr is captured near New Orleans and charged with treason. He is tried in a federal circuit court in Richmond and is acquitted. Later, with other charges pending, he escapes to England.

March 4, 1809: James Madison is inaugurated fourth President of the United States.

June 1812: At President Madison's request, Congress declares war against Great Britain (War of 1812).

August 1814: British attack the capital and burn the city, including many government buildings.

December 1814: Not yet known to President Madison, a peace treaty at Ghent, Belgium, has been signed. The war of 1812 is over.

Early January 1815: General Andrew Jackson defeats the British army at New Orleans.

January 1815: The U.S. government purchases Thomas Jefferson's library of more than 6,700 books to replace the Library of Congress that was burned in the War of 1812.

March 4, 1817: James Monroe from Virginia is inaugurated President of the United States.

October 6, 1817: The cornerstone ceremony for the University of Virginia takes place.

October 28, 1818: Abigail Adams (wife of John Adams) dies after 44 years of marriage.

1820: Thomas Jefferson compiles his wee-little book, later titled the Jefferson Bible.

March 1825: Thomas Jefferson's dream, the University of Virginia, opens with 123 students.

1825: John Quincy Adams becomes the sixth President of the United States.

July 4, 1826: On the fiftieth anniversary of the signing of the Declaration of Independence, Thomas Jefferson dies peacefully in his bed at Monticello; only hours later, John Adams dies in Massachusetts.

February 14, 1831: Dorothea Dandridge Henry (wife of Patrick Henry) dies.

June 28, 1836: James Madison (85 years old) dies quietly at his home.

July 12, 1849: Dolley Madison (wife of James Madison) dies.

1991: The monies that Benjamin Franklin leaves in his will, to be disbursed upon the 200th anniversary of his death, are given to the cities of Boston and Philadelphia and to the states of Massachusetts and Pennsylvania.

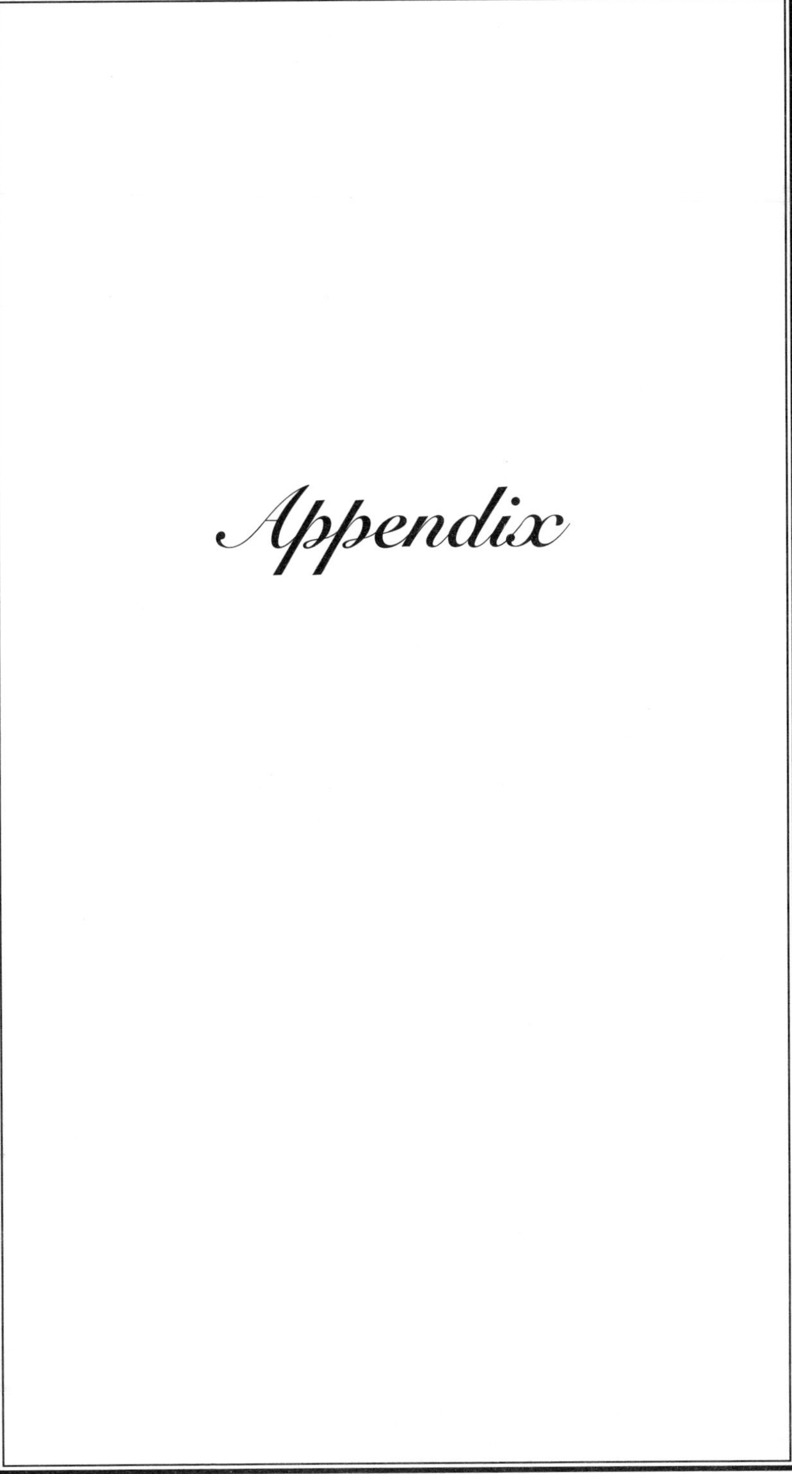

Appendix

APPENDIX

Debunking the Rumors

Ezra Taft Benson, former Secretary of Agriculture, made a powerful prediction concerning John Wesley, Christopher Columbus, and the Founding Fathers: "When one casts doubt about the character of these noble sons of God, I believe he or she will have to answer to the God of heaven for it.[1]

Tragically, and in spite of Benson's warning, many negative accusations have been made about the character and actions of George Washington, Benjamin Franklin, Thomas Jefferson, and other early American figures. It has become popular for recent history books to relate stories that "debunk" some of our most highly esteemed heroes.

The charge has been made that the dominant incentive of the Founders of the Constitution was to primarily benefit themselves and their class—the property owners—financially. Madison wrote: "There was never an assembly of men . . . who were more pure in their motives." And when their work was done, he added: "It is impossible for the man of pious reflection not to perceive in it a finger of that Almighty hand which has been so frequently and signally extended to our relief in the critical stages of the revolution."[2]

One historian, Charles Beard, recanted his expressed opinion that these men were only out to improve their economic status. But the harm had already been done. The earlier opinion found favor and was repeated over and over again. Unfortunately, it is now deeply entrenched in many books and histories.

George Washington

Some have claimed that Washington became involved in the Revolutionary War simply to accumulate more possessions or wealth. Rather than enriching himself through his war service, Washington actually lost several thousands of dollars. He asked only to have his actual expenses repaid. "Some have estimated that Washington's cumulative financial losses from the war—from neglect of his lands, noncollection from delinquent debtors and tenants, stoppage of exportation, and rapid depreciation of paper money—rose to some $120,000."[3] Since he refused any pay as President of the United States, it is extremely difficult to believe that he did *anything* to merely "accumulate more wealth."

Historians have examined the various accusations of graft or immorality that have been leveled at George Washington, and they have declared him completely innocent. In the last year of his life he could truthfully declare that he had "always walked a straight line and endeavored, as far as human frailties . . . would enable [him], to discharge the relative duties to [his] Maker and fellow man."[4]

One reappearing story concerns George Washington's supposed love for a neighbor's wife. However, history shows that Washington was strictly and unwaveringly faithful to Martha and to his marriage vows. One of his biographers, James Thomas Flexner, has said: ". . . no one has ever discovered any authentic evidence that he was unfaithful to Martha."[5]

Benjamin Franklin

Benjamin Franklin, also a leading figure in our nation's history, had scandalous stories concocted about him, circulating as gossip is often wont to do. There is no basis in fact for Franklin being described as immoral or unchaste.

Apart from William (who was treated as a legitimate son), there is hardly any explicit evidence to convict Franklin of either promiscuity or its opposite. But the rumors sprang up in his own lifetime and have gained ground ever since.

> The story of his "illegitimate daughter" is a case in point. In 1770, Franklin's close associate, John Foxcroft married Judith Osgood in England. Franklin gave the bride away and referred to her thereafter as his "daughter" because he had acted as surrogate father at the wedding, by no means an unusual practice. Many were the women he would call wife or daughter throughout his life, in a teasing or affectionate manner without suspecting, of course, that anybody would take him literally, then or later.[6]

Thomas Jefferson

Having written the inspired, undeniable truth in the Declaration of Independence, ". . . that all men are created equal," it is hard to comprehend the fact that Thomas Jefferson owned slaves. And in view of his high moral standards, how does one reconcile the recently resurrected story proclaiming that Thomas Jefferson had a slave mistress?

To a great extent, interest in this unsubstantiated story or myth is due to a recent biography by Fawn Brodie and to a popular novel entitled *Sally Hemings*, by Barbara Chase-Riboud. These ugly rumors cannot tarnish Jefferson's fame and glory as a scientist; an innovator;

a leader in government, law, architecture, agronomy, and other fields. However, the resurgence of these charges makes it imperative that they be examined.

The scurrilous story of Thomas Jefferson's mistress began with a disgruntled office seeker by the name of James T. Callender, who fled from Scotland to avoid being prosecuted for slander. When he came to America, he obtained employment with the *Philadelphia Gazette*, where he continued his slanderous practices by publishing lies that impugned the character of Alexander Hamilton. In 1799, Callender landed a job with *The Richmond Examiner*, where he referred to John Adams as "a repulsive pedant," a "gross hypocrite," and "in his private life, one of the most egregious fools upon the continent." Consequently, Callender was arrested and tried under the notorious Alien and Sedition Acts of 1798. He received a sentence of nine months in the Richmond jail and a fine of $200. However, because he believed his writings had helped the Republican Party elect Jefferson President, Callender thought he was entitled to a position in Jefferson's cabinet. He applied for the office of Postmaster General. Jefferson, knowing his true character, ignored his request.

Callender began to make threatening noises. If Jefferson wouldn't grant his request, he would release information damaging to the President. Jefferson was unperturbed. He said to his friend James Monroe, then governor of Virginia, Callender "knows nothing of me which I am not willing to declare before the world." Callender lost no time in making good on his threats. He began to write stories referring to Jefferson as a "lecherous beast." In 1798, in a letter to Samuel Smith, Jefferson explained his unwillingness to respond to Callender's many allegations:

> Were I to undertake to answer the calumnies of the newspapers, it would be more than all my own time,

> and that of twenty aids could effect, for while I should be answering one, twenty new ones would be invented. I have thought it better to trust to the justice of my countrymen that they would judge me by what they see of my conduct on the stage where they have placed me.[7]

Rumors had been floating around Charlottesville that Jefferson had fathered illegitimate children with a slave mistress at his mountaintop home of Monticello. Until Callender had gotten wind of these rumors, they hadn't amounted to much. Callender didn't bother to verify the rumors, or to even visit Charlottesville to make himself acquainted with those who spread them. He simply printed some stories of his own and treated them as fact. Jefferson was infuriated at these innuendos, but his responses remained mostly private. The stories began appearing in other papers that were hostile to Jefferson at the time.

Jefferson's alleged slave mistress was named Sally Hemings. Sally Hemings was the reputed daughter of the slave "Elizabeth (Betty)Hemings" and John Wayles. According to the common report, John Wayles took Betty Hemings as his concubine after the death of his third wife. John Wayles was the father of Martha Wayles, Mrs. Thomas Jefferson. Accordingly, Sally Hemings was ostensibly the half sister of Martha Wayles Jefferson. When John Wayles died, Martha inherited his plantation and the slaves that went with it.

> It is doubtful whether Mrs. Jefferson knew that her father supposedly sired these individuals, but Thomas Jefferson almost certainly did know. This would seem to explain why the Hemingses were given preferred positions at Monticello. All were house servants, and none was required to labor in the fields.[8]

Sally Hemings gave birth to at least five children. Some were said by Callender to bear a striking resemblance to Thomas Jefferson. Callender contended that Sally became Jefferson's mistress after the death of Martha. This is unsubstantiated innuendo. "The strong probability is that Thomas Jefferson and Sally Hemings had only the most conventional and proper relationship."[9] Jefferson took it upon himself to suffer in silence and make no response to the allegations. Thomas Jefferson Randolph, Jefferson's oldest grandchild, confirmed what others close to the family had said, that Sally Hemings was actually the mistress of Peter Carr, Jefferson's nephew.[10]

In recent years, DNA studies have been conducted which have also purported to show that Thomas Jefferson was the father of some of the children of Sally Hemings. The report of the study was published in *Nature* magazine, November 1998, pages 27-32, under the title: "Jefferson Fathered Slave's Last Child." A response to this article about the study came from Gary Davis at Evanston Hospital. He states:

> If the data [used in the DNA study] is accurate, then any male ancestor in Thomas Jefferson's line, white or black, could have fathered Eston Hemings . . . it is possible that Thomas Jefferson's father, grandfather or paternal uncles fathered a male slave whose line later impregnated another slave, in this case Sally Hemings.

The author of the *Nature Magazine* article later revealed:

> The title assigned to our study was misleading in that it represented only the simplest explanation of our molecular findings: namely, that Thomas Jefferson, rather than one of the Carr brothers, was likely to have

> been the father of Eston Hemings Jefferson . . . We know from the historical and the DNA data that Thomas Jefferson can neither be definitely excluded nor solely implicated in the paternity of illegitimate children with his slave Sally Hemings.[11]

More than a year after this study came out, another team of scholars issued their own findings on this report. Thirteen distinguished scholars, in a 563-page account, stated in a gentlemanly way that the earlier DNA report was "thin at best, and based on shoddy scholarship, improbable assumptions and even doctored documents."[12]

The Hemings kin are still not accepted as descendants of Thomas Jefferson by The Monticello Association. They heeded the recommendation of this panel of scholars that studied the paternity of the Hemings family.[13]

Ellen Randolph Coolidge, Jefferson's granddaughter, wrote a long letter to her husband Joseph Coolidge Jr., in which she said:

> I would put it to any fair mind to decide if a man so admirable in his domestic character as Mr. Jefferson, so devoted to his daughters and their children, so fond of their society, so watchful over them in all respects, would be likely to rear a race of half-breeds under their eyes and carry on his low amours in the circle of his family.[14]

The leading authorities on Jefferson acknowledge that he had his faults, but they are convinced that fathering Sally Hemings' children was not one of them. Callender's allegation against Jefferson was not proven when Callender printed it, and it has not been proven since. Perhaps Fawn Brodie and Barbara Chase-Riboud belong shoulder-to-shoulder with James T. Callender.

Jefferson's feelings about slavery are documented. Included in his first draft of the Declaration of Independence is a strong chastisement against King George III for bringing slavery to the colonies. Jefferson blamed American slavery on the King. This section dealing with slavery was removed from the final draft. Jefferson also wrote about slavery in his *Notes on Virginia*, concluding, "I tremble for my country when I reflect that God is just; that His justice cannot sleep forever."[15]

In 1784, in the Continental Congress, Jefferson proposed a bill that would have prevented slavery from being spread into any territory admitted to the United States other than the original 13 colonies. The measure was defeated by a single vote and Jefferson wrote: "heaven was silent in that awful moment."[16]

In 1820, in his last years, Jefferson wrote concerning slavery: "We have the wolf by the ears: and we can neither hold him, nor safely let him go. Justice is in one scale, and self-preservation in the other."[17]

Indeed, he had the "wolf by the ears."

> Since the number of slaves owned by Jefferson was in excess of two hundred at various periods, they constituted one of his principal assets. To have set them free would obviously have been a crushing financial blow. . . . In the end, following his death, Monticello and its contents had to be sold at auction, but the amount realized was insufficient to cover the obligations. Thomas Jefferson Randolph, Jefferson's grandson, paid the $40,000 deficit out of his own pocket. . . . Thus there were various reasons why the master of Monticello became less determined upon emancipation as the years went by. In addition to the overriding financial consideration affecting him

> personally, there was, on the national scene, the obvious problem of how to deal fairly with tens of thousands of illiterate and untrained free blacks who would suddenly be catapulted upon society. There were also the political implications of Jefferson's position as spokesman for the slave-holding South, with the possible jeopardizing of his influence through aggressive action. Hence it is clear that there were various plausible reasons for Jefferson's failure to press hard for emancipation.[18]

For the most part, the Founding Fathers quietly took the false tales about themselves and their character in stride, much as did Abraham Lincoln, who philosophized to his wife:

> Mary, if we were to try to read, much less answer, all the attacks made on us, this shop might as well close for any other business. Let's do the very best we know how, the very best we can; and keep doing so until the end. If the end brings us out all right, what is said against us won't amount to anything. If the end brings us out wrong, ten angels swearing we were right will make no difference.[19]

Benjamin Franklin, George Washington, John Adams, Thomas Jefferson, Patrick Henry, and James Madison were all great men. All of them were carefully raised up to play an important part in the drama of the American Revolution. All of them were imperfect men. But all of them were heroes. *Uncommon Heroes.*

Endnotes and Bibliography

ENDNOTES

Benjamin Franklin

1. Gelder and Co., "Benjamin Franklin, Williamsburg Sculpture," 1996, <http://www.williamsburgsculpture.com/benjamin_franklin.htm> (12 April 2002).

2. "Benjamin Franklin, Glimpses of the Man," The Franklin Institute Online, 1994, <http://sln.fi.edu/franklin/rotten.html> (12 April 2002).

3. Dean Walley, ed., *Poor Richard's Almanack, Benjamin Franklin's Best Sayings* (Kansas City, Missouri: Hallmark Editions, 1967), 5, 10, 16.

4. "Benjamin Franklin, Glimpses of the Man," The Franklin Institute Online, 1994, <http://sln.fi.edu/franklin/economist/economist.html> (12 April 2002).

5. "Benjamin Franklin and his Glass Armonica," the Franklin Institute Online, 1994, <http://sln.fi.edu/franklin/musician/musician.html> (15 April 2002).

6. Benjamin Franklin, *The Autobiography of Benjamin Franklin* (New York: Collier Macmillan, 1962), vi.

7. Andrew M. Allison, Dr. Cleon Skousen, and Dr. M. Richard Maxfield, *The Real Benjamin Franklin*, Vol. 2 of the *American Classic Series* (Washington, D.C.: National Center for Constitutional Studies, 1982), 6.

8. Franklin, 29.

9. Franklin, 34.

10. *Wives of the Signers, the Women Behind the Declaration of Independence* (Aledo, Texas: WallBuilder Press, 1977), 178.

11. *Wives of the Signers, the Women Behind the Declaration of Independence*, 178.

12. Allison, *The Real Benjamin Franklin*, 41-42.

13. George L. Rogers, ed., *The Art of Virtue* (Eden Prairie: Minnesota: Acorn Publishing, 1996), 80.

14. Franklin, 82.

15. Thomas Fleming, *The Man Who Dared The Lightning* (New York: William Morrow & Company, Inc., 1971) 85-86.

16. Franklin, 124.

17. Franklin, 25.

18. Franklin, 87.

19. Franklin, 87-88.

20. Franklin, 46.

21. Fleming, 28.

22. Fleming, 20.

23. Fleming, 221-222.

24. Albert Marrin, *The War for Independence—the Story of the American Revolution* (New York: Atheneum, 1988), 223.

25. Marrin, 223. During the next two centuries, this story found its way into American schoolbooks, keeping alive the story as if it were true.

26. H.W. Brands, *The First American* (New York: Doubleday, 2000), 611.

27. Fleming, 391.

28. Fleming, 297-298.

29. Franklin, 43.

30. Rogers, ed., 235-36.

31. Brands, 411.

32. David McCullough, *John Adams* (New York: Simon and Shuster, 2001), 155.

33. Brands, 380-81.

34. Brands, 399.

35. *Webster's Encyclopedic Unabridged Dictionary*; "venery:" gratification of sexual desire.

36. Allison, *The Real Benjamin Franklin*, 47-48.

37. Allison, *The Real Benjamin Franklin*, 191.

38. Brands, 645-646.

39. Franklin, 89.

40. Franklin, 90.

41. Brands, 709.

42. Franklin, 86.

43. Allison, *The Real Benjamin Franklin*, 258-259.

44. Allison, *The Real Benjamin Franklin*, 261.

45. Allison, *The Real Benjamin Franklin*, 262-263.

46. Catherine Drinker Bowen, *John Adams and the American Revolution* (Boston: Little, Brown and Company, 1950), 17.

47. Fleming, 492.

48. Allison, *The Real Benjamin Franklin*, 276.

49. Brands, 713.

50. Matthew 5:48, KJV.

George Washington

1. George Washington was born February 11, 1732, under the Gregorian calendar, but his birthday is now celebrated on February 22.

2. Jay A. Parry and Andrew M. Allison, *The Real George Washington* (Washington, D.C.: National Center for Constitutional Studies), xi.

3. Parson Mason Weems, *A History of the Life and Death, Virtues and Exploits of General George Washington* (Macy- Masuis Publishers 1927), 21-22.

4. This familiar "cherry tree" incident was possibly invented by Mason Locke "Parson" Weems, as it appeared in one of his books only after the death of George Washington. There is no available evidence that it was from any other source than Weems. Weems has been characterized as "a persuasive fictionalizer" who was "continually expanding his text with new imaginings." [James Thomas Flexner, *George Washington: The Forge of Experience*, 1732-1775 (Boston, Toronto: Little, Brown and Company, 1965)]. The story first appeared in the fifth edition (1806) of Weem's *Life of George Washington, with Curious Anecdotes Equally Honorable to Himself and Exemplary to His Young Countrymen*, which was originally published in 1800, the year after Washington's death. "This may be a disappointment to those of us who have grown up admiring the little fellow who supposedly declared, 'I can't tell a lie, Pa . . . I did cut it with my hatchet.' But the following observation by an eminent Washington scholar seems significant in this regard: 'It is not necessary to strain for effects in the story of George Washington. Everything for which documentary proof does not exist may be discarded without regret, for the provable facts that remain support a life and character more than satisfactory to the most ardent admirer.'" [Jay A. Parry and Andrew M. Allison, *The Real George Washington* (Washington, D.C.: National Center for Constitutional Studies, 1991), 834.]

Several of the most famous tales from Washington's youth are told by Weems. Parson Weems preached in Powick church for a while after the War for Independence. Washington attended this church, and he and Martha often entertained Weems in their hospitable home. Because of his acquaintance with the Washingtons, Parson Weems had a good opportunity to pick up many anecdotes about the great man's childhood. He was fond of a good story. Having a large family to support, he left off preaching to become a book peddler. He rode about the countryside in a gig, selling his own writing and those of others. He told so many stories and played the fiddle so well, he became a successful peddler. The Parson wrote a book about the life of Washington. It included several stories of Washington's childhood which Weems said he had learned from members of George's extended family. The stories are not improbable, but are doubted because they are told by this strange peddler who loved a good story too well. [Wayne Whipple, *The Story-Life of Washington* (Philadelphia: The John C. Winston Company, 1911), 21.]

5. Wayne Whipple, *The Story-Life of Washington* (Philadelphia: The John C. Winston Company, 1911), 1:54. There are 86 more "rules," making 110 altogether. Perhaps if the youth of our country would review them as often as George Washington did, we might raise a few young people of his caliber. You can find them in the small book *George Washington's Rules of Civility and Decent Behaviour* (Boston: Applewood Books, 1988). This book is sometimes available from the Mount Vernon Ladies Society.

6. Today, medicine recognizes no such ailment but speculates that it was probably a severe heart attack.

7. John Schroeder, *The Life and Times of Washington* (New York: Johnson, Fry, and Company, 1857), 19.

8. Many people would be surprised to discover that George Washington and Abraham Lincoln were about the same height. Lincoln wrote of himself: "I am six feet, four inches tall, nearly." The day Washington died, his attending physician measured the body: "In length, 6 feet, 3 and 1/2 inches, exact. Across the shoulders; 1 foot, 9 inches, exact." If these two great figures could come back and stand before us, Washington, who always stood very erect, would probably appear to be taller than Lincoln, who rarely stood in a position which disclosed his full height. Though the same height, Washington was a considerably larger man than Lincoln. The President of the Civil War era weighed 175 to 180 pounds, while Washington weighed between 215 to 225 pounds. Both of them were sparse, lean, powerful men. [Tobias Lear, *Letters & Recollections of George Washington* (Garden City, NY: Doubleday, Doran, and Company, Inc., 1932), 137.]

9. Nathaniel Parker Willis and William H. Bartlett, *American Scenery* (London: George Virtue, 1840), 63.

10. Having lived in England for 20 years, Stuart came to America in 1792 to paint Washington's portrait. Stuart was heavily in debt and saw the

Washington painting not only as a patriotic gesture, but an economic one. He did a full-length version, of which there are 3 copies in addition to the original. He also painted a half torso and the familiar face only. Stuart painted as many as 70 copies of his most famous portrait of Washington and sometimes referred to them as his $100 bills. The practice of making copies of original portraits was a common occurrence in his lifetime. Stuart went on to paint a number of the country's early Presidents, but none was as popular as Washington.

The "Lansdowne Portrait" hangs in the East Room of the White House and may be viewed on a tour. This portrait is the only object known to have remained in the White House since 1800 (except for a brief period during the War of 1812). The White House was burned in 1814. The painting was kept safely in New York until the restoration of the mansion was completed in 1817. [*The White House, An Historic Guide* (Washington, D.C.: White House Historical Association and National Geographic Society, 1987), 35-36.]

11. Since its arrival in Virginia, it has been on continuous display at the Capitol in Richmond. That state's legislature wouldn't even consent to its being moved to either New York or Washington, D.C., for display during the nation's bi-centennial. This statue is captivating! Go and see it if you can. [*The Virginia State Capitol* (Virginia: Virginia State Government, 1991), 6.]

12. *The Virginia State Capitol* (Virginia: Virginia State Government, 1991), 6.; see also Richard M. Ketchum, The World of George Washington (New York: American Heritage Publishing Company, Inc., 1974), 254.

13. "The Gl. [General] Showed us a plow of his own invention: in the middle on the axle itself is a hollow cylinder filled with grain; this cylinder is pierced with different holes, according to the size of the grain. As the plow moves ahead, the cylinder turns and the grain falls, the plowshare having prepared the furrow for it, and a little blade behind then covers it with earth." [Julian Niemcewicz, *Julian Niemcewicz Diary*, Published as Volume XIV in the Collections of The New Jersey Historical Society at Newark. New Jersey: The Grassman Publishing Company, Inc., June 5, 1798, <http://www.mountvernon.org/pioneer/sun/ julian.html>(April 22, 2002).]

14. A letter from George Washington to his brother John Augustine Washington, dated July 15, 1755, as quoted in David Barton, *The Bulletproof Washington* (Texas: WallBuilder Press, 1990), 47.

15. Barton, 50-51; Whipple, 1:188-190.

16. Whipple, 1:163.

17. Whipple, 1:162-163.

18. Albert Marrin, *The War for Independence* (New York: Atheneum, 1988), 3.

19. Whipple, 1:168-69.

20. The History of Mount Vernon. "The very name conjures up a mental picture of a White Mansion on a green lawn, peaceful, beautiful, a very desirable location next to a river surrounded by gardens and trees . . . and so it is. But, it is more! Mount Vernon is an integral part of our American History." The first Washington to own land at Hunting Creek (which later became Mount Vernon) was George's great-grandfather, John Washington (1632-1676). John was a partner with Nicholas Spencer in a transaction for 5,000 acres surveyed along Hunting Creek. A patent for the land was issued in 1674. John willed his 2,500 acres to his son Lawrence, who willed it to his daughter Mildred. Mildred sold it to Augustine, George's father. Augustine lived there from 1735 to 1738. Lawrence Washington, George's older half-brother, inherited the property in 1743. After Lawrence married Ann Fairfax of Belvoir, the couple lived at the site. The first cottage erected by Augustine burned in 1739. Lawrence rebuilt a new one, which became the nucleus of the present mansion. [James R. Westlake, "Washington's Mount Vernon," *The Sons of the American Revolution Magazine*, Spring 1999, 4-8.]

21. The Internet Public Library, "Early Political Activity." *Internet Biographies*, George Washington, Encyclopedia Americana. <http://gi.grolier.com/presidents/ea/bios/01pwash.html> (April 22, 2002).

22. Whipple, 1:206-207.

23. Robert Leckie, *George Washington's War* (New York: Harper Perennial, 1993), 177-180.

24. Henry B. Carrington, *Battles of the American Revolution* (Utah: The Ensign Publishing Company, 1979), 147-154.

25. Parry, *The Real George Washington*, 171.

26. George Washington to the Reverend William Gordon, May 13, 1776, as quoted in Parry, 171.

27. Jeff Jacoby, "The Christmas Crossing," *Reader's Digest Magazine*, December, 2000, 81-85; see also Marrin, 112-118; and Leckie, 315-320.

28. Jacoby, 82.

29. Jacoby, 83.

30. Jacoby, 83-84; see also Marrin, 112-118; and Leckie, 315-320.

31. Jacoby, 81-85.

32. Parry, The Real George Washington, 213 .

33. Jacoby, 81-85; see also Marrin, 112-118; and Leckie, 315-320.

34. Marrin, 121-123.

35. Marrin, 123.

36. Ron Carter, A *Cold, Bleak Hill* (Salt Lake City, Utah: Bookcraft, 2001), 446.

37. Carter, 446-47.

38. Washington's open acknowledgment of divine intervention was discovered by Charles Bracelen Flood in his research about the Revolutionary War.[W. Cleon Skousen, *The 5,000 Year Leap* (Washington, D.C.: National Center for Constitutional Studies, 1981), 99.]

39. BYU Library, Special Collections, Americana, M 208, Al #762. The vision of George Washington has been printed and re-printed many times—in books, magazines, and in pamphlet form. It was originally published by Wesley Bradshaw. This account was taken from a reprint published in the National Tribune, Vol. 4, No. 12, December, 1880.

40. BYU Library, Special Collections, Americana, M 208, Al #762.

41. Leckie, 438-439.

42. Leckie, 441-442.

43. Leckie, 442.

44. Whipple, 2:147-148.

45. Parry, *The Real George Washington*, 385.

46. As Washington resigns his commissions as Commander in Chief in a speech to Congress, December 23, 1783, as quoted in Parry, *The Real George Washington*, 434.

47. Parry, *The Real George Washington*, 472-474.

48. Parry, *The Real George Washington*, 485-486.

49. Enid La Monte Meadowcroft, *Benjamin Franklin* (New York: Scholastic, 1968), 181.

50. Although the language is that of Gouverneur Morris, it has recently been discovered that the Constitution itself was actually penned by a man named Jacob Shallus, the clerk of the Pennsylvania Assembly. [Andrew M. Allison, "Who Actually Wrote the Constitution?" *The Constitution Magazine*, May/June 1986, 33-35.]

51. J. Reuben Clark, Jr., *Stand Fast By Our Constitution* (Salt Lake City: Deseret Book Company, 1973), 21.

52. Speech given on September 17, 1796. Maureen Harrison and Steve Gilbert, ed., *George Washington In His Own Words* (New York: Barnes & Noble Books, 1997), 164-165.

53. Whipple, 2:297.

54. Whipple, 2:311.

55. Whipple, 2:314.

56. Whipple, 2:314.

57. Whipple, 316.

58. Parry, *The Real George Washington*, 608.

59. Richard Brookhiser, *Founding Father* (New York: The Free Press, 1996), 199.

60. Brookhiser, 162.

61. Roy P. Basler, *The Collected Works of Abraham Lincoln* (New Jersey: Rutgers University Press, 1953), 279.

John Adams

1. David McCullough, *John Adams* (New York: Simon and Schuster, 2001), 35.

2. Phyllis Lee Levin, *Abigail Adams—A Biography* (New York : Ballantine Books, 1987), 9.

3. Abigail Smith was born November 11, 1744, to the Reverend William Smith and Elizabeth Quincy Smith, in Weymouth, Massachusetts.

4. Levin, 7.

5. Levin, 27.

6. Irving Stone, *Those Who Love* (New York: Signet, The New American Library, Inc., 1965), 19.

7. Levin, xi.

8. McCullough, 61.

9. Catherine Drinker Bowen, *John Adams and the American Revolution* (Boston: Little, Brown and Company, 1950), 276.

10. Bowen, 330.

11. Letter from Abigail Adams to Mercy Warre, February 27, 1774. Jay A. Parry, "John Adams: New England's Bold Patriot", *The Constitution Magazine*, October, 1985, 26.

12. Wayne Whipple, *The Story-Life of Washington* (Philadelphia: The John C. Winston Company, 1911), 1:207.

13. Bowen, 534.

14. McCullough, 102.

15. McCullough, 103.

16. Bowen, 583.

17. Parry, *The Constitution Magazine*, October, 1985, 26.

18. Peter Shaw. *The Character of John Adams* (Chapel Hill: The University of North Carolina Press, 1976), 98.

19. Ezra Taft Benson, *The Constitution, A Heavenly Banner* (Salt Lake City, Utah: Deseret Book Company, 1986), 31-33.

20. Levin, 90-91.

21. Shaw, 2.

22. Letter from Abigail Adams to Mercy Warren, February 27, 1774. Levin, 167.

23. McCullough, 285.

24. Parry, *The Constitution Magazine*, October, 1985, 27.

25. December 7, 1787, Delaware becomes the first state to ratify the Constitution.

26. Benson, 32.

27. David C. Whitney, *The American Presidents* (Garden City, New York: Doubleday & Company, Inc., 1967), 23.

28. Whitney, 24.

29. Levin, 260-261.

30. Whitney, 25.

31. Parry, *The Constitution Magazine*, October, 1985, 28.

32. Levin, 377.

33. Levin, 378.

34. Richard B. Morris, *Seven Who Shaped Our Destiny* (New York: Harper & Row, Publishers, 1976), 72.

35. On July 11, 1804, Aaron Burr killed Alexander Hamilton in a duel. Whitney, 39.

36. Natalie S. Bober, *Thomas Jefferson, Man on a Mountain* (Atheneum, New York: Macmillan Publishing Company, 1988), 243.

37. Levin, 488.

38. John Quincy Adams won his election to the Presidency by only one vote. Since the popular vote had been evenly divided, the election had been thrown to the House of Representatives for a decision. The House had also been evenly divided on the issue, until one final vote had been taken. The Congressman from New York, in an attitude of prayer, had picked up a crumpled ballot and determined to vote for the name he found there. The name on the crumpled, discarded ballot had been esteemed a token and answer to prayer by the Congressman. And that is how John Quincy Adams became the sixth president of the United States. [Paul Aurandt, *More of Paul Harvey's The Rest of the Story*, (Toronto, New York: Bantam Books, 1980), 29.]

39. Correspondence between Adams and Mercy Warren, August 19, 1807. Shaw, 292.

40. Benson, 31-33.

41. Bober, 251.

42. From the song "Star Spangled Banner" by Francis Scott Key.

Patrick Henry

1. Moses Coit Tyler, *Patrick Henry* (Norwalk, Connecticut: The Easton Press, 1989), 15.

2. Henry Mayer, *A Son of Thunder: Patrick Henry and the American Republic* (Charlottesville: University Press of Virginia, 1991), 44.

3. Mayer, 45.

4. In 1628, Sir Edward Coke introduced his bill of liberties in the House of Commons. In it, he stated, "Magna Carta is such a fellow, that he will have no sovereign." His bill led to the Petition of Rights. [David Addy, "Magna Carta in Modern Times," St. Edmundsbury Website, August 1998, <http://www.stedmundsbury.gov.uk/modmcart.htm> (April 23, 2002).] Coke addresses the issue that the worst kind of oppression occurs when royalty usurps power under the guise of justice.["Coke's Institutes and the

Magna Carta," *Institutes of the Laws of England*, <http://kancrn.kckps.k12.ks.us/Harmon/breighm/ccntent.html#Of> (April 23, 2002).]

5. Tyler, 25.

6. Norman S. Ream, "Where are The Son's of Liberty?" *Where are the Son's of Liberty?* October 1990, <http://www.libertyhaven.com/personalfreedomissues/freespeechorcivilliberties/sonsliberty.html> (May 10, 2002) and Clarence B Carson, "The First American Crisis: 1763-66," *The Founding of The American Republic*, February 1972, <http://www.libertyhaven.com/theoreticalorphilosophicalissues/history/americancrisis.html> (May 10, 2002).

7. Jay A. Parry, "Patrick Henry Fearless Trumpet of Freedom" *The Constitution Magazine*, April 1986, 28-29.

8. Natilie S. Bober, *Thomas Jefferson, Man on a Mountain* (New York: Atheneum, Macmillan Publishing Company, 1988), 43.

9. Bober, 44.

10. George F. Willison, *Patrick Henry and His World* (Garden City, NY: Doubleday, 1969), 123.

11. Andrew M. Allison, *The Real Thomas Jefferson* (Washington, D.C.: National Center for Constitutional Studies 1983), 29.

12. Tyler, 97.

13. William Mead, *The Old Churches and Families of Virginia* (Baltimore: Genealogical Publishing Company, 1966), 220.

14. Parry, "Patrick Henry Fearless Trumpet of Freedom," 29.

15. Parry, "Patrick Henry Fearless Trumpet of Freedom," 29-30.

16. Willison, frontispiece and 9.

17. Mayer, 230-231.

18. Tyler, 214.

19. Mayer, 324-326.

20. Parry, "Patrick Henry Fearless Trumpet of Freedom," 30-31.

21. Parry, "Patrick Henry Fearless Trumpet of Freedom," 31.

22. Willison, 458.

23. Meyer, 370.

24. Meyer, 370.

25. Parry, "Patrick Henry Fearless Trumpet of Freedom," 31.

26. Tyler, 325-327.

27. Tyler, 331-332.

28. Tyler, 393.

29. Tyler, 391.

30. Willison, 418.

31. Willison, 444.

32. Tyler, 422.

33. Tyler, 395.

34. Norine Dickson Campbell, *Patrick Henry: Patriot and Statesman* (New York: Devin-Adair Company, 1969), 419.

35. Willison, 480.

36. Tyler, 391.

37. Parry, "Patrick Henry Fearless Trumpet of Freedom," 29-30.

Thomas Jefferson

1. Andrew M. Allison, *The Real Thomas Jefferson* (Washington, D.C.: National Center for Constitutional Studies, 1983), 14.

2. Natalie S. Bober, *Thomas Jefferson, Man on a Mountain* (New York: Atheneum, Macmillan Publishing Company, 1988), 9.

3. Bober, 11.

4. Bober, 51.

5. Allison, *The Real Thomas Jefferson*, 29.

6. Allison, *The Real Thomas Jefferson*, 35.

7. Allison, *The Real Thomas Jefferson*, 35.

8. Allison, *The Real Thomas Jefferson*, 36.

9. Allison, *The Real Thomas Jefferson*, 40.

10. Bober, 69.

11. David McCullough, *John Adams* (New York: Simon and Schuster, 2001), 113.

12. Maureen Harrison and Steve Gilbert, ed., *Thomas Jefferson In His own Words* (New York: Barnes & Noble books, 1993), 35-36.

13. Committees of Correspondence were organized by towns, counties, and colonies before and during the Revolutionary War. The first committee was appointed by the town of Boston in 1772, by Samuel Adams. The purpose was to keep in touch with other Massachusetts towns in their struggle to uphold the rights of the colonists. The first colonial committee in Virginia was appointed in 1773. The committees played an important part in drawing the colonies together.

14. Harrison, 173-174.

15. Harrison, 174.

16. Allison, *The Real Thomas Jefferson*, 63.

17. Thomas Fleming, *The Man Who Dared the Lightning* (New York: William Marrow and Company, Inc., 1971), 328-329.

18. Allison, *The Real Thomas Jefferson*, 71.

19. Allison, *The Real Thomas Jefferson*, 71.

20. Ezra Taft Benson, *This Nation Shall Endure* (Salt Lake City, Utah: Deseret Book Company, 1977), 29.

21. T.R. Fehrenbach, Greatness to Spare (Bridegwater, New Jersey: Replica Books, 1999), 18-19.

22. Rush H. Limbaugh, Jr., "The Americans Who Risked Everything," *The Limbaugh Letter*, July 1996, 5 & 15.

23. Allison, *The Real Thomas Jefferson*, 39.

24. Allison, *The Real Thomas Jefferson*, 107-108.

25. Allison, *The Real Thomas Jefferson*, 120.

26. Catherine Drinker Bowen, *Miracle at Philadelphia* (Boston: Little, Brown and Company, 1966), 279.

27. Allison, *The Real Thomas Jefferson*, 216-217.

28. Biography, President Thomas Jefferson <http://library.thinkquest.org/12587/contents/personalities/tjefferson/tj.html> (April 30, 2002).

29. Bober, 219.

30. Allison, *The Real Thomas Jefferson*, 223.

31. Allison, *The Real Thomas Jefferson*, 225.

32. Allison, *The Real Thomas Jefferson*, 247-248.

33. Allison, *The Real Thomas Jefferson*, 4-6.

34. Allison, *The Real Thomas Jefferson*, 270.

35. Alexander Garrett, *Outline of Cornerstone Ceremonies*, 6 October 1817, <http://etext.lib.virginia.edu/etcbin/toccer-new2?id=Jef1Gri.sgm&images=images/modeng&data=/texts/english/modeng/parsed&tag=public&part=47&division=div1> (April 30, 2002).

36. Ian Hoffman's Links: U.S. Government <http://www.aoc.nrao.edu/~ihoffman/ links.html> (April 30, 2002).

37. *Thomas Jefferson's Monticello* [pamphlet] (Charlottesville, Virginia), 14.

38. William Adams, *Jefferson's Monticello* (New York: Abbeville Press, 1983), 129.

39. Allison, *The Real Thomas Jefferson*, 306.

40. Allison, *The Real Thomas Jefferson*, 195-196.

41. Harrison, 214.

42. Harrison, 214-215.

43. Dickinson W. Adams, *Jefferson's Extracts from the Gospels* (Princeton, New Jersey: University Press. 1983), 364-365.

44. Allison, *The Real Thomas Jefferson*, 302-303.

45. Adams, *Jefferson's Extracts from the Gospels*, 376.

46. Allison, *The Real Thomas Jefferson*, 302.

47. Allison, *The Real Thomas Jefferson*, 312.

48. Allison, *The Real Thomas Jefferson*, 312-313.

49. Allison, *The Real Thomas Jefferson*, 316.

50. Bober, 150.

51. Allison, *The Real Thomas Jefferson*, 314.

James Madison

1. "The Past at Montpelier," The Home of James Madison <http://www.montpelier.org/ma-james.htm> (15 March 2002).

2. Ralph Ketcham, *James Madison* (Charlottesville: University Press of Virginia,1990), 31.

3. Ketcham, *James Madison*, 23.

4. Ketcham, *James Madison*, 35.

5. Ketcham, *James Madison*, 57.

6. Jay A. Parry, "James Madison, The Father of the Constitution," *The Constitution Magazine*, June 1985, 26.

7. Ketcham, *James Madison*, 65.

8. Ketcham, *James Madison*, 65.

9. Grolier Presents, "*James Madison Biography*," The American Presidency, 2000, <http://gi.grolier.com/presidents/ea/bios/04pmadi.html> (15 March 2002).

10. Ketcham, *James Madison*, 183.

11. The Articles of Confederation (1781-1789) were America's first attempt to govern itself as an independent nation. They united the states as a confederation—a loose league of states represented in a Congress. ["To Form a More Perfect Union," American Memory Library of Congress, February 2, 2001, <http://memory.loc.gov/ammem/bdsds/intro01.html> (March 27, 2002).]

12. Parry, "James Madison, The Father of the Constitution," 27.

13. Ketchum, *James Madison*, 188.

14. Catherine Drinker Bowen, *Miracle at Philadelphia* (Boston: Little, Brown and Company, 1966), 20.

15. Edmund Randolph had been an "Aide De Camp" to General Washington during the Revolutionary War. He was now the Governor of Virginia. Under President Washington he would later become the U.S. Attorney General, and then Secretary of State.

16. Parry, "James Madison, The Father of the Constitution," 27.

17. Jay A. Parry, "John Adams: New England's Bold Patriot" *The Constitution Magazine*, October 1985, page 27.

18. Ketchum, *James Madison*, 195.

19. Moses Coit Tyler, *Patrick Henry* (Norwalk, Connecticut: The Easton Press, 1989), 311.

20. Ketcham, *James Madison*, 189.

21. *A More Perfect Union, America Becomes a Nation*, prod. Peter M. Johnson and Nicholas J. Gasdik, dir. Peter M. Johnson, 1 hr. 52 min. (Washington, D.C.: National Center for Constitutional Studies, 1989).

22. Andrew Allison, *The Real Benjamin Franklin* (Washington, D.C.: National Center for Constitutional Studies, 1982), 258-259.

23. Andrew Allison, *The Real Benjamin Franklin*, 261.

24. Bowen, 242.

25. H. W. Brands, *The First American* (New York: Doubleday, 2000), 691.

26. Bowen, 263.

27. A *More Perfect Union*, America Becomes a Nation, VHS.

28. Parry, "James Madison, The Father of the Constitution," 28.

29. Ezra Taft Benson, *This Nation Shall Endure* (Salt Lake City, Utah: Deseret Book Company, 1977), 16.

30. Allison, *The Real Benjamin Franklin*, 263.

31. Paul F. Boller, Jr., *Presidential Anecdotes* (New York: Oxford University Press, 1981), 45.

32. The Bill of Rights was closely modeled on the Virginia Declaration of Rights which had been written by George Mason and adopted by the Virginia Constitutional Convention on June 12, 1776.

33. One of the amendments that Madison originally proposed in 1789 did not become part of the Constitution until 1992, when it became the 27th Amendment. It reads: "No law, varying the compensation for the services of senators and representatives, shall take effect until an election of representatives have intervened." This amendment was finally ratified by the majority of the states required, when Michigan became the thirty-eighth state to adopt it on May 7, 1992—and after only 203 years!

34. Dorothy Payne (also known as Dolley Madison) served as a hostess for many social functions in the White House for Thomas Jefferson. When Jefferson was President, he was a widower and requested her assistance.

35. John and Dolley Todd's house is now restored and open to visitors.

36. Elizabeth W. Watkins, "Dolley Madison, First lady of the Constituiton" *The Constitution Magazine*, July 1987, 25.

37. Ketcham, *James Madison*, 380.

38. Ketcham, *James Madison*, 381.

39. Ketcham, *James Madison*, 475.

40. Ketcham, *James Madison*, 511.

41. Thanks to Dolley Madison, the portrait now hangs in the East Ballroom at the White House.

42. Tracy Leininger, *Unfading Beauty, The Story of Dolley Madison* (San Antonio, Texas: His Seasons, 2000), 50-56.

43. Later Congress purchased Thomas Jefferson's personal library as a replacement.

44. John Adams to Thomas Jefferson, Feb. 2, 1817. Parry, "James Madison, The Father of the Constitution," 29.

45. Ketcham, *James Madison*, 626.

46. William O. Nelson, *The Charter of Liberty* (Salt Lake City, Utah: Deseret Book Company, 1987), 101-102.

47. Alexander Leitch, "James Madison, Jr." *Princeton Companion*, 1978, <http://mondrian.princeton.edu/CampusWWW/Companion/madison james.html> (28 March 2002).

48. Ketchem, *James Madison*, 667.

Appendix

1. Ezra Taft Benson, *This Nation Shall Endure* (Salt Lake City, Utah: Deseret Book Company, 1977), 18.

2. Benson, *This Nation Shall Endure*, 16.

3. Jay A. Parry and Andrew M. Allison, *The Real George Washington* (Washington, D.C.: National Center for Constitutional Studies), 442.

4. Parry, *The Real George Washington*, 593.

5. James Thomas Flexner, *Washington, the Indispensable Man* (New York: Signet Books, 1969), 371.

6. Andrew Allison, *The Real Benjamin Franklin* (Washington, D.C.: National Center for Constitutional Studies, 1982), 49.

7. Virginius Dabney, *The Jefferson Scandals, A Rebuttal*, (Lanham, New York, London: Madison Books, 1981), 10.

8. Dabney, 27.

9. Dabney, 73.

10. Andrew M. Allison, *The Real Thomas Jefferson* (Washington, D.C.: National Center for Constitutional Studies, 1983), 233.

11. E. A. Foster et al., "The Thomas Jefferson Paternity Case," *Nature Magazine*, Vol. 397, January 1999: 32.

12. "One More Visit to the Thomas Jefferson-Sally Hemings Controversy," *National Center for Constitutional Studies Newsletter*, June 2001: 4.

13. Michael Buettner, "Jeffersons won't accept Hemings kin," *East Valley Tribune Newspaper*, May 6, 2002. sec. A: 8.

14. Dabney, 79.

15. Dabney, 100.

16. Dabney, 35.

17. Dabney, 105.

18. Dabney, 111.

19. Irving Stone, *Love Is Eternal* (New York: Signet, The New American Library, Inc., 1954), 392-393.

BIBLIOGRAPHY

Adams, Dickinson W. *Jefferson's Extracts from the Gospels*. Princeton, New Jersey: Princeton University Press, 1983.

Adams, William Howard. *Jefferson's Monticello*. New York: Abbeville Press, 1983.

Allison, Andrew M. "Did Jefferson Have a Slave Mistress" *Freeman Digest*, November 1983.

Allison, Andrew M., Dr. W. Cleon Skousen, and Dr. M. Richard Maxfield. *The Real Benjamin Franklin*. Vol. 2 of *The American Classic Series*. Washington, D.C.: National Center for Constitutional Studies, 1982.

Allison, Andrew M. "Who Actually Wrote the Constitution?" *The Constitution Magazine*, May/June 1986, 33-35.

Allison, Andrew M. *The Real Thomas Jefferson*. Washington, D.C.: National Center for Constitutional Studies, 1983.

Aurandt, Paul. *More of Paul Harvey's The Rest of the Story*. Toronto, New York: Bantam Books, 1980.

Barbash, Fred. "A Man for the 90s." Liberty, January/February 1991.

Barnes and Noble. *The Wit & Wisdom of Benjamin Franklin*. New York: Barnes & Noble Books, 1995.

Barton, David. *The Bulletproof George Washington*. Aledo, Texas: WallBuilder Press,1990.

Basler, Roy P. *The Collected Works of Abraham Lincoln*. New Jersey: Rutgers University Press, 1953.

Beilenson, Nick, ed. *Thomas Jefferson, His Words and Vision*. White Plains, New York: Peter Pauper Press, Inc., 1998.

Benson, Ezra Taft. *The Constitution, A Heavenly Banner*. Salt Lake City, Utah: Deseret Book Company, 1986.

Benson, Ezra Taft. *This Nation Shall Endure*. Salt Lake City, Utah: Deseret Book Company, 1977.

Bober, Natalie S. *Thomas Jefferson, Man on a Mountain*. New York: Atheneum, Macmillan Publishing Company, 1988.

Boller, Paul F., Jr. *Presidential Anecdotes*. New York: Oxford University Press, 1981.

Bowen, Catherine Drinker. *John Adams and the American Revolution*. Boston: Little, Brown and Company, 1950.

Bowen, Catherine Drinker. *Miracle at Philadelphia*. Boston: Little, Brown and Company, 1966.

Brands, H. W. *The First American*. New York: Doubleday, 2000.

Brookhiser, Richard. *Founding Father*. New York: The Free Press, 1996.

Byrd, Max. *Jefferson, A Novel*. New York: Bantom Books, 1998.

BYU Library Special Collections, Americana, M208, Al #762.

Campbell, Norine Dickson. *Patrick Henry: Patriot and Statesman*. New York: Devin-Adair Company, 1969.

Cappon, Lester, ed. *The Adams-Jefferson Letters*. 2 vols. Chapel Hill University: North Carolina Press, 1959.

Carrington, Henry B. *Battles of the American Revolution*. Utah: The Ensign Publishing Company, 1979.

Carter, Ron. A *Cold, Bleak Hill*. Salt Lake City, Utah: Bookcraft, 2001.

Clark, E. Douglas Clark. *The Grand Design*. Salt Lake City, Utah: Deseret Book Company, 1992.

Clark, J. Reuben, Jr. *Stand Fast By Our Constitution*. Salt Lake City: Deseret Book Company, 1973.

Clark, Ronald W. *Benjamin Franklin*. New York: Random House, 1983.

Dabney, Virginius. *The Jefferson Scandals, a Rebuttal*. Lanham, New York, London: Madison Books, 1981.

Ellis, Joseph J. *Founding Brothers*. New York: Alfred A. Knopf, 2000.

Evans, Lawrence B., ed. *Writings of George Washington*. Putnam and Sons, 1908.

Faÿ, Bernard. *Franklin, the Apostle of Modern Times*. Boston: Little, Brown, and Company, 1929.

Fehrenbach, T.R. *Greatness to Spare*. Bridegwater, New Jersey: Replica Books, 1999.

Fitzpatrick, John C. *George Washington Himself*. Indianapolis: Bobbs-Merrill Company, 1933.

Fleming, Thomas. *The Man Who Dared the Lightning*. New York: William Marrow and Company, Inc., 1971.

Flexner, James Thomas. *George Washington: The Forge of Experience, 1732-1775*. Boston Toronto: Little, Brown and Company, 1965.

Flexner, James Thomas. *Washington, the Indispensable Man*. New York: Signet Books, 1969.

Franklin, Benjamin. *The Autobiography of Benjamin Franklin*. New York: Collier Macmillan Publishers, 1962.

George Washington's Rules of Civility and Decent Behaviour. Boston: Applewood Books, 1988.

Hamilton, Alexandar, James Madison, and John Jay. *The Federalist Papers*. New York: New American Library, 1961.

Harrison, Maureen and Steve Gilbert, ed. *Thomas Jefferson, In His Own Words*. New York: Barnes & Noble Books, 1993.

Harrison, Maureen and Steve Gilbert, ed. *George Washington In His Own Words*. New York: Barnes & Noble Books, 1997.

Jacoby, Jeff. "The Christmas Crossing." *Reader's Digest Magazine*, December, 2000.

Jefferson, Thomas. *The Life and Morals of Jesus of Nazareth*. Boston: The Beacon Press, 1951.

Jenkinson, Clay S. *Ethics with Thomas Jefferson*. State Bar of Arizona, 2001.

Ketcham, Ralph. *James Madison*. Charlottesville: University Press of Virginia, 1990.

Ketchum, Richard M. *The World of George Washington*. New York: American Heritage Publishing Company, Inc., 1974.

Lear, Tobias. *Letters & Recollections of George Washington*. Garden City, New York: Doubleday, Doran, and Company, Inc., 1932.

Leckie, Robert. *George Washington's War*. New York: Harper Perennial, 1993.

Leininger, Tracy. *Unfading Beauty, The Story of Dolley Madison*. San Antonio, Texas: His Seasons, 2000.

Levin, Phyllis Lee. *Abigail Adams – A Biography*. New York: Ballantine Books, 1987.

Limbaugh, Rush H., Jr. "The Americans Who Risked Everything." *The Limbaugh Letter*, July 1996.

Little, Shelby. *George Washington*. New York: Minton, Balch & Company, 1929.

Marrin, Albert. *The War for Independence*. New York: Atheneum, Macmillan Publishing Company, 1988.

Mayer, Henry. *A Son of Thunder: Patrick Henry and the American Republic*. Charlottesville: University Press of Virginia, 1991.

McCullough, David. *John Adams*. New York: Simon and Schuster, 2001.

Mead, William. *The Old Churches and Families of Virginia*. Baltimore: Genealogical Publishing Company, 1966.

Meadowcroft, Enid La Monte. *Benjamin Franklin*. New York: Scholastic, 1968.

A More Perfect Union, America Becomes a Nation. Prod. Peter M Johnson and Nicholas J. Gaskik, dir. Peter M. Johnson. 1 hr. 52 min. Washington, D.C.: National Center for Constitutional Studies, 1989. VHS.

Morris, Richard B. *Seven Who Shaped Our Destiny*. New York: Harper & Row Publishers, 1976.

Nelson, William O. *The Charter of Liberty*. Salt Lake City, Utah: Deseret Book Company, 1987.

Niemcewicz, Julian Ursyn. *Julian Niemcewicz Diary*. Published as Volume XIV in the Collections of The New Jersey Historical Society at Newark, New Jersey: The Grassman Publishing Company, Inc., June 5, 1798, http://www.mountvernon.org/pioneer/sun/julian.html.

Parry, Jay A. "John Adams: New England's Bold Patriot," *The Constitution Magazine*, October, 1985.

Parry Jay A., ed. "Patrick Henry: Fearless Trumpet of Freedom." *The Constitution Magazine*, April 1986.

Parry, Jay A. "James Madison: Father of the Constitution." *The Constitution Magazine*, June 1985.

Parry, Jay A. and Allison, Andrew M. *The Real George Washington*. Washington, D.C.: National Center for Constitutional Studies, 1991.

Rogers, George L., ed. *The Art of Virtue*. Eden Prairie, Minnesota: Acorn Publishing, 1996.

Schroeder, John. *The Life and Times of Washington*. New York: Johnson, Fry, and Company, 1857.

Seelye, Elizabeth Eggleston. *The Story of Washington*. New York: D. Appleton and Company, 1893.

Shaw, Peter. *The Character of John Adams*. Chapel Hill: The University of North Carolina Press, 1976.

Skousen, W. Cleon. *The 5,000 Year Leap*. Washington, D.C.: National Center for Constitutional Studies, 1981.

Stewart, John J. *Thomas Jefferson, Forerunner to the Restoration.* Bountiful, Utah: Horizon Publishers, 1997.

Stone, Irving. *Love Is Eternal*. New York: Signet, The New American Library, Inc., 1954.

Stone, Irving. *Those Who Love*. New York: Signet, The New American Library, Inc., 1965.

Thomas Jefferson's Monticello. (pamphlet) Charlottesville, Virginia.

Tyler, Moses Coit. *Patrick Henry*. Norwalk, Connecticut: The Easton Press, 1989.

The Virginia State Capitol. Virginia: Virginia State Government, 1991.

Walley, Dean, ed. *Poor Richard's Almanack*. Kansas City, Missouri: Hallmark Cards, Inc., 1967.

Watkins, Elizabeth W. "Dolley Madison: First Lady of the Constitution." *The Constitution Magazine*, July 1987.

Watt, G. D., ed. *Journal of Discourses*. 26 vol. Liverpool: F. D. Richards, 1855.

Weems, Parson Mason. A *History of the Life and Death, Virtues and Exploits of General George Washington*. New York: Grosset & Dunlap, 1927.

Westlake, James R. "Washington's Mount Vernon." *The Sons of the American Revolution Magazine*, Spring 1999.

Weymouth, Lally, ed. *Thomas Jefferson, The Man . . . His World . . . His Influence*. New York: G.P. Putnam's Sons, 1973.

Whipple, Wayne. *The Story-Life of Washington*. 2 vols. Philadelphia: The John C. Winston Company, 1911.

The White House, An Historic Guide. Washington, D.C.: White House Historical Association and National Geographic Society, 1987.

Whitney, David C. *The American Presidents*. Garden City, New York: Doubleday & Company, Inc., 1967.

Wiencek, Henry. *Mansions of the Virginia Gentry*. Birmingham, Alabama: Oxmoor House, 1988.

William T. Hutchinson, et al, eds. *The Papers of James Madison*. 14 vols. Charlottesville, VA: University Press of Virginia, 1982.

Willis, Nathaniel Parker and William H. Bartlett. *American Scenery*. London: George Virtue, 1840.

Willison, George F. *Patrick Henry and His World*. Garden City, NY: Doubleday, 1969.

Wives of the Signers, the Women Behind the Declaration of Independence. Aledo, Texas: WallBuilder Press, 1977.

110 Rules of Civility and Decent Behavior in Company and Conversation; 41, 44

A

A Defence of the Constitutions of the Government of the United States of America; 75

A Summary View of the Rights of British America; 155

Adams, Abigail; 84-88, 94, 98, 100-108, 110-111, 167

Adams, Charles; 88

Adams, John; 3, 26, 56-57, 75, 83-84, 86, 88-98, 100-106, 108-113, 131-132, 140, 143, 155, 157, 159-160, 166-167, 175, 181, 194-195, 200-201, 210

Adams, John Quincy; 85, 87, 111

Adams, Samuel; 57, 88

Adams, Thomas Boylston; 88

Africa; 210

Albemarle County; 152

Alden, John; 83

American Colonization Society, The; 210

Amsterdam; 100

Ancient and Modern Confederacies; 190

Annapolis Convention; 104, 190

Annapolis, Maryland; 71

Arnold, Benedict; 61, 135

Articles of Confederation; 72, 103, 136-137, 165, 191, 193-194

Art of Virtue, The; 21

B

Babel; 198

Barbados; 47

Bass, Hannah; 83

Beethoven; 6

Benson, Ezra Taft; 161

Bible; 13-15, 85, 139, 149, 178-179

Bill of Rights; 106, 137, 139, 155, 165, 202-203

Boston; 7-9, 24, 35, 55, 58-59, 83, 85, 87-88, 90-93, 104-105, 127-128, 155-156, 188

Boston Massacre; 92, 128

Boston Port Bill; 55, 127

Braddock, General Edward; 50

Braintree; 83, 87, 89, 93, 100-101, 105

Breed's Hill; 58

Brookhiser, Richard; 79

Brooklyn; 61

Brutus Speech; 143

Bunker Hill; 23, 57-58

Burgoyne, Johnny; 66

C

Canada; 21, 66, 134

Chamberlayne, Richard; 52-53

Charles the First; 125

Charlottesville; 135, 140, 171, 180

chastity; 28

cherry tree; 40-41

Chesapeake Bay; 67

Clark, George Rogers; 134

cleanliness; 25

Coke upon Littleton; 120, 123

Coles, Catherine; 206

Coles, Colonel Isaac; 204

College of New Jersey, The; 186-187

College of William and Mary at Williamsburg; 149

commander in chief; 44, 49, 56-59, 65, 67, 71, 93, 107, 130, 133, 192

Committee of Safety; 128, 130, 188

Common Sense; 62, 94, 160

Concord; 58, 102, 126, 156, 188-189

Constitution; 5, 32-33, 73, 75-76, 94, 103, 105-106, 109, 132, 135, 137-139, 165, 190, 194-195, 198-204, 206, 211

Constitutional Convention; 31-33, 39, 44, 55, 72-74, 105, 136-137, 165, 190, 193, 195, 197, 203, 209

Continental Army; 56, 61

Cornwallis, General Lord Charles; 70

Craik, Dr. James; 78

Custis, Daniel Parke; 53

D

Dandridge, Dorothea; 133

Declaration of Independence; 5, 23-24, 29, 60, 93, 96, 98, 110, 112, 120, 131, 143, 155, 157-162, 175, 179-181, 185, 195, 208, 210

Delaware; 61-64, 66, 73, 157, 167, 202

Dickinson, John; 73

Dorchester Heights; 58-59

E

Edison, Thomas; 3

Egypt; 173

Eisenhower, Dwight D.; 161

Electoral College; 74, 106, 166

electricity; 4, 20

England; 5, 7, 10, 13, 21, 29, 58, 75, 99, 101, 103-104, 107, 120, 124, 150, 156, 162, 189, 200

Episcopal Church; 180

Europe; 6, 21, 75, 99, 101, 194, 202, 211

Executive Mansion; 170

F

Fairfax, Lord Thomas; 46

Farewell Address; 76

Federalist Papers, The; 202-203

Federalist Party; 109, 166

Ferry Farm; 46

First Continental Congress; 55, 93

Folger, Abiah; 7

Fontaine, Martha; 141

Fort Washington; 61

Founding Fathers; 4-5, 20, 95, 113, 117, 142-143, 177, 181, 197, 211

Franklin stove; 3

Franklin, Benjamin; 3, 6-7, 12-13, 17-18, 27-28, 31-36, 69, 75, 94, 96, 99-100, 113, 132, 143, 159, 162, 164, 174, 177, 189, 194, 197-199, 201
autobiography; 7, 12-13, 30, 177

Franklin, Josiah; 7

Franklin, Sally; 34

Franklin, William; 13, 15, 23, 28-29, 157, 189

French; 4, 6-7, 21, 25, 48-50, 54-55, 70, 93, 99, 107, 110, 174, 179

French and Indian War; 48, 50, 54-55, 93

Frugality; 5, 18, 167

G

Galloway, Joseph; 189

Gates, General Horatio; 133

Ghent, Belgium; 210

Gladstone, William; 75

Glover, Colonel John; 64

Graff house; 158

Graff, Jacob; 158

Great Compromise; 74

H

Hamilton, Alexander; 65, 73, 105, 109, 166, 194, 199, 202

Hancock, John; 69, 89-91, 98, 105, 160

Hanover, Virginia; 117

Harvard College; 83, 85, 90

Henry County; 134

Henry, Edward; 126

Henry, John; 117-118

Henry, Patrick; 55, 96, 113, 117-118, 120-141, 143, 149-152, 163, 188, 190, 194-195, 202, 204

Henry, Patrick (Patrick's Uncle); 118

Henry, Ann; 126

Henry, Betsey; 126

Henry, Billie; 126

Henry, Johnny; 126

Henry, Martha (Patsy); 119, 126

Henry, William (brother); 118

Henry, William (son); 121

Hessians; 62, 65

Holland; 98-100

Hooper, William; 94

Houdon, Jean-Antoine; 49, 174

House of Burgesses; 54-55, 121, 123, 127, 133, 150-153, 155-156

House of Representatives; 74, 138, 166

Howe, Lord William; 26, 59-60, 62-66

humility; 29-30, 32-33, 155, 164, 196

I

ice cream; 168

Illinois; 134

Independence Hall; 31, 197, 201

Indiana; 134

industry; 5, 19, 23, 34, 121, 166

inventor; 3, 6, 20, 34-35, 171-172, 182

J

Jackson, Andrew; 209

Jay, John; 100, 156, 202

Jefferson Bible; 178

Jefferson, Jane Randolph; 156

Jefferson, Martha; 167-268

Jefferson, Mary (daughter); 110

Jefferson, Mary (sister); 148-150

Jefferson, Martha Wayles Skelton; 152-154, 163-164, 173, 181

Jefferson, Peter; 147-149

Jefferson, Thomas; 3, 27, 49, 55, 96, 98-99, 109-111, 113, 117, 120-121, 123, 125, 127, 130, 132, 134-135, 137, 140, 143, 147-148, 151, 153, 155-156, 161, 163, 165, 167, 169, 179, 181, 185, 187, 190-191, 194-195, 201, 207, 210-211

Jesus; 29, 122, 178-179

Johnson, Ben; 85

Johnson, William Samuel; 199

Jones, John Paul; 133, 174

justice; 23, 76, 92, 95, 119, 140

K

Keimer, Samuel; 10

Kentucky; 134, 171

King George III; 3, 58

King, Rufus; 199

Knox, Henry; 66

L

Lafayette; 48-49, 174

Lake Champlain; 61

Landsdowne Portrait of George Washington; 209

Leatherwood; 136, 139

Lee, Arthur; 195

Lee, Henry; 79, 139

Lee, Richard Henry; 55, 95, 131, 137, 157

Lewis and Clark Expedition; 167

Lexington; 58, 70, 102, 126, 156, 188-189

Liberty; 34, 69, 90-91, 94, 103, 129-130, 142, 144, 155-156, 161, 190

Library of Congress; 175, 209

Life and Morals of Jesus, The; 178-179

Lincoln, Abraham; 79

Little Hunting Creek; 46

Livingston, Robert R.; 96, 157

London; 6, 10, 15, 21, 102, 124, 189

Long Island; 60-61

Lord Dunmore; 127, 130, 133, 155, 188

Lord Kames; 13

Louisiana Purchase; 167

loyalist; 29, 64

M

macaroni; 168

Madison, Dorothy (Dolley) Payne; 167-168, 204-206

Madison, James; 72, 75, 105, 113, 131-132, 136, 138-139, 143, 165, 167, 185, 187, 190-200, 202-207, 210-212
autobiography; 187

Madison, Nelly Conway; 185

Manhattan Island; 61

Marbleheaders; 64

Marrin, Albert; 67

Marshall, John; 49, 195

Martin, Thomas; 186

Mason, George; 132, 137, 193

Massachusetts; 9, 35, 55-56, 59, 64, 83, 89-90, 93, 103-105, 131-132, 188, 203

Mayflower; 83

Michigan; 134

midnight judges; 110

Minnesota; 134

Mississippi River; 136, 195

moderation; 24

Monroe, James; 65, 137, 210

Monticello; 150, 154, 156, 171-176, 181

Morris, Gouverneur; 15, 75, 194, 199-200

Mount Vernon; 45-48, 52, 54-55, 71-72, 76-77, 192

Mount Wollaston; 85, 87

Mozart; 6

N

Napoleon; 3

New England Courant; 8

New Jersey; 28, 61-62, 64, 66, 157, 186-187, 189, 202

New Orleans; 209

New York; 9, 60-62, 66, 71, 73, 98, 104-105, 132, 156-157, 202-203

Nicholas, Robert Carter; 120, 127

Nicola, Lewis; 70

O

Ohio; 134

order; 16, 211

Otis, James; 89

P

Paine, Thomas; 62-63, 94

Paris; 4-5, 49, 100-101, 165, 174, 207

parsons' cause; 121, 123

Payne, John; 204

Payne, Mary; 204

Pendleton, Edmund; 120

Pennsylvania; 6, 35, 61, 66, 132, 157, 202

Pennsylvania Gazette; 5, 10

Philadelphia; 6, 10, 24, 26, 35, 55-56, 60, 62, 66-67, 72, 94-95, 104, 106, 127, 131, 136, 152, 156-158, 165, 188, 193, 195, 201, 204-205

Philosophy of Jesus; 178

Plymouth; 83

polygraph; 172, 175

Poor Richard's Almanac; 6, 18

Potomac River; 55

prayer; 31, 68, 127, 139, 141, 148, 155, 172, 180, 186, 197

Presbyterian; 14, 117, 180, 185-186

Preston, Captain Thomas; 92

Princeton, New Jersey; 62

Project of Arriving at Moral Perfection; 12, 36

Providence; 47, 51, 59, 64, 162

Q

Quaker; 30, 204-206

Quincy; 83

Quincy, Josiah; 92

R

Raleigh Tavern; 127, 156

Rall, Colonel Johann Gottlieb; 62, 64-65

Randolph, Edmund; 73, 105, 136, 191, 194

Randolph, Jane; 148

Randolph, John; 120-121

Randolph, Peyton; 120, 127

Randolph, Thomas Jefferson; 179

Randolph, William; 148

Rawlins, Doctor Albin; 77

Read, Deborah; 10

Red Hill; 139, 142

Reed, Colonel Joseph; 63

resolution; 17, 95-96, 98, 125, 131-132, 138, 143, 157, 159

Revolutionary War; 4, 29, 39, 47, 100, 134-135, 187-188

Richmond, Virginia; 49, 128

Robertson, Donald; 185

Romney; 90

Rush, Dr. Benjamin; 110

S

Savior; 36, 179

Scotchtown; 126, 131, 136, 204

Scotchtown Plantation; 126

Scotland; 13, 15

Second Continental Congress; 56, 93-94, 131-132

Senate; 74, 106, 128, 138-139, 196

Shakespeare; 85, 149

Shelton, Sarah; 118

Sherman, Roger; 96, 132, 157

silence; 15, 177

Silence Dogood; 8-9, 15

sincerity; 21, 32

Skelton, Bathurst; 153

slavery; 34, 129, 144, 197

Small, William; 187

Smith, Mary; 84-86

Socrates; 29

Sons of Liberty; 89

Spotswood, Alexander; 133

St. John's Church; 128

Stamp Act; 27, 89-90, 124, 126, 142, 186

Steuben, Lieutenant General Friedrich Ludolf Gerhard Wilhelm Augustin von; 69-70

Stuart, Gilbert; 49, 209

Supreme Court; 120, 140

Syme, Sarah Winston; 117

T

temperance; 13

Thomas, General John; 59

Thompson, Charles; 98, 160

Thompson, John; 159-160

Thoughts on Government; 94-95, 132

Todd, John; 205

Townshend Acts; 90-91

tranquility; 27

Treaty of Alliance with France; 5

Treaty of Paris; 5

Trenton, New Jersey; 61

Tufts, Dr. Cotton; 87

Two Penny Acts; 121-122

U

Union Fire Company; 6

United States; 5, 26, 29, 45, 53, 55, 65, 69, 83, 98-100, 102-103, 105-111, 138, 157, 165, 169, 171, 207, 211

University of Pennsylvania; 6

University of Virginia; 171, 182, 210

V

Valley Forge; 67-69, 134, 143

Virginia; 39, 41, 46, 48-50, 52, 55-57, 73-74, 85, 93, 95, 105-106, 117, 120-123, 125, 127-141, 147-148, 150-152, 155-156, 158, 163, 171, 177, 182, 185, 187, 190-195, 201, 203-204, 206, 210

Virginia Plan of Union; 193

Virginia State Capitol; 171

W

waffles; 168

Warren, James; 103

Washington, John Augustine; 48

Warren, Mercy; 112

Washington, Ann Fairfax; 45

Washington, Augustine; 39-40, 44

Washington, Captain William; 65

Washington, D.C.; 167, 208

Washington, George; 3, 7, 30-31, 33, 39-40, 42, 44-49, 53, 55-56, 58-59, 61, 66-69, 72, 75-76, 79, 93, 106-108, 113, 127, 133, 139-140, 143, 147, 152, 165, 174, 177, 192, 194, 200-201, 203-204, 206, 209

Washington, John; 39

Washington, Martha Dandridge Custis; 52-55, 68, 77-79,

Washington, Mary; 39

Wayles, John; 152-153

Weems, Reverend Mason Locke "Parson"; 40

White House Plantation; 53

Williamsburg; 52, 54, 95, 123, 127, 130, 132, 149-151, 153-154, 187-188

Wisconsin; 134

Wythe, George; 120, 150

X

XYZ affair; 107

Y

yellow fever; 205

Yorktown; 70, 100

Meet Steve

At the age of 21, having been overseas for two years, Steven W. Allen returned home to the United States. What a wonderful feeling to return to America. It was then Steve began to feel an overwhelming sense of patriotism.

Since that time, Steve has inspired thousands of people by sharing stories from the lives of the founding fathers at numerous civic and church groups. He has been asked to return year after year to Brigham Young University's "Education Week" to lecture about these great men. During the 12 years of these presentations, many attendees asked Steve where certain stories could be found. They requested he put these inspiring stories into a book to create one source of information.

And so Steve's book was born. His interest in the creation of The United States of America finally led him to write the popular book *"Founding Fathers – Uncommon Heroes."* In his book, Steve gloriously brings to life the heroes of the American Revolution. Senator Orrin G. Hatch was so fascinated by Steve's description of the lives of these Founding Fathers that he happily agreed to write a foreword to Steve's book.

An Estate Planning Attorney by profession, Steve lives in Mesa, Arizona with his wife, where his patriotism has not dimmed. His clients comment on the "patriotic art exhibit" in the law office, where paintings and prints of the Founding Fathers and beginning America adorn the walls. His office also heralds a statue replica of George Washington, Benjamin Franklin, and Thomas Jefferson.

Steve received his Juris Doctor degree from Arizona State University college of law. He is a member of the State Bar of Arizona, The National Lawyers Association, The National Association of Elder Law Attorneys, and the National Speakers Association. Let him inspire your group with amazing stories and anecdotes from some of the founders of this great country, who pledged their life, liberty, and sacred honor for the noblest cause on earth . . . freedom.

Quick Order Form

Founding Fathers—Uncommon Heroes

ISBN 1-879033-76-3

Fax Orders: (480) 644-0072

Telephone Orders: (800) 733-5297

Email Orders: orders@legalawareness.com

Postal Orders: **Legal Awareness Series, Inc.,**
1550 E. McKellips Road, Suite 111,
Mesa, AZ 85203

Name: ______________________________

Address: ______________________________

City: ______________ State: __________ Zip: __________

Telephone: ______________________________

email address: ______________________________

Sales tax: Please add 7.8% for products shipped to Arizona addresses.

Shipping:

U.S.: $4.00 for first book and $2.00 for each additional.
International: $9.00 for first book and $5.00 for each additional (estimate).

Payment:

☐ Check

Credit Card: ☐ Visa ☐ MasterCard

Card Number: ______________________________

Name on card: ______________________________

Exp. Date: ______________________________

Join our FREE monthly e-zine (electronic magazine) "Patriotic Salutes".

To subscribe go to www.uncommonheroes.us.

Quick Order Form

Founding Fathers—Uncommon Heroes ISBN 1-879033-76-3

Fax Orders: (480) 644-0072

Telephone Orders: (800) 733-5297

Email Orders: orders@legalawareness.com

Postal Orders: **Legal Awareness Series, Inc.,**
1550 E. McKellips Road, Suite 111,
Mesa, AZ 85203

Name: ______________________________

Address: ______________________________

City: ______________ State: ________ Zip: ________

Telephone: ______________________________

email address: ______________________________

Sales tax: Please add 7.8% for products shipped to Arizona addresses.

Shipping:

U.S.: $4.00 for first book and $2.00 for each additional.
International: $9.00 for first book and $5.00 for each additional (estimate).

Payment:

☐ Check

Credit Card: ☐ Visa ☐ MasterCard

Card Number: ______________________________

Name on card: ______________________________

Exp. Date: ______________________________

Join our FREE monthly e-zine (electronic magazine) "Patriotic Salutes".

To subscribe go to www.uncommonheroes.us.

Quick Order Form

Founding Fathers—Uncommon Heroes ISBN 1-879033-76-3

Fax Orders: (480) 644-0072

Telephone Orders: (800) 733-5297

Email Orders: orders@legalawareness.com

Postal Orders: **Legal Awareness Series, Inc.,**
1550 E. McKellips Road, Suite 111,
Mesa, AZ 85203

Name: ______________________________

Address: ______________________________

City: ______________ State: ________ Zip: ________

Telephone: ______________________________

email address: ______________________________

Sales tax: Please add 7.8% for products shipped to Arizona addresses.

Shipping:

U.S.: $4.00 for first book and $2.00 for each additional.
International: $9.00 for first book and $5.00 for each additional (estimate).

Payment:

☐ Check

Credit Card: ☐ Visa ☐ MasterCard

Card Number: ______________________________

Name on card: ______________________________

Exp. Date: ______________________________

Join our FREE monthly e-zine (electronic magazine) "Patriotic Salutes".

To subscribe go to www.uncommonheroes.us.